The Search for Society

ROBIN FOX

The Search
for Society

QUEST FOR A
BIOSOCIAL SCIENCE
AND MORALITY

RUTGERS UNIVERSITY PRESS
NEW BRUNSWICK AND LONDON

Library of Congress Cataloging-in-Publication Data

Fox, Robin, 1934–
    The search for society : quest for a biosocial science and
morality / Robin Fox.
        p.   cm.
    Includes index.
    ISBN 0-8135-1464-9 (cloth)   ISBN 0-8135-1488-6 (pbk.)
    1. Sociobiology—Philosophy.   2. Social sciences—Philosophy.
3. Ethics. I. Title.
GN365.9.F69   1989
304.5—dc20   89-10137
                                                                    CIP

British-Cataloging-in-Publication information available

*The author would like to thank the publishers for permission to reprint the
following:*

Chapter 1, "The Cultural Animal," in *Man and Beast,* ed. J. F. Eisenberg
    (Washington, D.C.: Smithsonian Institution Press, 1971)
Chapter 2, "Inhuman Nature and Unnatural Rights," *Encounter* 58,
    no. 4 (1982)
Chapter 5, "The Disunity of Anthropology and the Unity of Mankind:
    Introducing the Concept of the Ethosystem," in *Waymarks,* ed.
    Kenneth Moore (Notre Dame, Ind.: Notre Dame University Press,
    1987)
Chapter 6, "The Violent Imagination," in *Violence and Aggression,* ed.
    P. Marsh and A. Campbell (Oxford: Basil Blackwell, 1982)
Chapter 7, "The Inherent Rules of Violence," in *Social Rules and Social
    Behavior,* ed. P. Collett (Oxford: Basil Blackwell, 1975)
Chapter 8, "The Passionate Mind: Brain, Dreams, Memory, Evolution,
    and Social Categories," *Zygon* 21, no. 1 (1986)
Chapter 9, "Kinship Categories as Natural Categories," in *Evolutionary
    Biology and Human Social Behavior,* ed. N. Chagnon and W. Irons
    (Belmont, Calif.: Duxbury Press, 1979); reprinted by permission of
    the editors
Chapter 10, "Consciousness Out of Context: Evolution, History, Prog-
    ress, and the Post-Post-Industrial Society," Working Papers of the
    Committee on the Individual and Society of the University of
    Virginia

And to quote from the following:

W. H. Auden, "Archaeology," in *Selected Poems,* ed. Edward Mendelson
    (New York: Random House, 1979)
Bāṇa, "Poem 49," in *Sanskrit Poetry,* trans. Daniel H. H. Ingalls (Cam-
    bridge, Mass.: Harvard University Press, 1965)
Christopher Fry, *A Phoenix Too Frequent* (Oxford: Oxford University
    Press, 1949)

TO
MILES WHATMUFF
Sometime Senior History Master, Thornton Grammar School

Contents

THE SEARCH FOR SOCIETY

Man is locked inside his own consciousness and Nature has thrown away the key.

Friedrich Nietzsche

> In vain our pent wills fret
> And would the world subdue
> Limits we did not set
> Condition all we do;
> Born into life we are, and life must be our mould.

Matthew Arnold

Donnons donc au mot biologie le sens très compréhensif qu'il devrait avoir, qu'il prendra peut-être un jour, et disons pour conclure que toute morale, pression ou aspiration, est d'essence biologique.

Henri Bergson

Introduction: Bearing the Bad News

THIS book is about three things:

(1) The confusion over the nature of the subject matter of the social and behavioral sciences and the consequent confusion over *what* should be studied and *how;*

(2) the confusion over the nature of the moral system that may or may not be implicit in any definition or method that emerges;

(3) the confusion over the purposes and goals of any science or science-based morality that may result from the resolution of these issues.

I have held, contrary to the mainstream of social/behavioral science, that the subject matter (society, culture, behavior, action) must be a 'natural' phenomenon: as much a product of natural selection as our brains and bodies. Thus, it follows that its study is an empirical one whose methods should be those appropriate to the study of all forms of life.

This would mean a merger of natural and social science, and a study of human social behavior essentially no different from the study of the behavior of any other social animal. Like any such study, it would have to take into account the unique features of the species (*Homo sapiens sapiens*) in question.

This is where my position departs from the mainstream, which holds that these features of human uniqueness (however defined) render this species *in principle* incapable of study by the methods and assumptions of natural science. Thus, culture, or language, or symbolizing, are seen as qualitatively distinct emergent properties which require methods of study unique to themselves. Most of the current debate about the status of the social sciences rests upon a resolution of this issue.

I do not, with perhaps the exception of social categories, attempt any empirical demonstration here. Such demonstrations are being carried out and a large body of literature and research now exists. Here I am concerned more with what Robert Merton used to call 'sociological orientation' as opposed to 'sociological theory.' Things are mostly being done one way. I have argued for nearly three decades now that they should be done another way. The essays in this volume are the products of my reworking and rethinking that argument.

My concern with moral and ethical theory is also heterodox since (a) most social scientists do not consider it their business to thus indulge, and would cite the 'fact-value distinction' as routinely preventing such an enterprise (but not preventing them from expressing forceful ethical opinions), and (b) even if they admitted the possibility, they would object to any morality based on premises derived from natural science since it would commit the 'naturalistic fallacy' and hence be invalid *ex definitione*. Obviously, I do not accept either position and argue the case against them here with the proposal for an ethic that accepts the survival of life as a basic premise.

Finally, however, I am not convinced that the social and behavioral sciences, at least implicitly, do accept the fact-value distinction. I argue that they are committed to a utopian program by their history and by the expectations that keep them alive and funded, namely, that they will help to improve the future prospects of mankind. This is so taken for granted that many people will not see that there is an issue: of course these disciplines are intended for the future betterment of mankind; why else would we have them? One answer might be to look for the truth about human social nature whether or not the ensuing news be good or bad. In other words, it is certainly a logical possibility that there is no improvable future for mankind, that the news is indeed bad. At least the issue must be faced, not assumed to be settled. It is hard for the social sciences to face it, however; it is a poor basis for research proposals.

The result is that there is a tremendous bias in all the sciences towards the bearing of good news. It is inconceivable that any news refuting any part of the utopian program should be well received, however incontrovertible. The funds would immediately dry up. The bad news is, therefore, usually delivered by renegade philosophers (Nietzsche, Sartre), or by humanists (Orwell, Golding), or by theologians of an orthodox stripe, who can all be discounted by the social scientists of the academies. H. G. Wells spent his long and active life dutifully delivering the good news about the possibilities of a scientific utopia. But just before his death, and having witnessed World War II, he wrote the remarkable *Mind at the End of Its Tether* (1945), in which he concluded, "*Homo sapiens,* as he has been pleased to call himself, is in his present form played out." Certainly not a sound basis for a research proposal. Or Orwell's proposition that the vision of the future is a boot stamping on a human face; or Sartre's that evil cannot be redeemed (*What Is Literature?*); or Doris Lessing's that we have very little idea what is going on, and what idea we have is largely erroneous (*The Sirian Experiments*).

Yet this alternative message has been with us since the Greeks and the Prophets and perhaps we should pay it some respect. Very few of us do or dare to. Like the dean's wife with Darwinism, we hope that if it be true it not become generally known. Lately, the human sciences have become particularly strident in their collective condemnations of the bearers of bad news. Given the nature of the Enlightenment project of which they are the heirs, one can see why. If, for example, we were to treat Margaret Mead's *Coming of Age in Samoa* as utopia, not as ethnography, then we would understand it better and save a lot of pointless debate.

Occasionally, I find an anthropologist with the same information as mine making a similar point to the one that concludes this book (or that pervades my *The Violent Imagination.*) Thus Melvin Konner, in *The Tangled Wing,* quotes Shakespeare, Henry James, Goethe, and Malraux—all bearers of bad news, and continues:

Let us invite these, as it were, artists of the soul to a cocktail party. On one side of the room are a group of tinkerers arguing cheerfully about various strategies for making everything just fine. On the other side, a group of biologists are discussing, rather glumly, the unchanging facts of human nature. Which group would they join?

There is little doubt where they would feel more at home.

If the bearers of bad news have any hope to offer, it is that by facing the unpalatable truths we are better off than if we ignore them. They will continue to urge this morsel of wisdom on an ungrateful world. For even if mankind cannot achieve perfection, it can perhaps learn to live more tolerantly with its imperfections. But this rallying cry for moderation will never get the masses to the barricades, nor the tinkerers to cross the room to our side of the cosmic cocktail party.

The reader not familiar with the present state of sectarian fragmentation in the social sciences—anthropology in particular—may be baffled by some of the responses this book will provoke. The social sciences, unlike most of the natural sciences, do not have a consensus of 'normal science' to which appeal can be made in judging a contribution. What they have are competing ideologies. And as with all sectarian disputes, judgements are made on the basis of ideological purity versus heresy. It is almost impossible these days to get a reasoned discussion of issues in the social sciences. The dominance of neo-relativist, hermeneutic, critical, symbolic, deconstructionist, and interpretative versions of the social science enterprise involve a retreat from science and the very idea of objective knowledge. This book, therefore, represents an almost puritanical appeal for an attempt at a theory of social action based on the natural sciences. Obviously, it will be treated as heresy by those with contrary views. I have no idea where all this will end, except perhaps in the development of a natural science of society that simply bypasses the social sciences as we know them. This may become necessary, because while they are fiddling, Rome is burning, and someone has to attend to the fire rather than debate whether we can ever have sure and objective, nonrelative knowledge of the fire's existence.

The essays herein are not necessarily in chronological order except the first two. Numbers 3 and 4 have been in process of composition since the early 1970s, but I have never published them because they made such good lectures. Since I am not able to travel and lecture so much anymore, they have been organized into two chapters especially for this book. They could easily be expanded into a book themselves, and not always along the pathways usually followed by historians of social thought. Thus, there is much in that towering work of genius, Browning's *Sordello*, that bears on the 'individual and society' issue. Sordello is the Romantic child of nature whose very failure stems from his lack of socialization (literally). But, and this is the important thing, *he comes to understand this*, and it is the heart of his epiphany in book 5:

> . . . that collective man
> Outstrips the individual . . .

And he thus poses for us the question that Bradley (another of my heroes) fails to address: We are nothing without society and can only realize ourselves as part of a collective, but what if the collective in which we must realize ourselves is rotten, as was thirteenth-century Lombardy? Where then do we look for self-realization? Browning's immense poem was criticized for obscurity in its day and is virtually unread even now (Ezra Pound is one of the few to have read and sympathized); but its 'social psychology' is in many ways superior to anything produced by the behavioral or philosophical sciences since.

Another approach would be to examine the dramatic change that came over the attitudes of the New England Transcendentalists during the Civil War; an attitude change that had arch-individualist Emerson dismissing his recently dead friend and champion of rugged self-sufficiency, Thoreau, as nothing better than a picnic organizer. (I think his exact phrase was 'captain of a huckleberry party.') This same change drove Thoreau himself from the individualist seclusion of Walden to the pulpit in Concord to preach in favor of saving the Union—a decided collectivity. If the Franco-Prussian War was the catalyst for Durkheim's theories of social solidarity, the American Civil War (the first truly modern war) was similarly traumatic for the Transcendentalists. There are other examples of the same kind from literature and social thought that ought to be pursued (the interesting range of reactions, for example, to Charlotte Brontë's *Jane Eyre*, especially in France); but my task in these two chapters, as in most of the others, has been simply to point out the issues.

Most of the other essays have appeared in places where social scientists would not normally look, and so are usefully reproduced here for reference. Chapter 5 seems to follow on logically from 3 and 4 in that it picks up on the theme of Durkheim's individual-society distinction and the devastation it wrought, and continues the theme of the search for the location of social facts. The two essays on violence are grouped together, as are the two on categories. There has been so much gratuitous misunderstanding on the issue of the ethological approach to violence that it seemed worth restating the position here; a position that has nothing to do with 'innate aggression causing war' and other simple-minded and often perverse renditions. As to categories, this is the area where the antiscientific and pro-symbolic school make their stand, so it seemed useful to plant some banners in the heartland of the enemy. (For a fuller exposition of my position on categories—especially totemic categories and the origins of language—interested readers should see chapter 7 of *The Red Lamp of Incest*.)

Obviously, notes and bibliographies are relative to the times and occasions of the various essays. Science has not, however, stood still, and more up-to-date references should be consulted where appropriate. This book does not stand alone; it should be read as part of the ongoing enterprise, as a set of programmatic statements backing up the more detailed empirical studies, my own and others. To me, for example, it is interesting to see how far one has come from the somewhat simple ethological views of the first essay, to the sophistication of ecological ideas in the fifth, the detailed investigation of brain processes in the eighth, and the consideration of "sociobiological" theories in the ninth. (Sociobiology is in effect one branch of study in the wider conceptual scheme of biosocial science as I understand it.)

Also, primatology has come a long way since my first interest in it. I undertook what was perhaps the most extensive study of primate kinship systems to date in "Primate Kin and Human Kinship" (*Biosocial Anthropology*, 1975), but primate studies have moved on since then. I had to revise everything on the Great Apes, and on the role of female choice in breeding systems, for example, to write *The Red Lamp of Incest*. Recently I have written up, with Dieter Steklis, an account of a primate field study ("Menstrual Cycle Phase and Sexual Behavior in Semi-free-ranging Stumptail Macaques—*Macaca Arctoides*," *International Journal of Primatology*).

These items from my own work (they do not include, for example, the investigation of biosocial applications to constitutional, contract, and family law) help to show that this book is indeed part and parcel of a larger enterprise, and should be read for its specific contribution to that enterprise. In particular this book should be read for its demonstration of the philosophical and political foundations of the hostility to the innate in post-Renaissance European thought. The other essays set the scene for this analysis, and are developments of it, in the areas of ecology and universals, violence and aggression, social categories and natural processes, and the possible fate of mankind, which cannot be shirked even if dealing with it leads us into polemic and speculation.

If people wish to see this book as a kind of biosocial counterblast to Clifford Geertz's *The Interpretation of Cultures* (1973), another set of programmatic essays and one that seems to have become a kind of bible for the interpretative school, I would not object. I might point out, however, that one of the original inspirations for the first essay here was a piece by Geertz. The truly thoughtful will see, as Victor Turner did just before he died, for example, that the two positions are not irreconcilable. (See notes to chapters 5 and 8.) The final essay returns us to the more general theme of 'Consciousness out of Context' and thus brings us back to the bearing of, if not bad, at least uneasy news.

This is an appropriate place to say that while this final chapter uses Daniel Bell's *The Coming of Post Industrial Society* as a point of departure, my difference from Bell is not so great. The more I read of his complete works (and no one claiming to be a social scientist can afford not to) the more I see that I am pushing to its logical limit a position he holds on the immutable factors in human nature. Bell's formula of "optimism of the head, pessimism of the heart" pretty well sums up my own state of mind about the human condition.

There is some repetition in the essays; they often deal with the same themes looked at from different angles. Thus, in chapter 2, I introduce several themes in the context of the search for a rational ethic that are taken up in chapters 3 and 4 in the context of the history of ideas and its bearing on the present state of confusion in the social sciences. Some of these themes again, as we have seen, are taken up in chapter 5 in the search for a formula for cultural universals. Apart from restoring a few paragraphs that were cut for space reasons, I have not changed anything from the original versions of previously published pieces, except for spelling and other errors. If there are mistakes and wrong arguments it is as well to see how they developed, and where they are endemic and where correctible. Thus, we must rule out exactitude by hindsight. I shall also resist the temptation to use this introduction to make yet another programmatic statement. The whole book, after all, is introductory, and notes and scholarly apparatus are kept to a minimum so that the reader can receive the material unencumbered. I was tempted to include the introduction to my *Biosocial Anthropology* (which came out, interestingly, in 1975—the same year as E. O. Wilson's *Sociobiology*); but interested readers may look it up for the program announced therein, and judge for themselves how much of it has been realized. It did include, for example, a long essay by W. D. Hamilton, whose work was the foundation of Wilson's own effort. I shall here only quote the final paragraph:

> The ultimate message in all this is a response to the ultimate question of social anthropology and social philosophy: the question of the possibility of social order. And the response is that of Aristotle rather than Hobbes: that the nature of order is part of the order of nature. It is not that man is as culture does, but that culture does as man is. Thus perhaps we can return, by the biosocial route, to the only question that allows anthropology (social or otherwise) a distinct existence among the sciences: what is man?

It is usual for an author to end an introduction by acknowledging all the people who have helped. But in this case that would entail an intellectual autobiography of some length. It would be out of place here. (A brief version can be found in the introduction to my *Encounter with Anthropology*.) I have dedicated the book to a great teacher who introduced me to these ideas when I was only sixteen. Mr Whatmuff's sixth-form (college prep) history class unselfconsciously debated Hegel and Burke versus Spencer and Mill. We took it so much for granted. It is only now that I realize what an extraordinary education it was, and how grateful I should be to him and other teachers like him. I doubt he would have been altogether happy with the conclusions—he was a stout-hearted Methodist socialist; but he was a true teacher, and I know he would have applauded the effort. It's the best I can do to say thank you. His most severe criticism of me, and I remember it with embarrassing clarity, was that I was "inclined to let cleverness of writing substitute for soundness of argument." Guilty, Mr Whatmuff, guilty. I've tried to improve, but you knew that some things were incorrigible. Let me just mention, since they may think I have forgotten them in the interim, Ernest Gellner and Donald Macrae at the London School of Economics. Gellner and Watkins ran an 'alternative' philosophy seminar in their own time in the evenings, largely for graduate students. But Gellner asked me to come along, as he encouraged me in so many other ways, and I learned more from that experience than from all the conventional teaching. Donald Macrae introduced me to the Oxford Idealists while, appropriately, trying to teach me to punt during a conference in that city. This was held by the Rationalist Press Association, whose undergraduate essay prize (with his help) I had won that year. I never mastered the art of the punt pole, but I rushed off and read Bradley. Later, when we were colleagues at LSE, Macrae and I were the only two Gaelic speakers in the senior common room. It gave us a kind of bond, as did my hopeless attempt to emulate his massive and incomparable erudition. But these two teachers and colleagues are responsible for much of what follows, although I naturally exempt them from responsibility for all errors, omissions, and wrong conclusions.

The rest know who they are: my fellow students, my teachers and colleagues; the happy band of pioneers in biosocial science; the more helpful critics on the fringes who have goaded us to do better; and the institutions (especially Dear Old Rutgers) which have supported my efforts despite their often all too real misgivings about the possibilities of bad news. It isn't all bad; things could be a lot worse given our potential. If we can put survival of the species, and of life, back to the center of our scientific and ethical concerns—and there is evidence this is happening—then perhaps we may be permitted a glimmer of hope. Nature may have thrown away the key to human consciousness, as Nietzsche gloomily announces, but Darwin has shown us where to look for it, and we may yet open the door to these secrets without having to shoot off the lock. None of us would want our efforts to go for nothing, after all. That is very human. And to the righteous ones who are all too ready to attribute offenses against human dignity to those of us on the quest for universals, let me quote the Coda from W. H. Auden's last poem:

> From Archaeology
> one moral, at least, may be drawn,
> to wit, that all
>
> our school text-books lie.
> What they call History
> is nothing to vaunt of,
>
> being made as it is,
> by the criminal in us:
> goodness is timeless.

1

The Cultural Animal

> History itself is a *real* part of *natural history*, of the development of nature into man. Natural science will one day incorporate the science of man, just as the science of man will incorporate natural science; there will be one science.
>
> Karl Marx, *Third Paris Manuscript*, 1844

> Origin of man now proved. Metaphysics must flourish. He who understands [the] baboon would do more towards metaphysics than Locke.
>
> Charles Darwin, *Notebook M*, 1838

PRIMITIVE mythologies testify to man's enduring fascination with the problem of his own relationship to the natural world. For *Homo* is burdened with being *sapiens*, and one thing this *sapientia* drives him to is a ceaseless and almost passionate inquiry about his status—what T. H. Huxley aptly called *An Enquiry into Man's Place in Nature*. And, like Darwin and Huxley, the primitive seeks an answer to the eternal paradox: he is obviously part of nature, and in particular he is part of the animal world; yet he is set apart from nature by the very fact of knowing that he is part of it. Not only does no other animal know it is going to die, but no other animal knows it is alive. And no other animal concerns itself with the problem of its uniqueness. But man is obsessed with it. He is forever seeking to define himself—a task as yet uncompleted—and to do this he has to establish the boundaries between himself and the animal world.

In their mythologies the primitives solve the problem in various ways, usually by having man descend from various animals. It might be thought that this represents an anticipation of Darwin, but unfortunately most primitives believe in acts of special creation, so they must be disqualified. It is one of these acts of creation, however, that is usually the clue to the essential difference between man and animal. Language, fire, the art of cooking, rules about incest, and so on are the diacritics of humanity. We do not communicate, convert energy, eat, or breed quite like the animals, and hence we make that crucial breakthrough from nature to culture, and become the cultural animal.

Not only does man become cultural, he becomes divine. In many of his ego-boosting mythologies man does not differ simply in degree from the animals; he differs in kind. It is not some simple attribute—like the ability to make fire—but the possession of a divine spark that renders us *in essence* different, that carves out a gulf between man and 'brute creation.' Here again the matter remains stubbornly unsettled, and much argument ensues about where brute creation stops and the divine human starts. Any human group is ever ready to consign another recognizably different human group to the other side of the boundary. To be fully human, it is not enough to possess culture, one must possess *our* culture. Even universalist religions, which were happy to define man as an animal with a soul, were often not very certain how to define 'soul,' and categories of *Homo sylvestris* and *Homo feralis* were invented to take care of marginal cases. But at least in the Western world this definition sufficed (and for many still suffices) until the eighteenth-century savants began to look down on such arguments as perhaps too 'emotional,' and substituted reason as the defining characteristic of man. Linnaeus, to whom man owes his pretentious zoological title, *Homo sapiens,* was very much a child of the eighteenth century, when souls were not to be trusted because one never knew quite what they were up to, and animals may very well have them, too. But brute creation did not have reason and that was obvious enough. Soulful our furry friends might be, but rational they were not. They could probably adore God, but they could not understand Pythagoras.

Darwin undermined this stance as much as he undermined the position of the religiously orthodox. He noted what in fact many of his predecessors—including Linnaeus himself, and even Kant—had noted: the striking anatomical similarity between man and the rest of the order *Primates* and ultimately between man and the rest of the vertebrates. What Darwin added was a theory that could explain how this striking relationship came about, other than by some whim of the Almighty or by some Lamarckian effort of will. Now this caused many people other than Bishop Wilberforce to feel that human dignity and uniqueness were in danger. That great anticleric Samuel Butler castigated Darwin for 'banishing mind from the universe,' for blurring the distinctions that we had assumed were inviolable. Man had emerged gradually from the animal world by a natural process, not suddenly by a supernatural one. The moral was plain to the soul merchants and the reason merchants alike: man in fact differed only in degree, not in kind, from his cousins. The reaction was interesting. The anatomical argument was quickly adopted and became its own kind of orthodoxy. Despite a few skirmishes, the battle was over before it was fought.

The anatomist W. E. LeGros Clark said recently that it is astonishing to think people ever doubted the anatomical continuity between man and the other primates. And, indeed, it does seem absurd today, to the extent that when I am faced with an unrepentant fundamentalist I am unable to cope with him. I have no ready-made arguments for defending the self-evident, and so fare badly, thus confirming his worst fears about the conspiracy of the ungodly.

In the 130 years between the appearance of *The Origin of Species* and today, a large (although still too limited) amount of fossil evidence has come to light documenting the gradual transition that, even in the absence of direct evidence, Darwin realized *must* have happened. As far as anatomy was concerned, then, the case rested. But human behavior was somehow exempted from this rubric.

Whatever the opinion about Darwin's specific conclusions, his message was exceedingly clear. In many areas of behavior man shows great similarities to his cousins; their behavior, like their anatomy, has evolved through the process of natural selection—and so has man's. Anatomy and behavior, structure and function, were of course intimately linked, and what was true for one was true for the other.

Even in the biological sciences, the impact of this line of

thinking was not immediate, and it is only comparatively recently that biologists have been investigating in a serious way the evolution of animal-behavior systems. The reasons for this are not of concern here, although the historians of science should be working on them. But one reason should be noted: investigations of animal behavior really got going under the aegis of Pavlovian-style behaviorism, which is not evolutionary in orientation and has little respect for anything that is claimed to be 'innate.' There was a similar reaction (or was it even a reaction?) in the social sciences. Darwin had blurred the distinctions, all right, and even reason did not appear to be so firmly enthroned now; so anthropology became defender of the faith in human uniqueness and offered culture as the defining characteristic. Anthropologists, however, were never able to define very clearly what this was.

So, as in the older myths of the primitives, the nature of man's uniqueness remains something of a mystery. Roughly, 'culture,' in anthropological parlance, refers to traditional modes of behaving and thinking that are passed on from one generation to another by social learning of one kind or another. We get a little uneasy when told that animal communities also have traditions that get passed on, so we retreat into symbols. Culture is couched in symbols and it is by means of these that it is transmitted. Preeminent among the symbol systems is language, and, when all else fails, man can cling to language. By their speech shall ye know them.

The social and behavioral sciences thus sidestepped Darwin's challenge. This was easy to do at a time when behaviorism dominated psychology, and instinct theory had fallen into disrepute. Behaviorism was rigorous and 'scientific,' while instinct theory—primarily under William McDougall—seemed nothing more than a kind of thesaurus of human attributes. The eugenics movement, which put such store in biological aspects of behavior, became more and more entangled with racism, and the least attempt to show that there were important biological components in behavior was regarded as incipient racism, and still is in many quarters. In sociology, the Social Darwinists had also fallen into disrepute. They were not really Darwinians;

they simply used analogies from Darwinian biological theory and applied them, usually incorrectly, to social processes. Their wrongheaded use of evolutionary doctrines to support the excesses of laissez-faire capitalism eventually sent them into oblivion. With them, the proverbial baby went out with the proverbial bath water.

Henceforth, any explanation of a social phenomenon that was Darwinian or biological was ipso facto erroneous in the social sciences, and that was that. Marx and Durkheim dominated sociology, and while the latter had problems with the autonomy of the subject, his doctrine that the social must be explained in terms of the social and not 'reduced' to any lower level—like the biological, of course—held almost complete sway. Anthropologists continued to pronounce. Arthur Keith even set a limit below which culture was impossible: the brain, he said, had to reach a size of 750 cubic centimetres before any fossil primate could be considered a man. This gave substance to the anthropological belief that culture was, in the words of Malinowski, 'all of a piece.' People were never found with religion but no language, or law but no religion, and so on. If they had one they had them all. It must have happened at the point when the brain reached the size necessary for culture to 'occur.'

One can immediately see the similarities between this and the Catholic doctrine as annunciated in the encyclical *Humani generis,* which allows that man may have evolved in body, as described by Darwin, but insists that at some point an immortal soul was injected into the painfully evolving body. God would have had to wait, it seems, until his chosen primate had crossed Keith's 'Cerebral Rubicon.'

Anthropologists, also, were almost maniacally preoccupied with explaining cultural differences. They were really not very interested in what made men men, but in what made one lot of them different from another lot. As a student, I had the litany chanted at me: "Biological universals cannot explain cultural differentials." And, of course, at one level they cannot. Muslims, I was told, take off their shoes to go into church, while Christians take off their hats. Now find me a biological explanation for that! I was never sure I wanted to find any kind of explanation for it. It seemed to me a pretty arbitrary thing. And anyway, what explanation was I offered?

Even in those days I was plaguing my teachers with the question: If we do not really know what biological universals there are, how can we study the cultural differentials? How can we study the variables without the constants? I was told that biological universals were simply primitive drives, like hunger and sex; but the fact that sex was universal didn't explain why some cultures were polygynous and others monogamous. Maybe not, I thought, but it might explain why they were all adulterous. After all, might not behavior resulting from something as complex as sex produce more than just these rather grey and amorphous urges? Look at the courtship of birds and animals, for example. Ah, came back the answer, but that is *genetic*, whereas human courtship is *cultural*.

When all this was going on—in the early 1950s in London—I had no ready answer. It all depends, I thought to myself and in secret, upon what you want to explain. All human cultures have some kind of courtship ceremonies, and they all look very much alike despite the different cultural trappings. If all you want to explain is why in America girls wear their dates' fraternity pins while in Fiji they put hibiscus flowers behind their ears, that is fine. But (1) it does not seem worth explaining, and (2) there probably is no explanation, in any scientific sense; it is just what they do. These are simply ways of getting the same courtship job done, and the interesting thing to me is the universality of various similar symbolic devices. Has each culture independently invented the idea that the girl should declare her intentions in this kind of way? Or is there perhaps something more subtle about courtship than previously imagined— something uncultural, something unlearned?

Anthropology was undoubtedly fighting several real battles, often shooting at the wrong enemies. The no-links-between-biology-and-culture argument was partly an attack on the racists, who wanted to explain seeming inequalities between cultures as a result of biological differences. Again the baby went out with the soapsuds when anthropology strenuously opposed *any* connection between culture and biology, even at the universal level. At best—as, for example, in the work of Malinowski—culture could be seen as a response to a rather drab set of 'biological imperatives,' but then this kind of Malinowskian functionalism soon fell into disrepute as well, since it did nothing to explain cultural differences. While I am on my catalogue of complaints, let me add that as far as I could see, for all its obsession with cultural differences, anthropology did nothing to *explain* them. What it did was to take cultural differences as given and use them to explain other phenomena— largely, other cultural differences. All the things that might have explained cultural differences, such as racial variation, environment, history, and diffusion, were at one time or another ruled out of court.

All in all, for a variety of ideological reasons, anthropology, along with psychology and sociology, kept the world safe for humanity by refusing to allow that anything about culture could be 'reduced' to biology, and hence kept the gap between us and the brutes nicely wide. Man was the cultural animal, but stress was entirely on the *cultural;* the animal was relegated to a few odd things like blinking, sucking, feeling hungry, and copulating. It was held that 99 percent of human behavior was learned and hence cultural. And what was more, that there was no limit to what could be learned. The human infant was a tabula rasa on which culture imprinted itself, and the subsequent behavior of the infant was therefore wholly a matter of which particular culture had been imprinted on it. The differences between cultures, in their beliefs, behaviors, and institutions, were held to be so great that any considerations of common biological traits could be totally ignored.

This was all a great pity, since it was not the intention of the founding fathers of anthropology to create an unbridgeable gap between man and animal. E. B. Tylor, who is rightly credited with the invention of the anthropological concept of culture, was greatly interested in the behavior of animals. In his *Anthropology* of 1881, he included a chapter called 'Man and other Animals' in which he stressed continuities. (Leslie White, in his 'edited' version of this classic, cut out the chapter, since it was not, according to him, consonant with modern knowledge.)

Lewis Henry Morgan, whose work on kinship systems is indisputably the starting point of American anthropology, spent many years studying the beaver and wrote the standard book on its behavior. All his life he argued for a continuity of behavior between man and animal. It is ironic that Morgan, a special creationist, should be arguing for continuity, while his successors, supposedly believers in Darwinian natural selection, should have resurrected the doctrine of special creation.

What all this leads to is the crucial question: Weren't anthropologists suffering from 'ethnographic dazzle'? (I have adapted the term from linguistics, where 'orthographic dazzle' refers to the difficulty some people have of sorting out pronunciation from spelling.) In some respects and at some levels—of beliefs, of formal institutions—cultures are dazzlingly different from one another. Why are the Japanese the way they are, as opposed to the Americans, the Russians, the Hottentots, and so on? This is a fascinating question. But, as I have said, the answer from anthropology is a rather lame: "They are different because they do things differently." Anthropology mostly tells about the *consequences* of doing things differently, and tells it very well indeed. But are societies and cultures really so different at the level of forms and processes? Aren't they in some ways depressingly the same? Don't anthropologists, time after time in society after society, come up against the same processes carried out under a variety of symbolic disguises? I think they do, and if they can get past the cultural or ethnographic dazzle, they can see that this is so. Thus, if one looks at the behavior of what my colleague Lionel Tiger has called 'men in groups,' one finds that, whatever the overt cultural male-group behavior at the level of symbolism, actual practices, beliefs, and even emotions, one thing stands out: men form themselves into associations from which they exclude women. These associations vary in their expressed purposes, but in many of their processes they are remarkably uniform. Once this is grasped, a seemingly bewildering variety of male behavior can be reduced to a few principles.

Similarly, I have tried to show that the apparently endless kinds of kinship and marriage arrangements known to man are in fact variations on a few simple themes. The same can be said of political arrangements, which, despite their cultural variety, are reducible to a few structural forms. Once one gets behind the surface manifestations, the uniformity of human behavior and of human social arrangements is remarkable.

None of this should surprise a behavioral zoologist; the subject being dealt with is, after all, a uniform species divided into a number of populations. Since this is a species of rather highly developed mammals, one would expect many local differences in 'traditions' between the various populations, but one would expect these differences to reflect species-specific units of behavior. Thus, every species has a complex of social behavior made up of recognizable units—a complex that distinguishes it from other species—but these units may well be put together in different ways by different populations adapting to different environments. A baboon troop, for all its ingenuity, does not adapt in the same way as a herd of horses (and vice versa). The baboons can adapt only by using the material in their stock of behavior units, and the same is true of man.

The degree of flexibility is obviously greater among humans, but much of it is at the symbolic level. The story can be told in many different ways, but it is still the same old story. And if it is departed from too far—which is within man's capacity—the result may well be a truly dramatic chaos. For this is man's dilemma. Unlike the baboon or the horse, he can imagine things that are different from the plot laid down for him, and he can put his dreams into practice and watch to see if they will work. If man accepts that all behavior is culturally learned and that he can learn anything, he can invent any kind of society and culture for himself. If he believes that he has a species-specific repertoire of behavior that can be combined successfully only in certain ways, then there are definite limits to what this animal can do, to the kinds of societies he can operate, to the kinds of cultures he can live with. But there is no end to man's dreams and fantasies. His social behavior may have strict limits, but his imagination has few.

I mentioned earlier that language was the chief characteristic of the human species, the crucial distinguishing feature. It is now well established that the capacity for language acquisition and use lies in the brain and speech organs, and in the complex relations between the two. Linguists, like Noam Chomsky, and psychologists, like E. H. Lenneberg, argue that the capacity for grammatical speech is somehow in the brain and matures as the child matures. Thus every human child has the capacity for grammatical speech, and is ready, as it were, to be programmed with whatever actual grammar its culture provides. We know that these grammars are astonishing in their variety, and that their variation is arbitrary. There is no explanation for why the English say 'horse,' the French '*cheval*,' and the Germans '*Pferd*.' There is no explanation for why any particular pattern of sounds signifies a particular object or action (with the possible exception of onomatopoeia). This is all quite arbitrary. Nevertheless, the speech patterns of all languages operate on a few basic principles, which linguists have worked out, and the semantic patterns may also be reducible in this way, once what Chomsky calls the 'deep structures' of all languages are known. When they are, a 'universal grammar' can be written that will reveal the few principles upon which all actual grammars rest. Despite the enormous variety of 'surface grammars,' they are all not only doing the same job, but also are constrained to do it in a limited number of ways. Thus, no language exists that a linguist cannot record with the universal phonetic alphabet, and analyze with universally applicable techniques of semantic analysis. Artificial languages can be invented, based on binary signals, or other codes, which require different grammars, but natural languages can all be broken down, first into phones, then phonemes, then morphemes, then lexemes, and so on up to the higher levels of grammaticality.

The rest of culture is probably like this. The potential for culture lies in the biology of the species. Man has the kinds of cultures and societies he has because he is the kind of species he is. They are built of his behavioral repertoire and are analyzable into its elements and their combinations. Like language, the capacity for specific kinds of behavior is in man, but exactly how this will be manifested will depend on the information fed into the system. The system here is the behavior potential of the individual; the information is the culture he is socialized in. But in the same way that he can learn only a language that follows the normal rules of grammaticality for human languages, so he can learn only a grammar of behavior that follows the parallel rules in the behavioral sphere. Of course, in either case he can try departing from normal grammaticality, but he will then get gibberish, linguistic or behavioral.

People generally do not try to manipulate language because the matter is out of their hands, but with behavior they are continually producing gibbering illiterates, and until they understand the structure of the behavioral grammar within which man weaves his cultural variations, they will continue to do so. No one wants to produce linguistic gibberish, because verbal communication would break down; but behavioral gibberish is constantly being produced and then everybody wonders why social communication breaks down. The answer of those who believe that anything is possible since everything is cultural is: Try to invent yet more and more different languages with any kind of grammaticality you can think of. My answer is: Find out how the universal grammar works and then effect changes within that framework; invent new behavioral languages that do not violate the principles of basic grammaticality.

At least two monarchs in history are said to have tried the experiment of isolating children at birth and keeping them isolated through childhood to see if they would spontaneously produce a language when they matured. Both the Egyptian Psammetichos, in the seventh century B.C., and James IV of Scotland, in the fifteenth century A.D., did not doubt that untutored children would speak, although King James's hope that they would speak Hebrew was perhaps a little optimistic.

I do not doubt that they *could* speak and that, theoretically, given time, they or their offspring would invent and develop a language despite their never having been taught one. Furthermore, this language, although totally different from any known, would be analyzable by linguists on the same basis as other languages and translatable into all known languages.

I would push this further. If the new Adam and Eve could survive and breed—still in total isolation from any cultural influences—they would eventually produce a society that would

be likely to have laws about property, its inheritance and exchange; rules about incest and marriage; customs of taboo and
avoidance; methods of settling disputes with a minimum of
bloodshed; beliefs about the supernatural and practices relating to it; a system of social status and methods of indicating it;
initiation rituals for young men; courtship practices, including
the adornment of females; systems of symbolic body adornment generally; certain activities and associations set aside for
men from which women were excluded; gambling of some
kind; a tool- and weapon-making industry; myths and legends;
dancing; adultery; homicide; kinship groups; schizophrenia;
and psychoses and neuroses and various practitioners to take
advantage of or cure these (depending on how they are viewed).

In short, the new Adam and Eve would not only produce, as
the two monarchs suspected, a recognizable language, but a
recognizable human culture and society. In content it might not
be quite like any other. Its religious beliefs might be different,
but it would have some; its marriage rules might be unique (I
doubt it), but it would have them and their type would be recognized; its status structure might be based on an odd criterion,
but there would be one; its initiation rituals might be unbelieva-
bly grotesque, but they would exist. All these things would be
there because man is the kind of animal that does these kinds of
things.

In the same way, in a zoo one can rear infant baboons who
know nothing of how their ancestors and cousins lived in the
wild, and yet who, when they reach maturity, produce a social
structure with all the elements found in that wild, of which they
have no experience. Their capacity to produce a unique language is of course much more limited than that of our hypothetical naive humans, but in both cases the basic grammaticality of
behavior will be operating. In the same way that a linguist could
take our Garden of Eden tribe and analyze its totally unique
language, so an anthropologist would be able to analyze its totally unique kinship system or mythology or whatever, because
the basic rules of the universal grammar would be operating.

(In the interest of accuracy I should add that the experiment
might be impossible to perform. It is one of the ground rules of

the universal behavioral grammar of all primates—not just humans—that if young infants are deprived of maternal care at a critical period they will grow up to be seriously disturbed and may well perpetuate this error by maltreating their own children in turn. Thus the experiment might well produce a group of maladjusted adults. But at least this presents one element of the universal system: some method has to be found of associating mother and child closely and safely during certain critical periods. If isolated during these periods, the animal may be permanently damaged. It has to learn certain things at certain times—and this is true of language as of many other areas of behavior.)

What I am saying about the human tribe developed de novo in an experimental Eden may not seem particularly remarkable, but it does go against the anthropological orthodoxy. Without any exposure to cultural traditions the tribe would develop specific and highly complex patterns of behavior, and probably quickly—within a matter of a few generations, once they had got a language going. They would do so for the same reason that the baboons produce a baboon social system in captivity—because it is in the beast. And it is not just a general capacity that is in the beast—not just the capacity to learn, and to learn easily—which is all the culturalists bother to assume; it is the capacity to learn some things rather than others, to learn some things easily rather than others, to learn some things at one time rather than another, and to learn some rather specific things into the bargain.

This is an important point. I am not positing that initiation ceremonies or male rituals are instinctive, in any old sense of that term. I am positing that they are an outcome of the biology of the animal because he is programmed to behave in certain ways that will produce these phenomena, given a certain input of information. If this input does not occur, the behavior will not occur or will occur only in a modified or distorted form. The human organism is like a computer that is set up or wired in a particular way. The organism is thus in a state of readiness—at various points in the life cycle—to process certain kinds of information. The information has to be of a particular type, but the actual message can vary considerably. If the information is received, the 'computer' stores it and uses it to go on to the next task. If the system is confused, the 'machine' very easily breaks down, and might even blow the fuses. Of course, to push this analogy to its logical conclusion, there would have to be 'computers' feeding each other information. Only when they are synchronized would the total system run properly.

This, although crude, is a different model from that of the old instinctivists or the behaviorists. To the instinctivists, behavior resulted simply from the manifestation of innate tendencies that, in interaction, produced such things as territorialism, maternal behavior, or acquisitiveness. To the behaviorists the infant was a tabula rasa and behavior ultimately was the result of learning via conditioning. (Psychoanalysis leans to the instinctivist end, but is a special case in some ways.) I see the human organism as wired to process information about certain things, like language and rules about sex, and not about other things. It can process this information only at certain times and in certain ways. This wiring is geared to the life cycle so that at any one moment in a population of *Homo sapiens* there will be individuals with a certain store of behavior at one stage of the cycle giving out information to others at another stage who are wired to treat the information in a certain way. From the interaction of these individuals at various stages, certain typical relationships will emerge.

This may seem tortuous or obvious, but it *is* a different way of viewing human behavior and social structure from the orthodox one, which informs not only anthropology but the whole secular social ideology. The orthodox view says: When in trouble, change the program, because you can write any program you want to. What it should say is: When in trouble, find out what is in the wiring, because only then will you know what program you can safely write.

The culturalists acknowledge only a general capacity for culture, if they acknowledge anything at all about the general characteristics of the species. To them, all culture is pure human invention, and is passed on from generation to generation by symbolic learning. Thus, logically, it follows that if ever this store of culture should be lost, it is improbable that it would be invented again in the same forms. Something as specific as totemism and exogamy—that old anthropological chestnut—has to be seen in this view as a pure intellectual invention, and it would be unlikely that it would be invented again. But I think that my naive tribe, with no experience of any other human culture and no knowledge of totemism and exogamy, would produce both very quickly, and, moreover, that these phenomena would be immediately recognizable and analyzable by anthropologists. In fact, anthropologists who argued for the 'psychic unity of mankind' were acknowledging a similar position. They held that such customs had not been invented in one area and diffused throughout the world, but were stock responses of the human psyche to external pressures. They were reflections of 'human nature,' a phrase that anthropologists have been discouraged from using. The argument for psychic unity also had to face the constants-can't-explain-variables charge.

The psychic unity argument, however, was never pushed as far as I am pushing it. For these anthropologists the universal psyche had no specific 'content'—it was a capacity to do human things, but most of its proponents would have maintained that it was a general learning capacity and that culture was invented. At the level of specific content this is true—but there is a danger of being dazzled by this into ignoring those basic processes and forms that crop up with regularity, not to say monotony. (It is an error, however, to think that universal processes necessarily produce *uniform results*. Far from it. This is not true in the plant kingdom and is even less true in the animal.)

I can now return to the problem of the route by which I reached this conclusion. The question that had been plaguing me was really: How do we know what's in the wiring and how did it get there? For it is possible to find out what it is all about only if how it was constructed and to what end it was produced is known. It is no good trying to use an analogue computer as if it were a digital computer, because they were designed for different purposes. The answer to this should have been obvious, and soon became so. What is in the wiring of the human animal got there by the same route as it got into any other animal—by mutation and natural selection. These 'great constructors,' as Lorenz calls them, had produced remarkable end products in the social behavior of all kinds of animals, reptiles, birds, fish, and insects. And it is here that the message of Lorenz and his associates becomes important: behavior evolves just as structure evolves, and the evolution of the two is intimately linked.

Now we are back to Darwin's principle, from which anthropology so disastrously departed at the turn of the century. What the behavioral zoologists (in Europe usually known as 'ethologists') demonstrated was that units of behavior evolve on the same principle as units of anatomy and physiology—that a head movement that was part of a bird's innate repertoire of actions has an adaptive significance as great as the evolution of the wing itself. The head movement may be precisely what inhibits the attack of another bird, for example, and over the millennia it has become fixed as a signal recognized by the species as an inhibitor. Even if one does not accept that humans have 'instincts' of this kind (I think they have a few but not many), one should look at behavior as the end product of evolution and analyze it in terms of the selection pressures that produced it. If man has this marvellous flexibility in his learning patterns, then it must be a feature of the biology of the species. What should be asked is *why* he has it. What selection pressures operated to bring about this particular biological feature? The enormous dependence on culture as a mode of adaptation stands in need of explanation, for this, too, is a species-specific characteristic, and it drives man towards destruction as much as it raises him to glory. It is a two-edged weapon in the fight for survival, and the simple brutes with their instinctive head-wagging may well live to have the last laugh.

But the brutes, it has transpired, are not so simple. Man's cousins, the other primates, have an amazing complexity of social behavior. One thing the ethologist teaches is to compare the behavior of closely related species in order to get at their 'proto-behavior.' The flow of excellent material on nonhuman primates in the wild shows how many and subtle are the resemblances between them and man. Wider afield, the growing science of animal behavior shows that many mammals, and vertebrates generally, have social systems that duplicate features of human society, and in which similar processes occur—and even similar social pathologies. Lorenz showed how aggression was the basis of social bonding; V. C. Wynne-Edwards postulated that the 'conventionalized competition' that controlled aggression was itself rooted in the control of numbers; M.R.A. Chance demonstrated that among primates the elementary social bond was that between males rather than that between males and females, and so on. The politics of macaque monkeys suggests that Aristotle was right: insofar as he is a primate, man is by nature a political animal. (It is significant how often, when this is quoted, the phrase 'by nature' is omitted.) Ants can have societies, but ants cannot have politics. Politics occurs only when members can change places in a hierarchy as a result of competition. So man is more than social; he is political, and he is political because he is that kind of primate—terrestrial and gregarious.

As a consequence it becomes more and more obvious that man has a considerable animal heritage and hence a great store of comparative data to draw on in making generalizations about his own species. It forces upon us this observation: if man finds his own species displaying certain patterns of social behavior that duplicate those of other similar species, then he must conclude prima facie that these patterns are simply what would be expected from, say, a terrestrial primate, a land-dwelling mammal, a gregarious vertebrate, or whatever. Some aspects of these patterns and a great deal of their content will be unique, but this is only to say that they will be species-specific. Every species is unique because it is the end product of a particular path of evolution.

The real question—what is the nature of the uniqueness?—brings us back to where we started. And the question cannot be answered until it is known what man has in common with all other species, and with some other species, and with only closely related species. Thus the argument that man differs from all other species as a result of the triumph of culture over

biology I find false, because culture is an aspect of man's biological differences from other species. It is the name for a kind
of behavior found in the human species that ultimately depends on an organ, the brain, in which man happens to have
specialized. Man is different from other primates, not because
he has in some way *overcome* his primate nature, but because he
is a different kind of primate with a different kind of nature. At
the level of forms and processes man behaves culturally, because
mutation and natural selection have produced an animal that
must behave culturally—invent rules, make myths, speak languages, and form men's clubs, in the same way as the hamadryas
baboon must form harems, adopt infants, and bite his wives on
the neck.

But why culture? Why didn't man's simian ancestors content
themselves with a much less flexible, and perhaps at the time
less vulnerable, way of coping with nature's exigencies? This is
where another strand of evidence comes in—the material on
human evolution. In Darwin's day this was practically nonexis-
tent, and even now it is relatively meagre. But we can trace with
some confidence the general picture of man's evolution over a
period of at least five million years.

This is not the place for a detailed exposition of the accumulated knowledge; all I can do here is point out some of the implications of that new knowledge. Arthur Keith set the limit
of brain size below which was mere animal at 750 cubic centimetres. The modern human brain averages about 1400 cc.,
roughly twice that of Keith's minimum. The brain of the chim-
panzee is roughly 400 cc., that of the gorilla 500 cc. Modern discoveries have shown that true hominids have existed for at least
two million years and probably longer, and that at that early
date in their evolution they were indulging in activities that imply the existence of cultural traditions, even if of a rudimentary
form. The most striking evidence of this is the existence of toolmaking industries, first in bone and horn and then in stone
(wood does not survive but was undoubtedly used), among
small-brained hominids in East and South Africa. Two million
years ago, our ancestors with brain sizes ranging from 435 cc. to
680 cc.—only a little better than the gorilla—were doing hu-

man things, cultural things, before having reached the cerebral Rubicon. They were hunting, building shelters, making tools, treating skins, living in base camps, and possibly doing many other things (speaking languages perhaps?) that we cannot know directly, while their morphology was still predominantly apelike and their brains in some cases smaller than the modern ape's. What was not apelike about them was their dentition and their bipedal stance. In these features they were well launched on the road to humanity since both reflect the adaptation to a hunting way of life that differentiates these animals from their primate cousins.

I say these 'animals'; I might just as easily have said these 'men'—and this is the moral of the story. The record of evolution shows no sharp break between man and animal that can be pinpointed at a certain brain size or anything else. What it shows is a very gradual transition in which changes in locomotion led the way and in which the brain was something of a sluggard. The pelvis of the *Australopithecinae*—those ape men of South and East Africa—is strikingly human and totally unlike anything in an ape, because these were bipedal creatures; but the brain was, if anything, smaller than that of a gorilla—an animal not particularly noted for its cultural achievements.

The moral goes deeper. Once launched on the way to humanity through bipedalism, hunting, and the use of tools, man's ancestors became more dependent on their brains than their predecessors had been. If they were going to survive largely by skill and cunning and rapid adaptation to the changing circumstances of the Pleistocene epoch, a premium had to be put on the capacity for cultural behavior. Man took the cultural way before he was clearly distinguishable from the animals, and in consequence found himself stuck with this mode of adaptation. It turned out to be successful, although for a while it must have been touch and go. But because he became dependent on culture, mutation and natural selection operated to improve the organ most necessary to cultural behavior, the brain, and in particular the neocortex with its important functions of association and control. Those animals that were best able to be cultural were favored in the struggle for existence. Man's anatomy, physiology, and behavior are therefore in large part the *result* of culture. His large and efficient brain is a consequence of culture as much as its cause. He does not have a culture because he has a large brain; he has a large brain because several million years ago his little-brained ancestor tried the cultural way to survival. As cultural pressures grew, so did selection pressures for better brains; as better brains emerged, culture could take new leaps forward, thus in turn exerting more pressures.

This is an oversimplified account; the actual picture of the evolution of the brain is much more complex. But in essential outline it is true and, for immediate purposes, enough to make the point that man's uniqueness is a biological uniqueness and that culture does not in some mysterious sense represent a break with biology. The present human biological make-up is a consequence, among other things, of cultural selection pressures. Man is, therefore, biologically constituted to produce culture, not simply because by some accident he got a brain that could do cultural things, but because the cultural things themselves propelled him into getting a larger brain. Man is not simply the *producer* of institutions like the family, science, language, religion, warfare, kinship systems, and exogamy; he is the *product* of them. Hence it is scarcely surprising that man continually reproduces that which produced him. He was selected to do precisely this, and in the absence of tuition the mythical naive tribe would do it all over again in the same way. It is not only the *capacity* for culture, then, that lies in the brain; it is the *forms* of culture, the universal grammar of language and behavior.

This, then, is how it all got into the wiring of the human computer. These are the facts about human evolution, and there need be no great mystery about the production of culture by human beings and the relative uniformity of its processes. There are many mysteries of fact that will never be solved, since the behavior of fossil man can only be inferred. But, in principle, once it is accepted that culture is the major selection pressure operating on the evolution of human form and behavior, and that it has produced an animal wired for the processing of various cultural programs, the uniqueness of man becomes a problem on the same level as the uniqueness of any other animal species.

Combining the insights of the ethologists and the students of human evolution, we can scan the behavior of related species for aspects of behavior that are common to all primates and, beyond that, look to mammals and vertebrates for clues. For in the process of evolution man did not cease to be a primate or a mammal. Weston LaBarre has said that part of man's success lies in exaggerating certain mammalian tendencies rather than in losing them—length of suckling, for example. Much human behavior—in particular, social arrangements—can be seen as a variation on common primate and gregarious-mammalian themes. Certain 'unique' aspects—such as the use of true language—can be investigated for what they are, biological specializations produced by the unique evolutionary history of the species.

This perspective enables human society and behavior to be viewed comparatively, without any necessity to propound theories of the total and essential differences between man and other animals. It puts the obvious uniqueness into perspective and does not allow man's commonality with the animal kingdom to be lost sight of. Man is indeed the cultural animal, but both terms should be given equal weight; one does not contradict the other. Culture does not represent a triumph over nature, for such a thing is impossible; it represents an end product of a natural process. It is both the producer and the product of man's human nature, and in behaving culturally he is behaving naturally.

It is often said that man has lost all his instincts. I think this is a bit too extreme. If I may paraphrase Oscar Wilde: to lose some of one's instincts is unfortunate, to lose all of them smacks of carelessness. No species could afford to be that careless. But it is true that of instincts ('innate mechanisms which produce items of behavior complete at their first performance and relatively unmodifiable by experience') man has very few. Instead, it is often claimed, he has intelligence, foresight, wisdom, and the like, and the enormous capacity to learn. In rejecting instinct for intelligence he took something of a risk, since instinct does provide a sureness of response that has been evolved from trial and error over millions of years. Ant societies are much better organized and more efficient than any human societies and are driven wholly on instinctive mechanisms. But instinct has its costs. It is too rigid. Changed circumstances cannot be met by a rapid adjustment in behavior. Insects and animals heavily dependent on instinct have to wait for processes of genetic change to effect changes in the instincts themselves before they can adjust. The higher up the phyletic scale the less true this is, and with man it is least true of all. Thus, there is a cost-benefit analysis in the shedding of innate instincts in favor of more complex modes of behaving.

The crux of the matter is this: even if a species sheds its dependence on instincts, it still has to do the same things that instincts were designed to do. As Bergson saw so clearly, culture has to do the same job that instinct had been doing. This is another paradox, I suppose, but an intriguing one, because to get culture to do the same jobs that instinct had been doing, cultural behavior had been made in many ways like instinctive behavior. It had to be unconscious so that it did not require thought for its operation; it had to be automatic so that certain stimuli would immediately produce it; it had to be common to all members of the population.

How much of man's cultural behavior is in fact intelligent and conscious, and how much is at that unthinking, automatic-response level? Most human behavior is automatic, absorbed during socialization, and built into patterns of habitual thought, belief, and response. Indeed, habit is, as William James said, the great flywheel of society. Anthropologists speak of 'covert' or 'unconscious' culture to refer to this iceberg of assumptions, values, and habitual responses. And sitting over all of them is the great evolutionary invention of conscience, superego, moral sense, or whatever you want to call it. The sense of guilt, of having broken the taboos, the rules, the laws of the tribe, keeps most people in line most of the time. Conscience is an empty canister that culture fills; but once filled, it becomes a dynamic controller of behavior. Most of man's behavior, however, never even rises to the point where conscience and the sense of guilt need to step in. Man does what he does from habit, even down to the smallest details and gestures and twitches of the facial muscles. Most of this is never thought about; but people who do not behave 'normally' are quickly recognized—and are often locked up in asylums as lunatics. Think only of Erving Goffman's example of the man walking down the road in the rain without a raincoat, smiling, shoulders back, head facing the sky. Clearly a madman. He should be hunched, hurrying and looking miserable, with his jacket collar drawn up at least.

The genius of nature here stands revealed and the paradox is resolved. Of course most of man's learned cultural behavior operates almost exactly like instinct. This has to be the case. This is not foolproof, but neither is instinct itself. So the same effect is achieved, and those habits that have proved useful in survival become part of the behavioral repertoire. But these habits can be changed within a generation. It is not necessary to wait for the long process of natural selection to operate before these quasi-instinctual behaviors can be modified; they can be modified very rapidly to meet changing circumstances. Thus, man has all the benefits of instinctive behavior without its disadvantages. At any one time the rigidity of cultural habits will be just as invulnerable to change as instincts—as a moment's reflection on the persistence of traditions will confirm—and habits are extremely conservative. Since most of them are passed on by means other than direct tuition, they tend to persist for generations despite changes in deliberate education. But they can be changed relatively rapidly compared with the time span needed for changes in genetic material. Thus man can make rapid adjustments without creating anarchy (which does not mean that he always does so).

Here again cultural behavior can be seen as yet another kind of biological adaptation. At this level, other species also display behavior of the same kind, and the higher in the scale they are, the more dependent they become on habits transferred through generations by learning rather than instincts transferred in the genetic code. But it must always be kept in mind that this is not a sharp distinction. The code is not silent about learning and habits. Instructions about habitual behavior are as much in the code as instructions about instinctive behavior.

This model of behavior sees the human actor as a bundle of potentialities rather than a tabula rasa: potentialities for action, for instinct, for learning, for the development of unconscious habits. These potentialities or predispositions or biases are the end products of a process of natural selection peculiar to the human species. One consequence of this view is that much of the quasi-instinctive cultural behavior of man can be studied in more or less the same way and by many of the same methods as ethologists study the truly instinctive behavior of other animals.

I began with the theme of human uniqueness, and end with my point that it has to be interpreted in the same way as the uniqueness of any other species. Anthropologists have to ask 'How come?' How did culture get into the wiring? How did the great constructors operate to produce this feature, which, like everything else about man, is not antinature or superorganic or extrasomatic or any of the other demagogic fantasy states that science and religion imagine for him? Darwin did not banish mind from the universe as Butler feared; indeed, he gave man a basis for explaining how mind got into the universe in the first place. And it got there—as did every other natural and biological feature—by natural selection. The toolmaking animal needed mind to survive; that is, he needed language and culture and the reorganization of experience that goes with these. And, once he got the rudiments and became dependent on them, there was no turning back. There was no retreat to the perilous certainty of instinct. It was mind or nothing. It was classification and verbalization, rules and laws, mnemonics and knowledge, and ritual and art that pressed upon the precarious species, demanding better and better brains to cope with this new organ—culture—that was now essential to survival. Two related processes, thought and self-control, evolved together, and their end product is the cultural animal, who speaks and rules himself because that is the kind of animal he is; because speaking and self-discipline have made him what he is; because he is what he produces and was produced by what he is.

2

Inhuman Nature and Unnatural Rights

> Born into life—we bring
> A bias with us here,
> And, when here, each new thing
> Affects us we come near;
> To tunes we did not call our being must keep chime
> > Matthew Arnold, *Empedocles on Etna*, 1852

> Blushing, the idiot rose to his feet. He removed, with respect, his battered gray tam and stared down at his boots. "Logic only gives man what he needs," he stammered. "Magic gives him what he wants."
> > Tom Robbins, *Another Roadside Attraction*, 1971

> If man derives all his knowledge from the sensible world and from his experience of the sensible world, then this is to say that the empirical world should be arranged in such a way that man experiences and assimilates there what is really human, that he experiences himself as man.
> > Karl Marx, *Die Heilige Familie*, 1845

As an undergraduate student of anthropology and philosophy at London University in the 1950s I was faced with what seemed to be an irreconcilable conflict. The philosophers argued with compelling and urbane elegance that the naturalistic fallacy was just that: a fallacy. 'Ought' we were told, could never be derived from 'is.' Ought, in fact, could never be derived from anything, it seemed. On the one hand the logical positivists were firm in their assertion that any 'ought' statements were emotive or prescriptive and that was that; on the other, the existentialists were telling us much the same thing under a different guise: that all was contingent, not to say absurd, and that one made more or less bloody-minded choices and stuck to them. This was 'commitment.'

The one philosophy resulted in a kind of genteel north-Oxford inaction (as criticized by Gellner) and the other went off in all directions from left-bank gloom to the tortuous Marxism of Sartre's *Critique* and subsequent communist involvement, and this left at least one student with a sinking feeling that, while they might not be actively corrupting youth, these philosophers were not giving it much guidance either.

This was particularly so since in anthropology and sociology we were faced with analysis, prescription, and judgement which, if the philosophers were to be believed, was neither methodologically sound nor ethically viable. In effect, it was metaphysical nonsense and emotive assertions riddled with bad faith.

To the philosophical arguments—all the heirs of the amazing Hume—one could offer no answer, which was uncomfortable. It was as uncomfortable as one's failure to refute Berkeley's idealism: it was indeed irrefutable, but one knew it to be wrong. One also knew that even if prescriptions did not follow and could not follow from descriptions, they had to follow from something, and it was depressing to feel that they followed from nothing more than arbitrary likes, dislikes, or commitments.

Philosophy was equally scornful of 'natural rights.' There were 'rules of the game' that were human inventions, but in no sense could these be construed as given by nature. That would be to derive ought from is again—which would be, as we know, impossible and even distasteful.

The prime example of the naturalistic fallacy always quoted was the sin of advancing the more evolved as the best. One does not have to repeat all the elegant Oxfordian arguments here to the effect that if we equate more evolved with good, then we rob the language of a word—a worse sin than robbing the Bank of England. Granted. But in anthropology we were at the same time learning how, in a very positive sense, some organisms were better adapted to specific environments than others; how some gene pools contained greater fitness—all measureable; and how an organism like man was an all-round better adaptable risk than others because of its flexibility—and so on. Of course the concepts of good and better here had to be defined differently from adapted or fitness or we did impoverish the language and end in tautology. At the same time, it was clear that we were, in the study of evolution, making quite profound judgements about relative merits that were not simply emotive noises or esthetic preferences. It was better to be better adapted in the simple sense that otherwise the organism or species or population would likely vanish.

Equally in sociology, despite the rash of cultural relativism which would have had every culture and society as good as every other, we were constantly looking at patterns of social adaptedness, where it was clear that some cultures were less well able to survive than others. They 'functioned' less well in the jargon of the time. Again, it seemed that, as long as one accepted *survival* as a criterion, one was saying something more here than just a hurrah or boo.

But philosophy and ethics were implacable. One was simply stating preferences. There was nothing in nature that gave precedence. Cultures or species were simply there. To say that one was, for whatever reason, better or worse was to express approval and dislike; that was all.

The cultural relativist wing of anthropology aided and abetted this attitude, and was, perhaps, a child of the same conditions that bred this particular philosophy. All cultures were indeed equal, and to rank them was simply to express prejudice. This was a counter to ethnocentric Western European cultures automatically ranking themselves top, on some self-appointed scale of progress, with the poor benighted savages relegated to bottom place. What the relativists never seemed to realize, however, was that their logic did not abolish ethnocentrism, it simply *extended* the privilege to *all* societies!

None of these attitudes, embroidered into schools and disciplines, left room for absolutes, categorical imperatives, or natural rights—and none, certainly, with their heavy empirical bias in epistemology, would have had any room for instincts or innate ideas.

And it was not only the Viennese and Parisian biases that ruled out such considerations. Throughout the social sciences (and behavioral sciences generally) the innate was having a bad press. Darwin and evolution were definitely out of fashion; evolutionary ethics the last word in fallacious naturalism; and evolutionism a term of abuse which was only rendered less severe by the overtones of gentle ridicule it had acquired.

The social philosophers seemed as much the heirs of Mill as the philosophers of knowledge were the heirs of Hume. They shared a thoroughgoing, robust empiricism with a scorn of innate ideas and an indulgent fondness for the tabula rasa. Like Mill they would advance the argument (and still do) that to flirt with the innate was to flirt with reaction, racism, and finally fascism.

This led the sociological wing into some confusion. To be a thorough empiricist-individualist in the Utilitarian tradition was to deny the strength of Durkheimian collectivism—so necessary to the autonomy of the subject. It was also to deny such collectivism as Marx derived from Hegel. So, while espousing a modified collectivism, they drew the line at idealism (group minds were out), and shunned nativism.

The link they wished to both forge and sunder—and they did both with excruciating logical gymnastics—had bothered, for example, Hobhouse, in his critique of idealism and its dreadful consequences (*The Metaphysical Theory of the State*). It was a constant tension in sociology, although perhaps not always recognized as such; and as with all such tensions it was likely to produce pathological reactions in the patient when faced with an unpleasant stimulus. That such reactions were not always reasonable follows from the ambivalence of the subject—a known clinical condition.

The stimulus, of course, was any doctrine of the innate. Mill had declared such doctrines to be hopelessly reactionary of their very nature—for what was innate was not changeable and it was all too easy to point to what is and regularly has been, declare it innate, and hence unalterable; a position obviously anathema to reforming radicals. That Mill was wrong is obvious, but we must leave the exploration of the 'unnaturalistic fallacy' for a while and look further at the pathology.

Anything, then, that might link a doctrine of the innate

with an idealistic collectivism would obviously send shivers of horror down (or up) the collective spine of empiricist-relativist-reformist social thinkers; particularly, those social thinkers who wished to espouse a lukewarm collectivism while shunning the innate. To tell them that society (or 'the social') was indeed a reality sui generis and more than the sum of its individuals, but that this was because society was located in the gene pool of the species, was to produce panic bordering on terror. Yet, this is what that remarkable group of neo-Darwinian naturalists, the ethologists, had the intellectual impudence to do. Instead of floating lazily around in a haze of collective representations or even class consciousness, society had a definite material and wholly explicable location in patterns of evolved adaptive social behavior characteristic of a species, refracted into various versions by the local histories of each population. Marx would probably have been delighted: he and Engels would have had no trouble with sociobiology: only their lumpen-intellectual followers have that problem today.

The response, when the ethologists (and their few enthusiastic hangers-on from the social sciences) dared to suggest that this may be as true for man as for lesser beings, was a hectic attempt to deny man's animality, the method's validity, and the compassion and integrity of the scientists involved. No insult has been too much, no distortion or innuendo too extreme. When one is defending truth and goodness, any form of excommunication is permitted and even honored.

The anthropologists, who at least pay lip service to the importance of man's physicality and his evolution, might have been expected to cock a friendly ear in this direction. But they mostly reacted with even more incoherent indignation. For what was breached here was the distinction Lévi-Strauss has taught us is basic and sacred: that between Nature and Culture. Not only savage minds are overwhelmed when, as in the case of incest, this distortion is threatened, but the even more savage mentalities of post-Tylorian anthropologists are afflicted with grisly horror. For heirs to Huxley's disastrous distinction between cosmic and ethical evolution; Spencer's and Kroeber's between 'organic' and 'superorganic'; and that of Boas between 'genetic' and 'cultural,' they, like the savage, can only resort to incantation when the distinction is, however gently, declared irrelevent.

The bête noire here is racism and its sister-in-crime aggression. In the same way that all cultures are the same to proponents of this happy Weltanschauung, so are all races; and no one is aggressive but evil circumstances make him so. Mill would have been proud of them. But even he might have been hard put to explain how the evil circumstances came about in the first place. For which is worse, to have creatures who are inevitably aggressive or to have creatures who inevitably produce circumstances that inevitably produce aggression? No matter. To suggest the location of any profound behaviors in the biology of the creatures, and particularly in their more unsavory tendencies, was to offend against equality, progress, and human perfectibility, and so be the potentially reactionary, a priorist villain that Mill denounced in the unlikely person of Sir William Hamilton.

It is for the sociologist of knowledge to explore the paradox of liberalism which, at least in the United States and in scattered parts of Europe, has become coterminous with environmentalism and so the exact counterpart of Soviet doctrinaire Pavlovianism. In each case—reaching lunatic heights with Lysenko in Russia and Skinner in the United States—the innate is denied significance and the environment made prime mover. Behaviorism in psychology, philosophy, and the social sciences, dominates both East and West, and in the name of both liberal democracy and the dictatorship of the proletariat the completely manipulable man is made the model of explanation and practice.

That liberal-radical democrats in capitalist America should march ideologically hand in hand with communist-totalitarians in the Soviet Union might appear on the surface odd. But these people have more in common with each other than with beleaguered pessimists like myself, or even with the naturally conservative majority of mankind who are less likely to be intoxicated with their own rhetoric than those whose business it is to trade outrageous ideas for dubious action in that half-world between intellect and politics glorified by the name of theory. For the radicals are all dedicated to serious and cumulative change; change not only in social institutions, but—and they have at least the wit to see this—in the *very nature* of the people who support the institutions. For people must be motivated to practice the bright new institutions that either capitalist individualists or socialist collectivists wish upon them. Therefore, purveyors of either progressive-liberal or revolutionary-socialist solutions have to adhere to a doctrine of human perfectibility as a matter of principle. There is no old Adam in this philosophy; no original sin. There is only an infinitely perfectible human machine and a totally unoriginal virtue that will be implanted by the benign, self-appointed mentors. One understands their antipathy to doctrines of the innate. It is easy to follow the reasoning: the innate is what it is and is ineradicable; it is not subject to willful change; it is not at the mercy of ideologues, and is therefore suspect; if it exists, its existence is best denied. For an extension of the argument says that even if it *does* exist, then it is dangerous to admit of its existence, since this will *encourage* reactionaries!

Why this environmentalist doctrine should be so deeply entrenched in both communist and capitalist ideologies is, therefore, easy to see. Both are equally abandoning the feudal universe and the fixed order of nature; both are concerned to remold man in accordance with the dictates of a new environment, be it socialist utopia or capitalist production line. Both wish to erect an unnatural order; that is, an order made according to rational decision, not an order evolved from the needs of human nature. To this extent, then, 'human nature' must be denied, at least insofar as it appears to stand in the way of rational reformist action. It is not so much that human nature is repudiated (Mill reckoned men were incurably greedy and lazy), but that only those attributes that suit the reformist are allowed to exist in it.

One must also note a curiosity: that this hostility to the innate started as a hostility to the reactionary possibilities of innate *ideas*. Thus, John Locke attacked the doctrine for "the power it gives one man or another—to make a man swallow that for an innate *principle* which may serve to his purpose who teacheth them." (Italics mine). Thus, men's *natures* could well be seen as having fixed features (Mill's greed and laziness) but this did not matter as long as their *ideas* could be changed. It was with the waning of the Enlightenment overvaluation of ideas and reason—the rise even of Darwinism—that the hostility was extended beyond the limits of Platonic innateness—of ideas—to feelings, sentiments, predispositions—in short, to 'instincts' broadly conceived. This leads to endless ideological confusion. A great modern proponent of the anti-innate view, Ashley Montagu, can, on the one hand, insist that 97 percent (or is it 98 percent?) of human behavior is learned and not innate, and on the other insist that man is by nature good, kind, cooperative, altruistic, gentle, and so forth and so on. (But certainly not cruel, vicious, aggressive, sadistic: these are the product of evil circumstances, of course.) Even René Dubos, in his anxiety to defend the goodness of man, endorses a scurrilous and disreputable book with the same argument. Man's altruism, he says in one breath, is deeply rooted in his biological nature; but isn't it marvelous, he says in the next, that the author should point out how man has transcended his nature in order to be good and altruistic and shun war! Since Dubos is an honest biologist, he cannot deny the biological basis of this essential trait; but since he is also a profoundly confused humanist, he feels it necessary to sever the links with biology in case he might be tricked into admitting something nasty exists in the woodshed of human nature.

These examples could be multiplied, and one is alternately appalled by the viciousness of the proponents of human peacefulness like the author Dubos endorses, or saddened by the intellectual confusion that afflicts the basically humane people like Dubos who feel, like Mill, that to admit content to human nature might be to admit a Pandora's box of aggressive and malign intentions.

That altruism and aggression are not incompatible—and indeed might be necessary to each other—and that they are both, in their ultimate expression, a combination of innate propensities and environmental input, is obvious to students of the evolution of behavior, and virtually uncontroversial. It is only when these facts hit the heady realms of liberal ideology that otherwise intelligent men go haywire in their contradictory defenses of the manipulable man who both has no nature at all and is naturally good at the same time.

This all makes me follow with fascination and sympathy the dilemma of Noam Chomsky. No one, surely, can challenge *his* radical credentials, but, to the infinite puzzlement (and even greater embarrassment) of his left-wing colleagues, he espouses a vigorous doctrine of innate (linguistic) ideas. Since the radicals by now have accepted as a fact of the universe the total identification of this position with reactionary politics, Chomsky totally baffles them. His gentle and brilliant admonitions to examine the empty organism position rationally fall on unhappy and largely deaf ears. I can't decide whether this is tragic or hilarious (they're often not that different). But I do feel for Chomsky. (See his *Reflections on Language*, pp. 132–133).

For the record, I would rather hope that man has *some* nature, that it is indeed innate, and that it is aggressively concerned with the assertion of compassion, altruism, sharing, and other basic human virtues. I would rather hope for this than be stuck with a human tabula rasa on which any tyrants or do-gooders can write their (always benign) messages at will. And I think man *has* such a nature, that it is intensely social, and that it gives the lie to all sanctimonious manipulators from Mill through Stalin. Given the dilemmas of our technological hubris, I think it is also our only hope—certainly more so than the pious platitudes of the perfectionist liberals or the assertive prescriptions of socialism.

Lest this argument seem to be totally cranky and idiosyncratic, let me quote something from Lionel Trilling which is particularly appropriate, since he is rightly regarded as one of the great liberal critics. Here is Trilling on Freud:

> Now Freud may be right or he may be wrong in the place he gives to biology in human fate, but I think we must stop to consider whether this emphasis on biology, correct or incorrect, is not so far from being a reactionary idea that it is actually a

liberating idea. It proposes to us that culture is not all powerful. It suggests that there is a residue of human quality beyond the reach of cultural control. (*Beyond Culture*, p. 98)

But let us return for a moment to the calm waters of ethical theory where good and evil are elements in equations rather than problems of real life. Throughout the undergraduate period I was describing, an almost lone voice protested against the amoralism of the philosophers and the relativism of the anthropologists, that of Morris Ginsberg. He protested that moral argument was not largely emotive but factual; that men agreed on moral ends but argued about means; that there were indeed moral universals but there was no universal agreement about the range of their application. On the basis of these moral universals, then—universals which must surely reflect something in human nature—it was possible to erect a truly *rational* ethical discourse: essentially a discussion of means and applications. Thus all societies agree that murder is wrong and generosity good; they disagree about what constitutes murder and to whom one should be generous. We do not need to look further, he suggests, than the universal ends revealed by the comparative study of morals for a basis for a rational ethic.

Now, in such a position there seemed to be hope, although at the time I felt it did not go far enough, and feel so still. But it did suggest some basis in fact—the revelations of the comparative sociology of morals—for a rational code of ethics. The problem with it was, for me, that the prescriptions woven into moral codes were not necessarily representative of the whole range of human activities on which a social philosophy should be based. They were primarily negative, and concerned with what man feared in his own nature rather than what he exalted. A true attempt to base a rational ethic on human nature, or to formulate a natural basis for a system of natural rights, had to go further.

At the time, however, I could not see how to take it further. Clearly, in a theoretical sense, there must be a set of behaviors and their consequent social institutions that were more 'natural' to man than others—and one sincerely hoped that these would be congruent with one's liberal prejudices; but how to ascertain these? Aristotle could assert that slavery was natural, and Verwoed could do the same with apartheid, Spencer with laissez-faire capitalism, and Rousseau with equality. How did we decide? And having decided, on what basis did we assert that the natural was better?

One thing was certain, natural and instinctive were not one and the same thing, at least with *Homo sapiens*. Even then we could see that the old instinctivism would not do. It took the ethologists with their neo-instinctivism to teach us this, much as they are caricatured to the contrary. What we are equipped with is innate *propensities* that require environmental input for their realization. Thus, what we need to look for is a combination of the innate predispositions and the range of environments compatible with them. Any prescriptions would take the form: "We are programmed to do X and this requires environment Y; if we wish to see the maturity of X we must provide Y." Thus, for example, we know that there is no simple maternal instinct or even mating instinct but that an organism's capacity for a full display of maternal or sexual behavior depends on the organism itself having had a secure maternal relationship. Thus, the organism has, as it were, an output of energy in the early stages that demands the environment of maternal security. We know this as a result of the classic ethological 'deprivation experiment'—take away the environment and the maturation of the innate potential is thwarted. Instinct is the organism's demand for an appropriate environment.

The possibility was dimly emerging then, of a scheme whereby the innate demands and the necessary environmental stimuli could be catalogued so that we could eventually sketch the parameters within which human social arrangements had to operate *in order to be human*. Outside this, any demands made on the organism—any environments created for it—would be, literally, inhuman.

If we take an animal example, it is simpler and more obvious. A rooster crows, displays, struts, pecks, copulates, fights, and so forth. We do not feel we have to *justify* the rooster's crowing, for example; we need no theory of the rooster's *right* to crow. We recognize that if we prevent this we are taking away something intrinsic to being a rooster. We could say that all these things are a rooster's *needs:* things it has to do to realize fully its rooster-hood. The rooster, of course, lacking consciousness and imagination, cannot, like ourselves, have *wants* in addition to its needs. (We could almost define man as the animal that wants things.) The rooster cannot *want* things it does not need; humans can. And here they get into real trouble—but that is almost another story. We have touched on it in looking at the claims of those who *want* man to be perfectible. (I only want him to be human and, God knows, that is difficult enough.) One problem is that because of the dominance of wants—wishes, desires, aspirations, and utopias—we have lost touch with our needs; lost touch to the extent that we constantly sacrifice needs to wants like the animals in fables who have delusions of grandeur and end in disaster. This is surely in one sense a philosophy of caution, but, and contrary to Mill's expectations, it can turn out to be functionally quite radical. For in order to restore our humanity, in order to jettison outrageous wants and return to the satisfaction of basic needs, we may have to cut through a Gordian knot of 'civilized' behavior and industrial institutions that have outstripped our capacity to handle them. To restore the basic conservatism of the species may require the most radical action of all.

And here we must note another curiosity in the history of ideas. We have seen how the doctrine of innate ideas was hitched to reaction and why. But at least for the great conservatives of the eighteenth century, it was the proponents of innateness—of human nature—who were the dangerous revolutionary fellows, not the Lockeans and the Humeans and other empiricists. Take Burke's argument: we have to support the institutions of society as they stand, as we have learned them—since these are all we have. They are our rational bulwark against irrational (innate) passions. Burke quite consistently opposed the Rousseauistic French revolutionaries because they chose to upset established institutions (the social contract for Burke) with their claims for human rights based on human nature—hence natural rights. Thus, it was those with the doctrines of the innate who were seen as the dangerous revolutionaries—as indeed we are (Or at least *could* be. No political doctrine *follows* from either position, in fact; it is what you choose to make it.) Thus also, as Hofstadter and Burrow among others have pointed out, these conservative and radical labels slip about a lot in the nineteenth century and may or may not correlate with anyone's position on the innate. The nineteenth-century radicals were likely to be progressive, laissez-faire, Darwinian individualists, while their socialist counterparts were often agrarian conservatives, opposing change and progress (as conceived by the radical capitalists) as strenuously as Burke. In short, there is no *logical* connection between any doctrines of innateness or their opposite and any political stance: the connection is always forced.

But to return to the rooster. We can see that by depriving it of certain behaviors we would prevent it from being a rooster, since these behaviors define it as much as its anatomy defines it. At some point, sufficient deprivation could mean that it ceased to function as a rooster at all, which could mean its genetic death. If we did this to all roosters, the species would become rapidly extinct. Once one is up against this sheer fact of species survival, then the nature of the basic needs is obvious; and assuming that survival is accepted as a goal, the question of what to do about it is not difficult.

With man, we have, at least during the period since the Neolithic revolution, not been faced with any such problem: *as a species.* This or that population has faced the problem of survival, but the species as a whole has progressively expanded, filled the earth, changed the environment and radically transformed its own mode of existence. All this has happened, in evolutionary terms, virtually overnight. But during this 10,000-year period of unprecedented good weather and population expansion, wants have dominated needs to the extent that many behaviors and institutions that in the pre-Neolithic were simply *needs* that the community met, are now *rights* that can be extended or withheld, but above all, have to be justified.

We never feel we have to justify the cock's right to crow. We can scarcely even conceive of it as a right: it is simply what the cock does to be a cock. But we have elaborately to justify the 'right to work' or the 'right to vote' or the 'right to education'—

and, as we have seen, the philosophers will warn us of the naturalistic fallacy—of concluding that because men *need* to contrib-
ute to a group of which they are a part, that they *need* to be
involved in its power structure however indirectly, and that
they *need* to be informed of and initiated into its knowledge and
mysteries—because they *need* all these things this does not mean
they ought to have them. 'Ought' is a value judgement. We are
saying only 'hurrah work' or 'boo slavery.'

But—if as in our deprivation experiment with the rooster,
we progressively take away the satisfaction of these needs from
the majority of men, then whether we 'ought' to or not, we will
be faced with the consequence of extinction—or at least such
considerable malfunction that we might prefer extinction. Natural needs may not, in this abstract scheme, imply natural rights—
but then what does? Only a creature with wants would get so
confused: only a creature capable of making value judgements
would exercise them so badly.

In the natural, small, hunting communities in which we
evolved there were no ethical theorists. If there had been, we
would probably not have made it. It would have been as if the
roosters had spawned philosophers to tell them they had no
right to crow, fight, and breed as of nature, but had to justify
these things. Our ancestors were too busy surviving to care much
about wants or rights. They understood their needs (which included esthetic and spiritual needs) and they met these with
their communal and individual resources. They did not justify
hunting: they hunted to live and to survive and it was its own
justification. It was what men did. They had not much choice,
any more than the rooster. With the agricultural revolution and
the staggering population spurt, with the creation of a surplus
and a leisure class, wants came to dominate needs, theories to
confuse practice, and any sense of the immediacy of human
needs was lost. For even the peasant, on whom this fantasy structure that we call civilization rested, was himself as stripped of
major aspects of his humanity as the cultivated elite his tedious
labors supported. Even freedom had to be justified in this context—which is a little like justifying the rooster's crowing. The
Paleolithic hunter would not have understood.

What I am aiming at should be obvious: to understand the parameters of which I spoke, and which define our humanity, we must explore our evolutionary history and ask what are our inbuilt potentials, and what is the necessary environmental input for the realization of that humanity. Our ethic, then, would be avowedly naturalistic. It would state that all human action, that all social policy, should operate within human parameters and hence avoid the inhuman. To do less is to risk the survival of the species. To deprive human beings of their humanity beyond a certain point is to destroy the species or at least seriously distort it. To deny human beings the satisfaction of human needs is, by definition, to cut at the roots of being human.

Of course these are, stated thus, no more than the usual pious platitudes of good men everywhere. But with a difference. I want to define human not in terms of *wants,* not in terms of utopian expectations, Utilitarian formulas, theoretical possibilities or theological vistas, but in terms of what we know to be the repertoire of evolved behavior of the species *Homo sapiens.* I am not asking that we have a world in which all men will be good, perfect, socialist, angelic, or democratic, but that we have a world in which they are *human.* This need not be a totally pretty or pleasant world. It will likely contain, as well as the angelic qualities, its share of greed, jealousy, conflict, hate, killing, and exploitation. But—and this, I recognize is a statement of faith—we can work out a human scale for all these things. Exploitation among friends is one thing; among nations or classes, it is a disaster that could end everything.

All this assumes that we can indeed track down the essentials of human social nature, and having done so, we can act on this knowledge to produce an environment congruent with our needs. I am more sanguine on the first point than the second. The work of animal behaviorists, evolutionary geneticists, structural linguists, developmental psychologists, paleontologists, anthropologists, neurophysiologists, endocrinologists, and comparative ethnographers, promises, if treated in an evolutionary or biosocial framework, to yield the material we need. We can put together the information on our evolutionary past and physiological present, together with our knowledge of the range

of sociocultural experiments in which we have indulged, to establish the parameters of humanity. Many of us are, despite the
abuse of the good people, working to this end with growing success. But whether, having established the repertoire of human
needs and possible environments, we can cut through the morass
of wants that have turned into needs (jet travel, for example),
or through the theories based on the assumption that whatever
man wants to be he can be perfected into being, or through the
appalling consequences of the population-technology explosion that has overtaken this rather conservative, several-million-
year-old species, I do not know. One thing is certain: our evolved
repertoire was not intended for this environment. We may well
be evolved to fight, for example, but not at a distance with
weapons of ultimate destruction. We are certainly evolved to be
gregarious—but not in nations of 600 million, or in cities of 15
million. We are probably evolved to travel—but not around the
world in 80 minutes. We are an animal that has lost forever
the intimate scale of its natural evolution and lost its head in the
process.

But we can at least approach the unprecedented and truly
awful conditions that we have created for ourselves with a full
knowledge of what it is we are doing and are equipped to do. If
we know firmly what range of social contexts is required for each
and every human to realize his humanity, then we can strain in
that direction; as opposed to assuming that we can create whatever kind of humans we wish in whatever image our godlike
pretensions dictate. We are tampering with an old animal whose
behavior goes back to primate roots more than 70 million years
old, and to mammalian and even reptilian roots that are much
older still. We are a unique animal, but we were formed slowly
over several million years, and at least 99 percent of our existence—when our uniqueness was being molded on the African
savanna—was the existence of a small-scale hunter. This is
what established our parameters. The agricultural, sedentary
world is a mere 10,000 years old, and the industrial world with
its even more alarming transformation is only 200 years old.
Yesterday. We are an old animal coping with a startling new
world of its own creation that has gotten out of hand.

But we, no more than the rooster, can afford the luxury of an ethical theory that denies natural rights or rational ethics; nor can we afford a political philosophy or even working ideology that denies content to human nature. It is too late for that. It may be too late for anything. But, contrary to what Mill and his latter-day followers maintain, to look hard at, and accept the limitations of, human nature as a basis for political action, may turn out to be the least reactionary and most strenuously radical act of the twentieth century. But it will, in the nonpejorative sense of the word, be also a truly conservative act. So often we are told that man, because of his wonderful capacity for culture is able to say 'no' to his own nature (seen, one supposes, as brutish and nasty). But nature usually has the last laugh in these matters, and as one who is constantly shaken by the evidence of man's capacity to create truly hideous and revolting cultures, I would feel happier to think that something in human nature was always going to be able to say 'no' to human culture in the name of common humanity. I draw slight comfort from the evidence that that is so; that man cannot be indefinitely brainwashed by tyrants or liberals (and there are no worse tyrants than thwarted liberals), but that some of the old Adam resists the manipulation of the culture mongers, even violently. In this distastefully aggressive assertion of his natural rights, lies perhaps his last best hope.

But I doubt that the philosophers, relativists, behaviorists, radicals, liberals, socialists, and all the other products of human *wanting* will agree. If Jefferson said, "Always trust the people," perhaps I am saying, "Always trust our essential human nature." It is, after all, all we have in the end, if we will let it alone to do its natural business. It got by quite well without the theories until very *very* recently; and only since the theories has it gone astray.

We are now like roosters in some bizarre Aesopian tale, discussing whether crowing and pecking are in order; or, even worse, trying to find out if we really are an animal that crows and pecks, and if so, what we should do about it. Paradoxically, we might be forced to conclude that it is in our nature to create such quandaries for ourselves, so the situation is perfectly natural as it is. This smacks of the Cretan liar and his notoriously unsolvable paradox. But while it might be, in a sense, natural for us to create tragic dilemmas for ourselves, it is surely in some sense also unnatural—or at least literally inhumane—to create quandaries that negate our own nature. Even to be unnatural is not so bad; it is being inhumane that is the problem. Being bad is not so bad either; and being good is nowhwere near as important as ethical theory would have it be. The problem is to be human.

3

Darwin and the Donation of Durkheim 1: Liberalism and the Legacy of Locke

> Man was destined for society. His morality, therefore, was to be formed to this object. He was endowed with a sense of right and wrong, merely relative to this. This sense is as much a part of his nature as the sense of hearing, seeing, feeling; it is the true foundation of morality.
>
> Thomas Jefferson

SOMETHING went wrong about the end of the seventeenth century. Louis XIV was stamping his autocracy on France and threatening to export it to the rest of Europe. The British had already demonstrated, through both violent revolution and regicide, and a 'glorious' but (except for poor Ireland) largely peaceful constitutional revolution in 1688, that they wanted no more of the old régime. The Restoration had had its philosophical defenders, and the shock of the puritan fury had led authors like Filmer to try to reassert the divine right of kings and Hobbes the naturalness of hierarchy. But these were not the dominant trends. Bolingbroke's *Idea of a Patriot King* expressed British feelings much better, and constitutional monarchy was entrenched. Even the German Hanoverians took thoroughly to this, despite attempts to blacken the reputation of George III, who was in fact a thoroughly constitutional ruler and perhaps understood the constitution better than most monarchs before or after.

We can only understand the fury loosed on poor George from both sides of the Atlantic if we understand how determinedly the British (and even more so their American cousins) opposed any kind of return to even the suggestion of absolute monarchy. It was not so much that George really attempted this but that it made a perfect stick with which to beat him and the policies of his ministers. The Whig oligarchy or ascendancy or whatever wanted its version of the balance of powers to prevail—that is, the balance to stay in its favor. The Whigs, aristocrats, and street radicals alike (and here we must throw in the American independence movement) wished to preserve the individual liberties enshrined in the Glorious Revolution.

They wished to preserve much more. Their revolution had been based as much on a battle of ideas as a clash of arms. They had defeated the powers of reaction in the field, and although they allowed a return of monarchy, it was a very limited one. Monarchy was popular, but it was there by the will of the people, not by divine right. The king could be head of the Church of England, that was fine for social stability—much valued by the Whigs, but he was not put there by God but by the constitution. There was not necessarily a total consistency to Whig thought, but there was a conspiracy theory that held it together: the forces of reaction were ever ready to reverse these 'progressive' gains and go back to the old ways. Hence, the hysteria over George and the supposed plot to undo the constitution that dominated the Whig view of history until quite recently. (Even Bolingbroke's book, which must seem rather mild to us now, was revived as a supposed evil influence on the king, although there is no evidence that he ever read it. That didn't stop the conspiracy theorists who insisted that Lord Bute taught him its precepts!)

Part of the reversal would involve a reversal of philosophical doctrine. For the 'glorious revolution' had established that the ideas of the ancien régime had been overthrown along with the regime itself. Most pernicious among these was the doctrine of 'innate ideas.' Even Hobbes was an empiricist who attacked the innate ideas doctrine. Although he favored despotism over democracy, he wanted it to be a secular despotism, or at least not a Catholic one. But that he could move, in his mind logically, from a vigorous empiricism to an advocacy of despotic government, should have shown from the start that there was no necessary connection between the theory of knowledge and the form of the constitution.

John Locke became the intellectual hero of the Whigs. What Locke did was to steal Hobbes's empiricism and turn it to the service of constitutional democracy. He thus became the perfect exponent of Whig doctrine in his famous statement that there was nothing in the mind that was not first in the senses. Knowledge was not born in us, but came into us with experience. This was not an original position but was merely a restatement of Occamite nominalism: *nihil est in intellectu quod non pruius in sensu fuerit;* a doctrine that seems so natural to the English temperament. Not only was Locke not original in stating it (as we have seen, Hobbes was just as vigorous), but his opening chapter of the *Essay on the Human Understanding* (1690) is one of the strangest in the history of philosophy, for its polemical insistence on the pernicious nature of the doctrine of innate ideas, including many versions of this that no one is known to have held. No. What makes Locke special is, as we have seen, his taming of Hobbes: his appropriating the doctrine of the tabula rasa and turning it to Whig uses by making it the basis of liberal democracy.

We have to understand what this was opposing. Stated baldly to a neutral observer it does not seem a necessary proposition: it is something that has itself to be empirically demonstrated. Why should there not be innate ideas? Plato had thought there were, and on the continent other philosophers like Leibniz were to argue for them. But the doctrine of innate ideas was, for the Whigs, bound up with certain *particular* innate ideas: for example, the divine right of kings and the natural deference of slaves (Aristotle). It included also the whole theological baggage of original sin and guilt and the knowledge of God himself, inherited from the Catholic (and hence abhorrent to the Protestant ascendancy) middle ages. This again was tied into the domination of the church-state through the divine-rights doctrine. Henry VIII had got rid of the domination of an *external* church, but the special position of the 'Defender of the Faith' in the church-state hierarchy was reinforced by his taking on the position of local pope himself. After the Civil War and the defeat of the divine kingship it was going to be impossible for anything like it to assert itself again. The Restoration was welcomed after the grimness of the Commonwealth, but there was

to be no restoration of the old system, at least in the minds of
the Whigs.

A new alliance had come about during all of this political, religious, and intellectual turmoil, an alliance that brings us to the
other two crucial names that contributed to the mistake: Bacon
and Newton. Bacon more than Newton influenced the growing
Whig consensus. He was the culmination of the Renaissance
humanism that led to modern science. His thinking was a curious mixture of Platonism and empiricism, but his notion of
science was fundamentally empirical. In *The Advancement of
Learning* and the *Novum Organum* there could be no appeal
to innate knowledge as far as knowledge of the external world
was concerned; all knowledge had to come through induction.
Newton added the convincing proof that such knowledge could
lead to a correct view of the mechanisms of the universe: "God
said 'let Newton be' and all was light." Bacon carried this further. He was the next great writer (in English) of a utopia, after
the Catholic and humanistic Thomas More. And his utopia
(*New Atlantis,* 1627), usually totally ignored in histories of philosophy, was scientific, technological, and educational. It was
also immensely popular. It showed that a society could be constructed de novo without the baggage of medieval scholasticism
or theology. We did not need to live according to the church's
version of reality in order to be saved, and certainly not in
order to be happy, we needed only to live according to science
inculcated through education. No one wanted to throw God
over at this point, but what the Whigs did was to substitute
the God of Newton, the Divine Watchmaker, for the God of
Augustine or Thomas. Deism was born; this was a God the
builders of the new regime could live with. The innate 'original
sin' here was simple ignorance and salvation was through education. It was from now onwards that the science of pedagogy
got going in real earnest and most future philosophers felt it
necessary to write on the subject to fill out their schemes: if one
could not depend on innate ideas, then one had to say what was
going to take their place. To the progressives of the seventeenth
century there was no doubt that this was to be inductive science

and this in turn *required* the doctrine of the human mind as a blank slate.

They did not entirely get away with it. These luminaries of the newly founded Royal Society (the King was suitably involved in the enterprise as a kind of benevolent chairman—even if he did play jokes on the rather serious members) became the targets for one of the most brilliant satires penned in modern times. In *Gulliver's Travels,* the cynical Tory Jonathan Swift pillories them as the scientists of the Flying Island and the Grand Academy of Lagado in "The Voyage to Laputa." While some of the scientists are engaged in suitably potty projects like extracting sunshine from cucumbers, the astronomers on the Flying Island are so wrapped up in their perusal of the heavens that they ignore the use of their island by the king to put down subversion among his subjects. This connection between science and technology and the powers of despotism (with even the use of flying machines) was frighteningly prophetic; but it was not a connection that would have occurred to the Bacon-Locke faction. The only danger to subjects, for them, came from the existence of despotic, ecclesiastical, and antiscientific regimes, supported by the pernicious doctrine of innate ideas.

But the links were being forged, and there was not an effective philosophical opposition until Rousseau and Kant started the attack on empiricism later in the eighteenth century. And let us remember in advance that Rousseau, who had his own strong notions about what was innate in human nature, is credited with helping to start the French Revolution, which owed so much to the two English revolts—the Parliamentarian and the American—but which failed to produce the same equable results. This would not have been predicted by those who made the original mistake, however. For what was forged in the aftermath of the 'glorious revolution' was a series of wrong philosophical links, totally understandable in their time, but devastating in their long-term effects.

Essentially, the combination of Locke and Bacon with the political interests of the Whig constitutionalists led to the following connection of ideas: If we are to have a progressive society that will achieve the ultimate happiness of man, then it must be a society based on inductive science and education; to this end it must oppose all those things that threaten such a program and in particular any theory of knowledge that is not empiricist, such as the doctrine of innate ideas. As Locke plainly stated it (*Essay on the Human Understanding,* 1.iv.25)

> For having once established this tenet, that there are innate principles, it put their followers upon a necessity of receiving some doctrines as such; which was to take them off from the use of their own reason and judgement, and put them upon believing and taking them upon trust, without further examination: in which posture of blind credulity, they might be more easily governed by and made useful to some sort of men, who had the skill and office to principle and guide them.

This puts it in the proverbial nutshell: even if the doctrine of innate ideas is true, it should not be believed, because unscrupulous rulers can use it to plant the inevitability of their own institutions in the minds of the credulous. That unscrupulous rulers either did not care a fig about ideas, innate or otherwise, or could just as easily use the tabula rasa doctrine to the same end, was ruled out in the Whig scheme of things. We should not be too hard on them. They were fighting after all for things we now cherish and even take for granted, and they killed such dragons as appeared, and often appeared rightly, to threaten these fragile notions of liberty, equality, and progress. But by the same token we should no longer be bound by what they saw, wrongly, as a necessary connection.

What happened after Locke is interesting. In England (and America) his doctrine of empiricism and its necessary connection to science and democracy, became so quickly entrenched, that it was never effectively challenged throughout the eighteenth century. While empiricism as a theory of knowledge was taken to its logical (and hence impossible) extremes by Hume and Berkeley, it was not used as the conscious basis of a political philosophy. Hume, in any case, was a Tory, and Berkeley a bishop. The opposition if it can be called that was really from the Scottish philosophers who preached the doctrine of moral sense: the existence of an innate faculty of the mind that was responsible for the possibility of moral judgements. But even these philosophers (notably Hutcheson, Kames, Reid, and Adam Smith) were epistemological empiricists in all other matters than moral.

And to make matters more complicated, the arch-empiricist Hume seized on Hutcheson's theory in toto as the acknowledged basis of his own theory of morals. This is not well understood by philosophers. Hume separated, for them, fact from value, 'is' from 'ought,' reason from moral passion. The logical development of this has been the rejection of an empirical basis for morality by all his descendants who dominate modern philosophy. But Hume, in recognizing this, turned to his only alternative if he was to have a basis for morals at all, which was the moral sense doctrine of his partners in the Scottish Enlightenment. Since there was no empirical basis for morality, but since we clearly had it and lived by it and did not want to think it merely arbitrary taste, it had to have a basis elsewhere than in induction. Among others, this idea (derived from the wave of Scots who went to teach in America) greatly influenced Jefferson—more so than the doctrines of Locke. It enabled him to declare with conviction that all men were created equal (in all having the moral sense)—something that Locke certainly did not believe.

The net result of this happy accommodation was, as we have seen, that there was no particular emphasis on the empiricist basis of democracy in eighteenth-century England. The doctrine was in a sense so enshrined in the constitution as agreed upon by all parties, and in the English temperament itself, that it needed no affirmation. This does not mean that it was never affirmed, since philosophers like Gay and Hartley did indeed defend it against the moral sense school, but simply that it was never seriously challenged as the philosophical orthodoxy in England. The need to enter into a vigorous defense of the orthodoxy came later when Napoleon's exporting of the French Revolution caused a wave of real reaction in England, and roused the liberal-progressive-democratic wing to philosophical action.

But before the revolution in France, things were very different. The ancien régime persisted under the Bourbons, and
therefore the philosophical opposition to it had also to make its
case, particularly against the Catholic clerical orthodoxy. To
this end, the doctrines of Locke were to the forefront of the
thinking of the French materialists who paved the way for the
Encyclopedia and the ideology of the revolution. The great connection, either assumed or circumvented in England, was made
and remade by such French thinkers as Condillac, Bonnet,
Helvétius, Mettrie, Diderot, and d'Holbach. If we look at
Helvétius, for example, we see taken to its extreme another
basic principle of Lockean thought, individualism. This is more
implicit than stated in Locke, but follows from the empiricist
position since all 'knowledge' is the individual's sensations, and
the original social contract was made between individuals (as
was true for Hobbes). The English never stressed this as a basis
for political action, again since Locke was really only restating
what was accepted in Anglo-Saxon thought from way back: the
primacy of the individual. On the continent, however, this was
by no means the case, and so the French rebels had to make it.
Helvétius, for example, stressed that all differences between
men were the result of chance and outward circumstances. The
greatest good is the greatest personal pleasure, for him. Self-
love and self-interest are the only motives of conduct. This is
taking empiricist-based individualism to its logical conclusion—
something the wary English and Scots were not inclined to do.
But we see in it the basis of future Utilitarianism: the grand
radical response that put individualism and empiricism back at
the center of political philosophy and progressive activism in
nineteenth-century England.

Other influences from the more active French front served as
catalysts for the English radicals, more particularly Rousseau
and romanticism, Saint-Simon and socialism, and Comte and
Positivism. But the radicals remained stubborn individualists,
and resisted the collectivist tendencies in all these developments. Comte, in particular, following on the devastations of
the revolution, sought to find a sociological basis for the integration of society. He maintained the inductivist, empiricist, sci-

entific strain of his materialist forebears, but played down the individualism. The Rights of Man (i.e., of individual men), assumed in England (habeas corpus) and proclaimed in France, were giving way to the Rights of Society. Already Kant, aroused from his dogmatic slumbers by Hume and galvanized by Rousseau, had attempted the most ambitious philosophical answer to empiricism, including its political implications. His doctrine of 'disagree but obey' was a radical departure from the individualist position, as was the emphasis on duties as opposed to rights. He was making another connection, which we can loosely phrase as that between innatism and collectivism. In other words, the collectivity (society, state, culture, Volk, race, class, humanity) took some kind of moral precedence over the individual, since it created him in the first place and he existed as an individual only by its grace, as it were. This went along with an epistemology that stressed the creative role of a priori 'categories of understanding'—organizing principles that were, if not specific ideas, at least 'innate' principles by which our ideas of the world were organized.

Again, we should stress that there was really no *necessary* connection here. Let us not forget that the first modern apologist of the dominance of the state over the individual, Hobbes, was a rigorous empiricist. But even so, one can see how the Whigs and materialists would react with horror to what looked like a resurrection of the hated principle of innate ideas, linked to a political doctrine that was anti-individualist, thus confirming their worst fears about the necessary connection between the two. We shall come to the details of their reaction, but first let us note that the philosophico-political waters were becoming muddied. Thinkers like Comte, for example, were sticking to science and progress and its inevitability—one wing of the Locke-Bacon program, while at the same time declaring the necessity for social integration, even through a form of religion, that sharply opposed the individualism of that program. Thus, it is interesting to see the individualist Utilitarians tussling with Comte, whom they wanted to admire and follow but at the same time could not swallow his collectivism. They had less trouble with the ultimate development of Kant in the statist philosophy of Hegel, and there was an immediately out and out war there between the children of Locke and the heritors of Hegel.

This war was equally fiercely fought between the Lockean Whigs, who were now essentially the intellectual voice, not so much of the classical Whig ascendancy as the rising bourgeoisie, and those other materialist-collectivists the Marxist socialists, those standers-of-Hegel-on-his-head, left-wing radicals. For here too was a strange development. While Comte had gone to a neo-religious solution for his principle of social integration (albeit a religion incorporating science), and Hegel and the right wing had reasserted the primacy of the state, Marx and the other socialists opted for a secular version which asserted the rights of a collectivity over the individual, but essentially a collectivity that *opposed* the state as constituted: the class, either as the proletariat or the self-conscious party that would lead them. And it would lead them into another form of collectivism, even though, in the Marxist version, the state would wither away. Other socialist versions, stemming more from Saint-Simon than Marx, still led to the expectation of a socialist *state*, in which bourgeois individualism would have no place. Indeed, one of the functions of the state would be to see that it didn't.

Hence, the growing intellectual confusion. On the one hand, the philosophical liberals were railing against the revival of the 'right wing' innate-ideas-plus-collectivism model in the name of individualistic empiricism; on the other hand, both 'right-wing' (Comte) and 'left-wing' (Marx) versions of collectivism were arising, which were nevertheless empiricist as far as their epistemology was concerned. That Marxism was a philosophical derivation of Hegelianism, and that the greatest radical individualist of the nineteenth century, Herbert Spencer, should base his whole philosophy on the idea of society as an organism, helped to confuse matters even further. But since we are ultimately interested in the philosophical confusions that founded social science, let us just stick to this point: that in the aftermath of the French Revolution there grew up a school of thinking that considered itself in the materialist, empiricist tradition, but which did *not* necessarily link this to democratic individualism. Rather, it preached a new form of sociological collectivism radically opposed to the idea of society as merely the sum of its individuals. Thus, it was committed to the linking of two ideas that had traditionally, in liberal-progressive-scientific thinking, been declared incompatible.

The problem is, that it has never really recognized this as its basic problem. The social sciences are still dominated by Lockeans who want at the same time to be Hegelians. No wonder there is confusion. But the confusion was worse confounded in the birth of modern sociology and anthropology. Durkheim took the Positivism of Comte and the socialism of Saint Simon, and mixed these with a desire to solve Kant's problems of the origins of the *authority* of moral dictates (the conscience). He was a Frenchman in the line of both the materialists and the reconstructionists, and faced with the devastation of France after the Franco-Prussian War and, hence, a concern, not with radical progressivism but with social solidarity, he gave to social science its definition and method.

Durkheim, in the 1890s, established the autonomy of sociology as the study of 'social facts.' These were to be 'treated as things' because they were 'things-in-themselves' that had three general characteristics: they were exterior to the individual, they exercised constraint on him, and they were general in the society. Law, custom, and religion were examples of domains of social fact, and embodied the 'collective representations' of a society from which 'individual representations' were derived. The collective representations in turn were embodied in the 'collective conscience' of the society, which was prior to individual consciences and more than the sum of these.

Sociology then should find its subject matter in the study of collective representations, the clues to social facts. These were irreducible to individual 'representations' and individual 'facts.' The latter were the province of psychology and biology, and any explanation of social facts that regarded individual (i.e., psychological or biological) facts as basic or prior, was self-evidently erroneous and did not have to be examined. Durkheim's examples of religion, law (division of labor), and suicide are well enough known to require no elaboration. His declaration that the explanation of social facts must be found in other social facts (not in psychological or individual facts) became the cornerstone of European and later American social science. Durkheim's doctrines of the autonomy of sociology, of the irreducible nature of social facts, his collectivism, and his index of solidarity have left their mark on the social sciences. The problem of relating the individual to society (or rather the individual to the social) has remained a standing one in the social sciences, and various unsatisfactory attempts have been made to resolve it.

Some form of the Durkheimian doctrine of social 'autonomy' then, was always useful to sociologists wishing to stake out a claim to territorial exclusiveness in the scramble for bits of reality as subject matter that took place from the end of the nineteenth century on. Thus psychology and biology got 'the individual' and sociology got 'society.' Vague fringe disciplines were created to explore the relations between the two elements defined as different. 'Social psychology' and 'culture and personality' represent the sociological and anthropological wings of this enterprise, and no one seems very satisfied with either.

The 'collectivism' of Durkheim—the doctrine that society is more than just the sum of its individual actors and is a reality sui generis, is not new. Durkheim was to collectivity what Darwin was to evolution: he did not invent it, but he told us where to look to find it. Durkheim pointed us to collective representations and social facts, and Darwin to natural selection. We shall return to Darwin later, but in the meantime we must look at a necessary corollary of Durkheim's collectivism; necessary in the sense that Durkheim thought it followed. If collective representations are prior—individuals come and go but society goes on forever—then whatever is in the individual mind must derive from the social. This would include the individual's categories of thought and perception and of course his moral values. Thus, he thought to solve the Kantian problem of the *authority* of all such judgments—their seemingly absolute character to the individual who felt them 'acting through him'—by pushing the Kantian a priori back from the individual into his society. Durkheim and Mauss carried this to its logical conclusion in *Primitive Classification*, where it was maintained that all the categories of thought—time, space, cause, motion, and so on—were socially 'caused' and in some way assimilated by the individual.

One can easily take exception to this and argue that Durkheim and Mauss do nothing to show that the organizing principles of thought are not generically present in the mind even if particular notions of time, space, and so forth are fed into this 'program' by the society. But this raises the interesting issue that we have seen is at the heart of the confusion of modern social science. To Durkheim and Mauss, *some form of empiricism* was a necessary concomitant of the autonomy of the social. Nothing could be in the mind that was not first in the senses, and nothing could be in the senses that did not derive from the social collective. It was thus that the *socius* of Comte was possible—the forms of association that caused common, unreflective behavior in society and so ensured its cohesion. We incorporated society into ourselves through socialization, and hence we all had a slice of the collective pie, sufficiently like everyone else's slice to ensure a commonality of values and action. The doctrine finds its most extensive expression in the work of Parsons (who is still our best commentator on Durkheim) and has echoes in the linguistic theories of Sapir and Whorf and the 'culture and personality' of, for instance, Linton and Kardiner. It is a doctrine in tune with behaviorist psychology as well as with the Freudian emphasis on early learning and the 'repressive' nature of civilization.

But Freud would have thought that the organism brings something to the social situation rather than simply takes something from it. This can be a matter of degree, or a firm line can be drawn and an absolute dichotomy made: either nothing is in the mind that was not first in society or everything that is in society becomes an expression of mind (in the former the mind is a reflection of society). As in the case of the nature versus nurture debate, the truth is probably that there is a complex interaction between each side of the dichotomy—but that is jumping ahead. It is enough to note at this point that Durkheim found it hard to be consistent in this view. He was an honest thinker and had to face the obvious problem that social definitions of reality could not become too bizarre or people would not be able to survive in the real world. The 'reality' that was defined and redefined by different societies, was, after all, the same for all of them. One can redefine, for example, categories of eatable and uneatable, but one *must* have an 'eatable' category or one would starve to death. Strangely, despite the possibility of limitless variation, all societies have a large category of eatables. (This is my example, not Durkheim's; he didn't give any that I can find.) He was forced to admit, therefore, that categories had to conform to 'nature' in some sense, and that they exhibited a 'degree of artificiality' that was highly constrained.

But if they came from society (the collective conscience) and if societies did endlessly vary, then how come that categories did not endlessly stray? Durkheim's answer was to say that society was a 'natural' phenomenon, therefore it would follow that categories derived from it would follow nature very closely. This view he adopted, like so many others, from his mentor, the remarkable Alfred Espinas, who produced in 1877 *Des Sociétés Animales*—the first thesis accepted for a doctorate in sociology by the University of Paris. One might have thought, therefore, that Durkheim would have made the further leap into accepting that society was a *biological* phenomenon—a product of evolution in the same way that the body was. But he had already argued that it was not: that its reality was of a different kind than biological reality. (He used the doubtful analogy of 'mind versus brain' to help make his point—fair enough for a spiritual descendant of Descartes). Thus, like Espinas himself (a Comtean influenced by Spencer) he did not make the logical transition into a Darwinian view of the nature of society. He had defined this as impossible. That ended the matter. Social science has accepted this definition, and other versions of it by Kroeber, Huxley, Boas, and others as gospel. But it is important to point out that from the beginning it was not a necessary proposition but one *ex definitione*.

Durkheim's collectivism was not new, and neither was the Durkheim-Mauss argument that empiricism was a necessary corollary of it. It is a kind of Rousseauistic argument and finds its echoes in other French thinkers. Saint-Simon and Comte have their own versions of it and Durkheim, of course, derived much from both. All were collectivists of one sort or another, and all were empiricists. They had to be—or so they thought. To reform society in the direction of collectivist socialism, one had to show that men were reformable. If men were what their institutions made them, and if the very structure of their thought was determined by these institutions, then change the institutions for the better and men would likewise be perfected. Notions of the perfect society differed, and there was not much in common between the return to noble savagery of Rousseau, the sober guild socialism of Durkheim, and the positivistic secular religiosity of Comte—but in their collectivism they were united, whether this manifested itself in the 'general will,' the 'collective conscience,' or 'humanity'. The chain of causality that these collectivist thinkers saw as necessary led from collectivism to empiricism to some form of statism or guild socialism. They felt it necessary to deny individualism, subjectivism (innatism, nativism, intuitionism, a priorism) and laissez-faire.

But it by no means follows that all collectivists need be socialists or empiricists—nor that individualists need be subjectivists. The early part of this argument has been devoted to showing how a supposedly necessary connection was forged between individualism and empiricism, for the same ends as those Durkheim was pursuing: the general improvement of society through education. (Durkheim taught 'education' at Bordeaux for a good part of his life.) The confusions rampant in philosophy, politics, and the social sciences over this issue are still with us, and their resolution is perhaps no nearer than it was for Durkheim. But it is to this resolution that we are addressing ourselves, and we must proceed by examining some alternatives to the Durkheimian 'necessary' connections.

The idea that social reformers must reject what we shall continue for convenience to call subjectivism—any suggestion that human nature was given or that ideas were innate, has, as we have seen, a long history. The need for anyone interested in changing the status quo to embrace empiricism as an epistemological theory was beautifully stated in John Stuart Mill's autobiography, where he explains his need to attack the ideas of Sir William Hamilton.

The difference between these two schools of philosophy, that of Intuition, and that of Experience and Association, is not a mere matter of abstract speculation; it is full of practical consequences, and lies at the foundation of all the great differences of practical opinion in an age of progress. The practical reformer has continually to demand that changes be made in things which are supported by powerful and widely-spread feelings, or to question the apparent necessity and indefeasibleness of established facts; and it is often an indispensable part of his argument to show how those powerful feelings had their origin, and how these facts came to seem necessary and indefeasible. There is, therefore, a natural hostility between him and a philosophy which discourages the explanation of feelings and moral facts by circumstances and association, and prefers to treat them as ultimate elements of human nature; a philosophy which is addicted to holding up favorite doctrines as truths, and deems intuition to be the voice of Nature and of God, speaking with an authority higher than that of our reason.

In particular, I have long felt that the prevailing tendency to regard all the marked distinctions of human character as innate, and in the main indelible, and to ignore the irresistible proofs that by far the greater part of those differences, whether between individuals, races, or sexes, are such as not only might but naturally would be produced by differences in circumstances, is one of the chief hindrances to the rational treatment of great social questions, and one of the greatest stumbling blocks to human improvement. This tendency has its source in the intuitional metaphysics which characterized the reaction of the nineteenth century against the eighteenth, and it is a tendency so agreeable to human indolence, as well as to conservative interests generally, that unless attacked at the very root, it is sure to be carried to even a greater length than is really justified by the more moderate forms of intuitional philosophy.

This is a latter-day restatement of Locke's objections that were quoted earlier. But as with so much of Mill, it is a matter of 'what oft was said but ne'er so well expressed': the case has rarely been better put. Many who today are attacking 'biologism' for much the same reasons would do well to study Mill's arguments before they become too intoxicated with their own originality. What Mill was objecting to was the form of intuitionism deriving supposedly from Plato and the medieval neo-Platonists, finding its modern expression in Descartes and Kant, and, with a friendly push from Byron, Coleridge, and Goethe, ending up in the intense subjectivist/idealist doctrines of Schopenhauer and Hegel and the near lunacy of Fichte. What Mill feared was the spreading of this doctrine to England, with adverse consequences for reform. Hence, his anxiety to nip it in the bud—even so unpromising and obscure a bud as Sir William Hamilton—and substitute a robust and scientific empiricism. The latter, he obviously hoped, would give conservatives, reactionaries, and tyrants no excuses for maintaining the status quo on the ground that it simply reflected human nature. Several objections immediately come to mind.

(1) While grosser forms of intuitionism may have the faults Mill imputes, reasonable and firmly argued philosophies of subjectivism do not make the claims he objects to. Neither Descartes nor Kant, for example, exalted intuition over reason, even when they argued for the innateness of ideas or categories.

(2) It does not follow that a reformer need embrace empiricism in order to combat a regime claiming to be merely a manifestation of human nature. Mill does not consider the obvious alternative: that a reformer can simply reject the claim. He can maintain, presumably on the basis of evidence and argument, that the version of human nature put forward by the regime is faulty and distorted; his own version will then be a goal towards which reform can aspire. Rousseau, for example, could maintain that inequality was not the natural condition of man, and hence civilization should be removed to allow man's natural goodness to assert itself. Many reformers in fact take this line. If one is to argue that something is inhuman one has to have a theory—at least implicitly—of what is indeed human. Mill himself frequently insists on maintaining strict adherence to empiricism because of the need to counter natural human indolence (he adds greed), so even empiricists can have some notions of innate qualities. Mill's science of 'ethology' was indeed to consti-

tute a search for these by stripping away the products of local circumstances. But this was not, to empiricists, a stumbling block as long as *ideas* were not innate. One could not perhaps change greed and indolence, but as long as one changed the ideas people lived by one could change society.

(3) We can counterargue that the logical conclusion of Mill's doctrine leaves us with no yardstick by which to measure reform. If all institutions are the outcome of particular circumstances, then on what grounds are we to change them? What is the ideal state of affairs—except a purely negative relief from suffering? Mill's answer was the Utilitarian 'greatest happiness of the greatest number' principle, with all its attendant difficulties—difficulties never satisfactorily resolved. The tyranny of the majority is still a tyranny, as Mill saw, and his idea of a cultivated elite making decisions for the rest is a desperate device that belies his own principles. For a strict empiricist, radical Utilitarian, there is no escape: pushpin *is* better than poetry.

(4) We can criticize Mill for not seeing that empiricism can logically be as good a friend of reaction as subjectivism—always assuming, of course, that tyrants and reactionaries need philosophical justifications or even care a damn about them. A subjectivist would make just as good a dictator as an empiricist. And it could be argued that empiricism was an even better tool for tyrants. Given an intuitional ethic, anyone could claim his version of human nature as the true one as against the regime's version. But empiricism logically leaves no way out. The regime sets up the 'particular circumstances,' these in turn determine the ideas and characters of the subjects, and what basis is there then for revolt—even ideological revolt? That man is ultimately completely malleable, and his ideas and predilections are the product entirely of 'circumstances,' is a doctrine to be welcomed by dictators and reactionary regimes as earnestly as it is embraced by reformers like Mill. Empiricism is as much a two-edged weapon as subjectivism in the world of practical opinion and political action.

(5) Mill also ignored the possibility that there may be some kind of not-so-obvious interaction between innate, a priori categories of thought and action on the one hand, and social cir-

cumstances on the other, each exercising its own influence and only in combination producing the 'phenotypical' result. As Chomsky observes, some such position has to be held by any but the most frenetic empiricist.

(6) A confusion exists here between intuitionism, which declared that only individual intuition counted or only the ego was real, and a priorism, which maintained that ideas or categories were innate—but not necessarily that they were free from rational scrutiny.

More important than these considerations for our immediate purposes is the connection Mill makes (ultimately following Helvétius's version of Locke) between empiricism, radicalism, and individualism. For the Utilitarians there is no supraindividual collective. There is no 'general will,' but simply the counting of heads—that greatest number whose happiness is to determine the course of radical action. The greatest number is arrived at by simply counting. It is the sum of its parts and no more. All social action is on the same model—it is the sum total of individual actions. Any counter doctrine of mysterious collectivities was as abhorrent as subjectivism itself, with its worship of society or the state or the racial unconscious or whatever. Collectivism was for conservatives—like Burke for example—or for socialists. The Utilitarians spoke for the newly rich but politically peripheral industrial bourgeoisie; it was not coincidence, therefore, that the queen of sciences for them was economics—not, as for Comte, sociology.

Political economy, through Adam Smith's 'hidden hand,' provided what empiricist individualists had previously lacked: a coherent account of how coordinate social action could be accomplished without coercion or conscious intervention. And this takes us to the heart of our problem—the heart of sociology itself: How is society possible? How is it that a mass of individuals, all seemingly pursuing their own interests, can produce coordinated, like activity, share like values, harmonize interests, and so on? Why is there not endless chaos? For even though there are periods of anarchy, society mostly functions, and not simply because of coercion. One answer to this problem, pro-

posed by Aristotle, was simple: society is a natural phenomenon; in other words, it is in man's nature to be social. But this
was not enough for thoroughgoing empiricists, since it left
open the possibility that a good deal else was innate, and such
a position was not tenable. Hence, the answer, before Smith,
Ricardo, and Marshall, was in the form of that social-contract
theory we saw earlier as the solution proposed in the seventeenth century to counteract notions of the divine origins of
feudal social order. Society came not from God and his divine
regent the monarch; it was a human and rational *invention;* and
it was the invention of rational *individuals,* acting on an *empirical*
assessment of their situation in the 'state of nature.'

In pre-contract times, in Hobbes's version, men pursued a
zero-sum policy without respect to the wishes and interests of
their neighbors—a very nasty, not to say brutish and short,
situation. Rousseau's state of nature (at least his second step
after the languageless prehuman acquired speech—however
mysteriously) was more benign—but the outcome was the
same: whether men were good at all costs or evil at all costs,
they sank their individuality in a contract and surrendered
individual sovereignty in return for collective security, either
embodied in a despotic sovereign as with Hobbes, or in an os-
tensibly democratic but potentially totalitarian collectivity as
with Rousseau, or in some form of constitutional democratic
government as with Locke.

The various versions of the contract theory are too well
known to need laboring here. The point to establish is its relationship to individualism and empiricism. The main logic of the
connections lay in reconciling extreme empiricism and individualism with the obvious existence of civil society. The contract
theorists went a stage farther back than Durkheim and asked
how the civil institutions that were the bases of individual experience came to exist in the first place, if all that was ultimately
real was individual experience itself?

The contract was the answer. Society was not the natural outcome of human nature, but a conscious artifice to overcome the
anarchistic tendencies of human nature. No one has been any
happier with contract theory than with lumpen-Utilitarianism;

perhaps the only modern exponent was Freud in *Totem and Taboo*, until John Rawls came along with his 'original position' theory. (*A Theory of Justice,* 1971) But the latter is not intended to describe an actual historical state. It is a hypothetical state that a rational observer must assume himself to be in in order to choose a fair social system. The problem with it is that the rational human being proposed as the chooser is so stripped of any vestiges of humanity except a disembodied, sexless, ageless, and kinless rationality that it is impossible to see how it could ever make a human choice. It simply doesn't work as a theory, but the reasons will have to be spelled out elsewhere. Freud's Primal Horde is if anything more satisfactory.

What we must grasp here is that despite its seeming scientific rigor and rationality, empiricism-individualism did not seem destined for great success as a theory of sociality—and despite its connections with philosophical liberalism, it was as likely as its subjectivist counterpart to take the totalitarian road. Indeed, one could agree that the romantic school against which Mill protested (even if reading Wordsworth saved his sanity) could just as well take the road to anarchism as to reaction—in its subjectivist-individualist version. This culminated, perhaps, in existentialism after World War II, before Sartre's extraordinary sideways shuffle into Marxism. The necessary connection between subjectivism and conservatism on the one hand, and empiricism and radicalism on the other, that Mill proposed, was, as we have seen, not so necessary as he imagined. And it is worth noting that conservative political collectivism, as in Burke and St. John, or radical individualism as in Paine and Fox, for example, could be adopted without any necessary theory of knowledge attached to it. Implicit assumptions about human nature were there to be sure—but radicals as well as conservatives held these more or less coherently. Indeed, as I have argued elsewhere, Burke could be seen as an empiricist arguing for the power of institutions to guide us in the absence of innate moral tendencies.

If anything, one could argue that there was an intellectual gap between the extreme empiricism-liberalism-individualism of Locke and its revival by the Utilitarians. The empiricism survived as the major theory of knowledge: it was not seriously challenged. But it did not dominate as a theory of morality and society. And here I am only talking of the Anglo-Scottish school, not of the continental developments, which included Descartes and Leibniz, for example. Nevertheless, the tone set by Locke and Bacon (with Newton looming in the background) was still seen as a dominant force in revolution: the throwing off of the ancien régime and clerical authority and the divine rights of kings and all the baggage of innate ideas. Empiricism was still the basis of science if not of morals, and the philosophical liberals (Utilitarians) sought precisely to make of morals a science and thus complete this agenda. Their real intellectual ancestor was perhaps as much Sir William Petty, as John Locke, since Petty was one of the first actually to try to quantify the calculation of pain and pleasure that was to be the linchpin of Utilitarianism.

But philosophical liberalism needed something other than the contract origin-myth, and it got this in the rise of scientific political economy through Smith, Mill, and Ricardo, reaching its zenith under the great Alfred Marshall. As in so many other things, Hume grasped the essential problem here. If we have a thoroughgoing empiricist and individualist doctrine, how do we account for social cohesion without coercion? Hume's answer was not that we establish a contract, but that we establish *conventions,* and not necessarily by conscious enactments at all.

> I observe that it will be to my interest to leave another in the possession of his goods, provided he will act in the same manner with regard to me. When this common sense of interest is mutually expressed and is known to both, it produces a suitable resolution and behavior. And this may properly enough be called a convention or agreement betwixt us, though without the interposition of a promise, since the actions of each of us have a reference to those of the other, and are performed upon the supposition that something is to be performed on the other's part. (*A Treatise Of Human Nature,* III.ii.2.)

He draws the analogy with two rowers in a boat who, without any agreement or precise determination, nevertheless, out of a common interest to move the boat forward, row in rhythm. The 'adjustment of interests' without conscious agreement (although of course such agreement could take place) gives rise to conventions that can become laws or customs. It is also what lies behind the economic theory of price, and the behavior of unrelated persons in a market who are constantly making such adjustments without any explicit agreement. Since these adjustments are arrived at naturally, it follows that one should not interfere with them, and hence laissez-faire becomes the obvious social policy deriving from this model of behavior. Similarly, the individual entrepreneur and the 'economic man' with his economic rationality and 'market mentality' became the elementary units of analysis.

In anthropology we recognize that these doctrines are debatable largely through Malinowski's attack on the one, and Polanyi's bitter polemic against the other. Also, as the heirs of Durkheim, we have learned to be suspicious of arguments deriving from individualism. Leslie White, perhaps, represents our major anti-individualist polemicist, although his targets are sometimes a little bizarre. His collectivity is 'culture'—which he claims is what Durkheim was talking about anyway, and in the form of the superorganic this has held sway from Kroeber on. (Strange, however, that the term itself derives from that great laissez-faire individualist Spencer. But more of that later). The individualists have also had their say and issued their replies. However, the strongest voices of individualist doctrine have come from sociology and psychology, with perhaps Homans as the best example of a rigorous empiricist whose rugged individualism would have warmed Mill's heart. The whole tradition of behaviorist psychology from Pavlov and Watson, to Hull and Skinner, is firmly empiricist, and while not usually taking a stand on collectivism or individualism, it nevertheless is almost by definition individualist. It can, however, serve various political masters, from Stalinist Russia to capitalist United States.

That behaviorist-empiricist individualism is the perfect ideology for a capitalistic system is not often mentioned—but it is a case for sober consideration on the part of those who too readily equate neo-Darwinism with neo-fascism, or at least with support of the status quo in the manner of Mill. As with Sorokin's 'new Columbuses of the social sciences,' the contemporary critics and proponents of either individualism or collectivism often behave as though the debate sprang newborn from their imaginations. But indeed, as we have seen, it has a long history and it still is not resolved.

4

Darwin and the Donation of Durkheim II: Bradley and the Benison of Bergson

> For society to exist at all, the individual must bring into it a whole group of inborn tendencies; society therefore is not self explanatory; so we must search below the social accretions, get down to Life, of which human societies, as indeed the human species altogether, are but manifestations.
>
> Henri Bergson

Even throughout the nineteenth century, individualism had been under attack from the collectivists. After Durkheim, on the continent, collectivism held sway, but in the Anglo-Saxon world the opposite was the case. Here the villain I suppose is Herbert Spencer, although he is difficult to place. But he must be counted a strict individualist, laissez-faire liberal, whatever his theory of knowledge. The title of his most famous popular book, *The Man Versus the State* (1884), says it all. In fact, although it is buried in his complicated 'organic analogy' his epistemology was perhaps the first really great attempt to make evolutionary sense of the Kantian position on categories. Spencer argued, in his *Principles of Psychology* (1855), that although all knowledge in its origins came from outside and through the senses, as a result of the process of evolution it was incorporated into the organism thus becoming 'innate.' The problem here was Spencer's Lamarckism. Obviously 'knowledge' as such is not incorporated into the organism, either by use and disuse or any other mechanism. But if Spencer's dictum is rewritten in proper Darwinian terms, then it becomes the ideal formula for the evolution of behavior: selective retention of traits—including those involved in the higher faculties of cognition—that lead to greater reproductive success. Darwin, as we shall see, saw this point, but a real Darwinian psychology based on its understanding—one that would once and for all settle the empiricism-subjectivism debate—is still only being developed more than a hundred years later.

The dominance of Spencer, of economics, of individualism, was assailed from two sources (or perhaps it was only one): Idealism and Marxism. Insofar as both drew on Hegel and both were collectivist they differ only in the idealist versus materialist bias of their epistemology. While Marxism—with the 'class' as the collective—was to have the most effect on the social sciences, Idealism had the most effect on philosophy. Perhaps it would have been all to the good if it had been the other way round. But while it could be said that the individualistic-empiricism of Mill—which held sway for half a century—had been chased from the field of philosophy by 1900, it continued to dominate Anglo-Saxon sociology through the erroneously labelled Social Darwinists, and psychology first through associationism (from Hartley) and then through the behaviorists. The Anglo-Saxons seem congenitally averse to idealist thinking when it comes to the practical business of dealing with the world, and since they were mostly interested in social science because of what it might *do* rather than what it might *explain,* the idealists exerted almost no influence. Not only that, but they came under severe attack from the liberals for a kind of guilt by association with Hegel and hence Prussian militarism.

Indeed, the greatest exponent of this view, L. T. Hobhouse, touchingly dedicated his attack, *The Metaphysical Theory of the State* (1918), to his son serving in the RAF, saying that, inadequate as it may seem, a book denouncing German Idealism was also a way of carrying on the fight against the continental evil. It is easy to see, however, that Hobhouse is really attacking the British disciples of Hegel, and in particular, Bosanquet, for the same reason Mill attacked the same disciples of Kant; he wanted to stop the spread of the pernicious doctrine in his own homeland. This guilt by association, while containing more than a kernel of truth, was unfortunate, since it meant that doctrines not slavishly Hegelian, even if influenced by Hegel, were swept away along with the offenders. Hegel failed to apply consistently a crucial distinction—the very same error that vitiates the work of Locke, for example: the distinction between the nation/culture/volk or people/race/society on the one hand, and the state, as the organs of law and government, on the other. Hegel certainly made the distinction—between Sittlichkeit versus Recht for example; what we would now distinguish as perhaps custom or culture versus law (deriving from the state). But it was all too easy having established that freedom was only possible in subjection to the one, to transfer this principle to the other. Herder, for example, had not made this mistake. In spite of being the father of German romantic nationalism and hence taking some of the blame for what followed, it is fair to say that he always made the separation to the extent of positively hating 'the state' and seeing it as antithetical to the Kultur of the people. If these idealists had a collectivity, it was not the state and certainly not the Prussian militaristic state. The greatest of the English idealists was not a state worshipper and certainly not a militarist, and Hobhouse does not deal with him or seem to see his relevance. He was not alone.

Perhaps the saddest intellectual failure of the nineteenth and early twentieth centuries was the failure of social scientists to appreciate the brilliant and conclusive arguments of F. H. Bradley (brother of the great Shakespearean commentator, A. H. Bradley). In his *Ethical Studies* (1876), published when he was only thirty years old, the essay entitled, "My Station and its Duties," not only demolishes the stark individualism of Mill—'individuals do not exist,' says Bradley—but puts forward a view of the relation of individual and society, remarkably like that of G. H. Mead, that foreshadows almost all later work in status (station) and role (duties), and is certainly more satisfactory than Durkheim's. Social science, however, got its collectivism from Durkheim—an empiricist socialist; had it got it from Bradley, a subjectivist conservative, it might have had a different history. On the subject of individual and society, Bradley insists that there is no way in which individuals could be prior. From the beginning the so-called 'individual' is a mixture of its two parents who are in turn the repositories of their ancestry, and hence of the 'race.' This latter term was loosely used in Bradley's day. But his point is clear: the individual is from birth the product of many others. Modern genetics would make this point even clearer. But from that point on, through what we would now call socialization, he receives the imprint of his society. What is individual, that is, unique to him, is nothing, says Bradley:

> We say that, out of theory, no such individual men exist; and we will try to show from fact that, in fact, what we call an individual man is what he is because of and by virtue of community, and that communities are thus not mere names but something real, and can be regarded (if we mean to keep to facts) only as the one in the many.

He wishes to 'keep the subject to what is familiar' and not to invoke 'the life of animals, nor early societies, nor the course of history.' But it is worth noting that he saw the relevance of calling these to his aid. He takes an Englishman, and points out that apart from what he has in common with others he is not a man at all:

> What we mean to say is, that he is what he is because he is a born and educated social being, and a member of an individual social organism; that if you make an abstraction of all this, which is the same in him and in others, what you have left is not an Englishman, nor a man, but some I know not what residuum, which never has existed by itself, and does not so exist. If we suppose the world of relations, in which he was born and bred, never to have been, then we suppose the very essence of him not to be; if we take that away, we have taken him away; and hence he is now not an individual, in the sense of owing nothing to the sphere of relations in which he finds himself, but does contain those relations within himself as belonging to his very being; he is what he is, in brief, so far as he is what others are.

Geertz could not have put it better; indeed he never has. But to all those devotees of Geertzism who insist on quoting almost identical passages from the master to me, let me point out where Bradley takes his argument:

A man owes his individuality to his ancestors who made his

society. "The ancestors were made what they were by the society they lived in."

> If in answer it be replied, 'Yes, but individual ancestors were prior to their society,' then that, to say the least of it, is a hazardous and unproved assertion, since man, so far as history can trace him back, is social; and if Mr. Darwin's conjecture as to the development of man from a social animal be received, we must say that man has never been anything but social, and society was never made by individual men. . . . They at all events have been so qualified by the common possessions of social mankind that, as members in the organism, they have become relative to the whole.

Thus Bradley takes the step that Durkheim was unwilling to take: he asserts that society is not merely natural in some sense that it is a human product, but it is natural because it is an evolutionary product, in Darwin's sense. We descended from social animals; we were always social. Thus, society *as such*—as opposed to this or that society—is something that developed in evolution. Our sociality is a property of our evolved animal status: it is a biological phenomenon. The philosopher need then only take a small step to the investigation of sociality on Darwinian lines: an investigation of the evolution of social behavior to parallel the investigation of the evolution of the individual organism. The particular forms of this or that society are what will mold the little organism and make it the individual it becomes, but the propensity for sociality itself is rooted in evolution.

Bradley concentrates on the effect of a particular society in shaping an individual organism, since the ethic he derives from his position is that we can only live a moral life in such a society by adhering to 'our station and its duties.' (A position that becomes more and more difficult to maintain as society becomes more Weberian, individualistic, fragmented and impersonal, and above all, large.) Without society we are, as he has argued, nothing. But our capacity to be social at all and hence to benefit from our society's ministrations is innate; it is inherent in our very natures as evolved animals. If it were not so, we could not be social at all and would be indeed the struggling, pre-social individuals of contract theory. Essentially, Bradley is only reviving basic Aristotelian doctrine: that man is by nature a social animal and that he can only live a virtuous life by achieving his *telos* as a member of the social organism. But this bowing to the Greek original only helped to ensure that he would not receive a hearing from the burgeoning social sciences. All the New Philosophies of the late Renaissance had abjured Aristotelianism. Since Aristotle had been The Philosopher of the medieval Catholic schoolmen, it followed that he was persona non grata to the new sciences. Empiricism, science, and individualism formed their alliance almost consciously against the influence of Aristotle. (See the denunciations in Hobbes, for example. But see also the works of Montesquieu for an eighteenth-century assertion of the naturalness of society in the classical tradition.)

But Bradley, like Aristotle, leaves the way open for an exploration of the biological basis of sociality and the innate qualities that enable us so easily to assimilate ourselves through socialization to the social organism that gives us our being. He does no more than give us this hint. Durkheim, on the other hand, gave us numerous heavy volumes, all based on the insistence that the social could not be reduced to the biological, which, of course, he equated with the individual. It was the latter mistake that Bradley did not make: he did not equate the individual with the biological leaving the social with some disembodied sphere of its own; he equated the social with the biological through its evolutionary past.

Both men—writing at much the same time—were collectivists: they both agreed that society was a reality in itself not reducible to individuals. But Bradley, as a Hegelian idealist, was not pressed into some form of empiricism. He could allow for the existence of innate social qualities, and thus welcome Darwin's assertion of their evolutionary and hence biological base. The individual organism came prepared by evolution to embrace the collective; it came into the world needing the collective to make it whole; it actively sought out the definition of itself through the collectivity; its only possibility of a moral life was through the collective. Thus, its biology was essential to its existence as part of—product of—society. But for Durkheim, the individual had to be set in stark contrast to society; a contrast almost as stark as that of the most rigid contract theorist. Society was a different order of reality from the individual, who was a biological and psychological reality.

For Bradley this contrast did not exist; society and individual were not divisible in this way. There was, in effect, no such distinction since individuals did not exist. Society—a biological reality—was *all* that existed; individuals were a theoretical abstraction. Durkheim, in contrast, hoisted himself on his own theoretical petard; the arch collectivist enshrined the 'individual versus collective' distinction by assigning each to different spheres, with the social, like the mind, having an emergent reality of its own quite distinct from the individual, which was biological like the brain. It was the ultimate triumph of Cartesian dualism—the curse of French intellectual life—in the realm of social thought.

It is hard for us now to understand that an avowed idealist like Bradley should have been essentially more commonsensical and pragmatic than our acknowledged fathers of empirical social and behavioral science, whether sociological collectivists, scientific behaviorists, or cultural realists. For the edifice of empiricist behaviorism cannot stand before the developments of modern evolutionary biology, while Bradley's Idealism accommodates them quite logically and easily. It is sobering to ponder how the most obviously authoritative of yesterday's orthodoxies so easily turn out to be massive mistakes. Durkheim was right to insist on the priority of the collective, society; he was simply mistaken, as a result of his misplaced empiricism, on where to locate it. The search continues, but thanks to Darwin, we now know where to look.

The insistence on linking a collectivist sociology with an empiricist epistemology is at the root of our dilemmas—and derives, as I hope to have shown, not from any necessary connection between these but from a socialist/radical/liberal need for a doctrine of reform. Let us pause and take stock. We have seen that collectivism and individualism, and empiricism and subjectivism, have been variously associated. There are just four possible combinations, of course.

> collectivist—empiricist
> collectivist—subjectivist
> individualist—empiricist
> individualist—subjectivist

We have seen how the 'necessary' connection has been made largely on the basis of the political beliefs of the connector. Some typical examples:

> collectivist—empiricist—socialist (Durkheim)
> collectivist—subjectivist—conservative (Bradley)
> individualist—empiricist—radical (Mill)
> individualist—subjectivist—nihilist (Nietzsche)

This is obviously oversimplified and schematic. It is often difficult to place people in hard categories like this and a *relative* positioning along the two axes might be more profitable. Some writers, at different stages of their thought, can occupy more than one position, and others, while taking a stand on one issue, do not necessarily take an overt stand on the other. The reader can envisage various thinkers as occupying a position somewhere in one of the four quadrants produced by the intersection of our two 'factors':

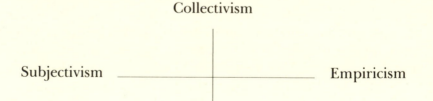

Also, while there may be a connection between the political beliefs and the philosophical position, we have seen that there is no *necessary* correlation. Thus, many current right-wing polemicists would be individualist-empiricist reactionaires, despite Mill's claims; while a radical Tory of the Bow Group stamp or a liberal Republican could be almost any of the combinations! Insofar as we in social anthropology are heirs to the legacy of Durkheim (and in America to its Boasian and Kroeberian counterpart), then, we are struggling with the problem that started this part of the discussion: If we combine empiricism with collectivism, then we have an insoluble problem about the nature of the collective and the relation of the individual to it. This becomes especially problematical when 'lower' levels of explanation, for example, those from biology, are relegated to the individual and declared irrelevant to the social. Much sociology is still dominated by Mill's view of the necessary relation of empiricism to reform; and this has its own problems. We are halfway to a solution—with our collectivism; we need to examine the other half—our empiricism.

The legacy of Locke was the indissoluble marriage of empiricism to reform, science, and individualism. The donation of Durkheim was the correct rejection of the individualism, but the creation of another indissoluble marriage that followed from Locke's position on science, empiricism, and reform: that of sociological collectivism with empiricism. Even if, in the name of social solidarity, individualism had to go, the entrenched prejudice in favor of an empiricist epistemology ensured that this would be retained. It was unthinkable to return to any subjectivist position to solve the problem of solidarity. After all, if Durkheim had taken that step, he would have been back to Aristotle. So, even though his mentor Espinas showed the way, and Darwin provided the means, this was too much of a leap to expect from an heir of the French Enlightenment. We should be grateful that Durkheim at least took us as far as he did; our distress stems from the inability to make the logical leap that Bradley saw was inevitable. And this inability itself stems from our Lockean heritage (since we are all by and large decent people who want a better world) and its equation of progress—material and moral—with an outright rejection of subjectivist positions of whatever flavor.

One name has figured only lightly in this discussion so far, despite its prominence in the title of the piece: Darwin. Darwin's position is ironic: he was potentially the man to solve the problem in favor of the collectivist-subjectivist school, and yet he was taken up by the individualist-empiricists and Darwinism was the banner nailed to their masthead. In effect, these so-called Social Darwinists were Spencerians and not Darwinists; they were believers in individualism and laissez-faire, and progressive, cumulative social change loosely (and wrongly) labelled evolution; wrongly if it was intended to be Darwinian, since no such implications were present in Darwin's theory. Their main sources were the French philosophers of the Enlightenment and the Scottish social evolutionists (Ferguson, Millar, McLennan) rather than Darwin. Like Spencer, and unlike Darwin, their major preoccupation was the application of analogies supposedly drawn from nature—the survival of the fittest, the struggle for existence, and so forth—to social life. There is no warrant for this in Darwin's theory where fitness is measured solely by the ability of an organism to leave viable offspring, and that is all. It says nothing about fitness being measured in terms of wealth or worldly success in the capitalistic jungle.

What were Darwin's own views? He never espoused a particular political position, and hence, by default becomes a kind of conservative. Recent attacks on his doctrine of 'gradualism' in evolution have linked it to the urging of only gradual, rather than revolutionary, change in society. But here the mystery of the reception of Darwin begins, for at first this was certainly not how he was regarded by the establishment, civil or religious. At a time when religion—regarded by the bourgeoisie as the bulwark of social morality—and the European aristocratic ascendancy were on the defensive, Darwin's materialism, pessimism, and obvious incompatibility with biblical notions of origins and species, were seen as frighteningly dangerous. Darwin himself sensed this and was consequently cautious about expressing himself on political or religious issues. He was not a philosophical radical; he was an English country gentleman who had, early in life, seriously considered the church as a vocation. Not the stuff of which revolutionaries are made. Nevertheless, he was enthusiastically taken up by the left as well as the right. Both viewed the consequences of his doctrines in much the same way, but the left (including, after a slow start, Marx himself) welcomed the implications, while the right was horrified by them.

What the Social Darwinists did to Darwin was much what Locke had done to Hobbes: they took a doctrine with one set of implications and derived the opposite. In the same way that Locke took Hobbes's empiricism and turned it into the basis of Whig democracy rather than royal despotism, so the Social Darwinists took Darwin's materialism and turned it from a doctrine that seemed to strike at the roots of bourgeois moral and social order into one that was supportive of the basic Spencerian principles of that order: individualism and laissez-faire economics. But throughout, there was a strong left-wing Darwinism that modern critics forget. There was even an anarchist version, under Kropotkin, that saw as much *mutual aid* implied in evolutionary theory as 'nature red in tooth and claw.' In short, there was no one political philosophy to be derived from Darwin, but as in the earlier derivations of political philosophies from empiricism that we have been examining, philosophers sought to make *necessary* connections where there were none. It could be argued either way.

But back to Darwin's own views. He certainly took up the cudgel in some of the intellectual wars we have been exploring. And his chief targets were the empiricist-individualist Utilitarians. In *The Descent of Man* (1871), for example, chapter 4 is devoted, appropriately, to a consideration of "The Moral Sense." He starts by restating Kant's question about the authority of *ought,* and suggests that the problem with the failure to resolve it is that 'no one has approached it exclusively from the side of natural history.' He continues:

> The following proposition seems to me in a high degree probable—namely, that any animal whatever, endowed with well-marked social instincts, the parental and filial affections being here included, would inevitably acquire a moral sense or conscience, as soon as its intellectual powers had become as well, or nearly as well developed, as in man.

Thus the moral sense is inevitable in a social creature able to reflect on its own sociality. It does not need to be derived from generalizable rationality, or from self-love, or from the greatest happiness of the greatest number, which, he rightly points out, is a 'standard not a motive of conduct.' The moral sense is rooted in sympathy—in this he agrees with most of the Moral Sense school—but this sympathy is partial; it does not extend to all members of the species. Enmity is as rooted in social being as deeply as sympathy. Darwin argues directly against Mill in a significant footnote to the above quoted passage:

> Sir B. Brodie, after observing that man is a social animal, asks the pregnant question, "ought not this to settle the disputed question as to the existence of a moral sense?" Similar ideas have probably occurred to many persons, as they did long ago to Marcus Aurelius. Mr. J. S. Mill speaks, in his celebrated work, "Utilitarianism," (1864, pp. 45, 46), of the social feelings as a "powerful natural sentiment," and as "the natural basis of sentiment for utilitarian morality." Again he says, "Like the other acquired capacities above referred to, the moral faculty, if not a part of our nature, is a natural outgrowth from it; capable, like them, in a certain small degree, of springing up spontaneously." But in opposition to all this, he also remarks, "if, as is my own belief, the moral feelings are not innate but acquired, they are not for that reason less natural."

He picks up Mill's ambivalence here, and notes the devious argument, so similar to Durkheim's, that the 'categories'—in this case moral categories—while not innate are in some sense natural to us. Like Durkheim, Mill does not say what this sense is. Darwin continues, with what looks suspiciously like mild sarcasm:

> It is with hesitation that I venture to differ at all from so profound a thinker, but it can hardly be disputed that the social feelings are instinctive in lower animals; and why should they not be so in man? Mr. Bain and others believe that the moral sense is acquired by each individual during his lifetime. On the general theory of evolution this is at least extremely improbable. The ignoring of all transmitted mental qualities will, as it seems to me, be herewith judged as a most serious blemish in the works of Mr. Mill.

And, we might add, in the works of all committed empiricists, collectivist or individualist. Moral feelings derive from social feelings. The latter are inherited qualities peculiar to the species, acquired through evolution not education. Thus, he argues, if bees or any other social animals were to acquire consciousness, the moral sense they developed would not be the same as man's. But the moral imperative we feel, is authoritative for the same reason that the urge to eat or copulate is authoritative. We feel with urgency the need to obey those social impulses that have been selected for in the course of evolution. Of course, these will differ in exact expression from locale to locale in time and space. Darwin is well aware of this and gives many examples, but the basic form of the feelings of sympathy and obligation are rooted in the natural history of the species. A truly social animal is a moral animal by its nature: it follows imperatives of action that have been selected because those who followed them left more offspring. The authority of 'ought' is simply that. A social animal endowed with self-consciousness and powers of reflection is going to act morally in the sense of following *some* set of moral imperatives; and these will be imperatives that direct it away from selfish and towards social ends: not because it calculates the greatest happiness of the greatest number or the rational generalizability of its actions, but because it has no choice but to act this way. And, says Darwin, there could have been no other evolutionary outcome.

How different is this socially derived innate moral sense approach of Darwin's from the individualistic pleasure-pain calculus of the Utilitarians, or the hidden hand of the economists producing order mysteriously from the chaos of human selfish choices, or the rational decisions of the social contract man. There is no question that for Darwin the species is a collectivity and is innately social and moral. Any society is a local population of the species expressing its local version of this species-specific moral-social heritage. He still takes a developmental rather than a relativistic view of the local differences. The moral sense is universal, but it can become more refined with civilization. We may today wonder to what degree this refinement is the special property of few thinkers rather than a general improvement in the moral condition of mankind, but Darwin was a man of his times and he wanted a hopeful outcome from his theories even if he must have realized that no such result was warranted. ('There is a grandeur in such a view of life.')

But from the point of view of our argument here, Darwin's is a materialist version of the subjectivist-collectivist position. We can now see why he was so attractive to Bradley, the conservative idealist, as well as to Kropotkin, the revolutionary anarchist. For the anarchists, while being in a way individualists in rejecting the power of the *coercive* state over the individual, nevertheless wanted to establish the essentially social and cooperative nature of man as more basic than its individual-competitive counterpart. Darwin certainly thought that individual competition (struggle) was at the basis of natural selection, but he equally thought that in the social animals those individuals that were 'more social'—ultimately with man more 'moral'—would succeed better than those that were more 'self-regarding.' By a paradox, therefore, social morality would serve individual ends better than self-love, even in the basic game of propagating one's own genes. The asocial creature of contract theory or Utilitarian calculation, who had to wait for 'education' to acquire motives for morality, would simply be an evolutionary failure. Such 'individuals'—as Bradley so clearly saw—do not exist 'outside of theory.'

Finally, in response to the Kantian question he posed, Darwin locates the authority of 'ought,' as we have seen, not like Durkheim in the social collective divorced from any biological foundation, but in the moral propensities of the species, of which specific societal examples are simply local expressions. We obey the imperative 'ought' not because of socialization or social pressure—this merely tells us which 'ought' to follow; we obey because natural selection has implanted the urge to obey 'ought' as surely as the urge to obey 'reproduce.' As to the fact-value distinction so much touted in the twentieth century, Darwin anticipated a very modern objection to it. We do in fact derive 'ought' from 'is' in any statement of a 'natural function.' Thus, a pointer's 'job' is to point at game; therefore, we argue quite naturally, a pointer 'ought' to point at game. A man's job is to live in society, therefore he 'ought' to do this, in a simple and direct sense where 'ought' means 'fulfill his natural function.'

Hence a father 'ought' to care for his children from the very fact that he is a father. These moral imperatives do follow from these factual statements in a simple logical way. But the resolution lies in the statement of function, and in this case natural function.

In the search for society Darwin told us where to look and how. The 'where' had been implicit in all former naturalistic theories, from Aristotle onwards. The answer lay in the naturalness of society, and given that this could be 'approached from natural history,' that is, subject to scientific investigation, verification, and falsification, it became an empirical rather than a philosophical problem. One could investigate, for example, what Darwin himself set out to do in *Descent* and in *The Expression of the Emotions in Animals and Man,* namely, the comparative evolutionary development of the social instincts. This would lead to the same investigation of the 'higher mental powers'—or as we would now say, the evolution of cognitive processes. This would eventually enable us to say with some accuracy just what the 'innate social qualities' were in both man and animals. The 'collective' here is a real and tangible entity— measurable and capable of empirical investigation. The 'innate' propensities of social behavior can be uncovered. Scientific empiricism does not imply epistemological empiricism at all. We can investigate the innate; we no longer need to banish it in principle before we start. We can investigate the collectivity; we no longer need to assert the primacy of the individual as a methodological, political, and ethical premise. Things seem set for a happy reversal of the mistake made towards the end of the seventeenth century. What went wrong? Why are the issues still as virulently with us?

To answer this fully would require an entire rewriting of intellectual history since 1859. I am not up to that task. I can only point to what seems to me to have been the more salient developments, leaving it to others to fill in the details.

One of the most paradoxical and sad of these is what we might call the persistence of vitalism. This took many forms. Ironically, the Marxist insistence—through Engels's *Dialectics of*

Nature—of an application of dialectical materialism to all natural processes was one of the most virulent. But all took off from the intolerable nature of the basic Darwinian truth: that natural selection operated by chance. Nietzsche was one of the few who could face this and without flinching accept the consequences (in *Beyond Good and Evil*):

> You desire to live "according to Nature?" Oh, you noble Stoics, what fraud of words! Imagine to yourselves a being like Nature, boundlessly extravagant, boundlessly indifferent, without purpose or consideration, without pity or justice, at once fruitful and barren and uncertain: imagine to yourselves *indifference* as a power—how *could* you live in accordance with such indifference?

The plain answer was: nobody could and probably nobody can. Even many of those who accept Darwin still seek for some first principles in some view of nature that allows us then to operate on the basis of something other than accident. Huxley was the first Darwinian disciple to scuttle to a happy haven with his insistence that 'ethical evolution' had overtaken 'cosmic evolution' so we were in control of our own destinies. Accident was simply not acceptable to those who wanted some purpose in the universe; a purpose in which man and human society—in some form or other—were the pinnacle of the developmental process. This Spencerian-Hegelian doctrine found many outlets, of which the Marxist materialist version was but one.

The idealist wing was just as active in the once widely popular doctrines of Henri Bergson and the idea of 'creative evolution,' passing through the passion for the *élan vital* of George Bernard Shaw's *Man and Superman,* and ending in the frankly religious version of Teilhard de Chardin. Had Bergson, for example, understood and accepted Darwin fully, then there might have been in his social theory the germ of the Darwinian social science we are looking for. As in the epigraph to this chapter, we see that Bergson had, in his direct criticisms of Durkheim, reached a point similar to ours. It is worth looking in detail at his extended criticism in *The Two Sources of Morality and Religion* (1932):

> According to Emile Durkheim, there is no need to try and find out why those things which such or such a religion asks us to be-

lieve "appear so disconcerting to individual minds. This is simply because the representation of those things by religion is not the work of these minds, but that of the collective mind. Now it is natural that this mentality should see reality differently from our own mind, since it is of another nature. Society has its own mode of existence peculiar to it, and therefore its own mode of thinking." (*Année sociologique, Vol. II, pp. 29 sqq.*) So far as we are concerned, we shall readily admit the existence of collective representations, deposited in institutions, language and customs. Together they constitute a social intelligence which is the complement of individual intelligences. But we fail to see why these two mentalities should clash, and why one should be able to "disconcert" the other. Experience teaches nothing of the kind, and sociology appears to us to afford no grounds for the supposition. If we held the view that nature stopped short at the individual, that society is the result of an accident or a convention, we could push the argument to its conclusion and maintain that this conjunction of individuals, similar to that of primary elements united in a chemical combination, has given rise to a collective intelligence, certain representations of which will be puzzling to the individual mind. But nowadays nobody attributes an accidental or contractual nature to society. If sociology is open to criticism, it would rather be that it leans too much the other way: certain of its exponents tend to regard the individual as an abstraction, and the social body as the only reality. But in that case, how could it be that the collective mentality is not prefigured in the individual mentality? How can we imagine that nature, having made man a "political animal" so disposed human intelligence that it feels out of its element when it thinks "politically?" For our part we believe that in the study of the individual one can never overestimate the fact that the individual was meant for society.

And again, following on this:

Common sense, or as it might be called, social sense, is innate in normal man, like the faculty of speech, which also implies the existence of society and which is none the less prefigured in individual organisms. It is indeed hard to admit that nature, which placed social life at the extremities of the two great lines of evolution ending respectively in the hymenoptera and in man, while regulating beforehand the detailed activity of every ant-hill, should have neglected to give man any guiding principles, however general, for the co-ordination of his conduct with that of his fellow men. Human societies doubtless differ from insect societies in that they leave undetermined the actions of the individual, and indeed those of the collectivity also, but this is equivalent to saying that it is the actions which are preordained in the insect's nature, and that in man it is the faculty alone. The faculty is nonetheless there, being so organized in the individual that it may function in society.

The point has rarely been so brilliantly and persuasively put. It would appear that here was the possibility of taking Bradley's insight and developing it into a real inquiry into the way in which the social collective is, to use Bergson's favorite and beautifully descriptive word, 'prefigured' in the individual consciousness. In short, how exactly the individual was made for society. But it was not to be. By the time Bergson made this plea, theories of élan vital were already totally outmoded in the scientific world, and Bergson was already an anachronism. Accurate as his criticism of the Durkheimian autonomy of the social was, it was no use if hitched to a teleological philosophy which had no way of linking up with the developing life sciences that were in the midst of creating the new neo-Darwinian synthesis of the 1930s; a synthesis that had absolutely no room for such vitalist metaphysics. Not that it would much have mattered, since no one involved in the synthesis had much concern with the theoretical problems of sociology; they had little enough concern with the problems of closely related sciences. For this was the great age of specialization, and this requires us to take a step back.

There were, God knows, enough ideological reasons acting against the possibility of the idealist-Darwinian synthesis and we shall return to them briefly. But within the life sciences themselves problems abounded. Our regret is that the life sciences and the behavioral sciences did not link up—but the life sciences were at war with each other. Darwinism was not wholeheartedly embraced within the life sciences by any means, and in France in particular there was opposition or indifference. Well into the twentieth century, French thinkers took their evolutionary biology from Spencer or Lamarck. Equally, the very developments that should have clinched the Darwinian theory of natural selection, that is, Mendelism and mutation theory (Morgan, De Vries, etc.), were used as arguments *against* natural selection.

What Darwinism needed was a strong population/evolutionary genetic theory, and what it got was Galton, Pearson, and eugenicism, and a lot of wrong turnings in hereditarian theory that were not only bad science (although they virtually invented statistics) but drove Darwinism into the corner from which it is still trying to get itself out: racism and selective breeding. Again, there was no necessary connection here, but it is the way things went. And within the life sciences there came to be other splits as the scientific paradigm leaned more and more to the proven and successful experimental method. The need to ape the successes of physics to be truly 'scientific' meant that the observational sciences were relegated to 'natural history' and all but dropped out of college curricula, being left to the devoted amateurs by and large. There was a tradition of careful animal observation that later became ethology, and developed under both amateur and professional auspices under Spalding in England and Heinroth in Germany. William James picked up on Spalding's research and wrote some of the most intelligent words ever on the nature of instinct in his *Principles of Psychology* (1890), virtually discovering the theoretical mechanisms of imprinting. But this branch of observational zoology had little prestige and was cut off from other developments. When Lorenz was told how courageous he had been in pursuing his 'instinctive' studies in the teeth of the prevailing orthodoxies of the behaviorists, he had to admit that he had never heard of the behaviorists; he was just doing what Professor Heinroth told him to do!

It is easy to see with hindsight that all these and other branches of study should have been in communication, and that the social sciences should have been in communication with them in turn. But that is not how it happens in science. Combinations of orthodoxy and ideology and sheer ignorance kept them all apart. Physical anthropology, for example, which should have taken up the Darwinian challenge, was obsessively concerned with racial classifications and was faced with a paucity of, and either contradictory or fraudulent, fossil evidence. The 'natural alliance' with ethology in the study of the evolution of behavior never occurred. It is doubtful if either camp knew the other existed, and neither was paying much attention to the new population genetics that under Fisher, Haldane, and Sewall Wright was revolutionizing our approach to evolution.

Ideology ensured that this state of affairs should continue. I mentioned behaviorism. This should perhaps come under the heading of 'the persistence of empiricism' as I have already indicted 'the persistence of vitalism.' There were two aspects to this: the strength and success of the empiricist paradigm and the weakness of any innatist response. We have seen that Western reformist progressive thought was peculiarly susceptible to empiricism as a doctrine of knowledge, and we have seen the reasons for this. There was a tendency therefore to seize on that theory of behavior most compatible with empiricism. And since, as we have seen, the latter was coterminous with 'science' only truly empirical theories could claim scientific status. The unqualified environmentalism of Pavlov in Russia and Watson in the United States won the day, not only because of its ideological soundness in both cultures but because it provided a sternly effective *experimental* method of arriving at results. Lorenz and Tinbergen were to introduce experiment into ethology, but this was later, was ignored, and was pioneered in Nazi Germany, none of which was helpful. The behaviorists captured the scientific high ground, and Russell rewrote the empiricist theory of knowledge, and Bloomfield theoretical linguistics, to accommodate them. Neither the philosophy of mind nor theoretical linguistics can today in any sense be considered behavioristic. But for four or more decades, it dominated.

Behaviorism, it turns out, while describing some limited factors of the learning process, simply does not work as a total theory of behavior. There are inherent limits to conditioning, and this is now firmly established. But even so thousands of behaviorist psychologists go on as if nothing has happened. When conclusive counter evidence was produced, one leading exponent maintained colorfully that he would believe these results when they found bird shit in cuckoo clocks. None of the major journals would accept them. (We should note, however, that consistent with the developments in linguistics and philosophy, much of psychology has turned to the study of cognition, and here there is a more ready acceptance of innate constituents.) Even the advent of Freud did not disconcert the behaviorists who either rejected him in toto or rewrote Freudianism in various ways to suit their own paradigm.

Freud is ambiguous—try to fit him on the two-factor diagram. In some senses he was an instinctivist and a collectivist, but at the same time he saw the collectivity 'civilization' as a repressive intrusion into the individual libido in almost Rousseauistic fashion. But there is no question that he wrestled with the same questions that we have seen are basic and tried to put the issues of individual and society into an evolutionary framework. The problem here, I believe, is that the therapeutic framework of his theories overtook the intellectual effort to build up a theory of man and society, and that his essentially antagonistic view of man and civilization could not lead to a satisfactory social theory at all. But his remains one of the most serious efforts in the twentieth century to explore the instinctive nature of social man and its evolutionary history. That it has never developed into the social theory that should have followed Darwin is one of those episodes in intellectual history that needs more detailed scrutiny. We have stressed the therapeutic dominance which distracted from such a development, and must add what was mentioned earlier: that the prestige of the scientific paradigm was from the start either dead set against Freud or was intent on taking over his theories and rendering them acceptable to the empiricist doctrine. Thus the instinctive aspects of human nature were played down, and the theory of early learning as a determinant of later personality played up. The whole enterprise of 'culture and personality' in anthropology can be seen as a quite explicit attempt to rewrite Freudian theory in terms of the effects of socialization on a blank-slate infant; something Freud would not have recognized. The power of Freud was certainly felt and accepted, but the need to tame this power in the service of the dominant environmentalist-behaviorist ideology was overpowering. His attempts at phylogenetic explanation, as in *Totem and Taboo,* suffered equally from a lack of sound evolutionary material both theoretical and factual. It is only recently that their prescience has been acknowledged (see my *Red Lamp of Incest*).

This taming of Freud's phylogenetic-instinct theory (in anthropology—psychology was doing its own hatchet job) of course stems from the dominance of the Kroeber-Boas doctrine of the superorganic with which I have dealt elsewhere. It was, in effect, nothing other than Durkheim's 'autonomy of the social' given a twist as the 'automony of the cultural,' thus preserving some corner of behavioral reality for the growing science of cultural anthropology.

In Europe, anthropologists took their doctrine either straight from Durkheim or, as in England, from him through Radcliffe-Brown. (Tylor's version of culture was not incompatible—for him too culture moved in mysterious sui generis ways of its own, and Tylor was an impeccable empiricist who declared anthropology to be a 'reformer's science.') In America, it was an autonomous development stemming more from Germanic influences such as Humboldt and Herder. But in essence it was the same, as later commentators like White so perceptively point out. The full history of this cannot be related here. It is enough to know that it existed and that it simply added to our growing (and groaning) list of forces that prevented the development of a Darwinian social theory or even a Darwinian psychology. There had been attempts at such and one could reel off names—James and the pragmatists, Carveth Read with his prescient notions of 'lycopithecus' the wolf-ape, William McDougall with his development of instinct theory and the 'group mind'—but they all fell before the strength of the prevalent behaviorism, and, to be fair, from their own inherent weakness.

If only there had been a coming together. If Carveth Read, for example, could have met Dart, and discovered that the 'missing' link—the possibly predatory primate—really existed in *Australopithecus* (but millions of years earlier than he could have imagined), and if they could have teamed up with the ethologists who had a real theory of how behavior could evolve, and if these in turn could have linked up with the genetical theory of natural selection that Fisher was developing. . . . But, as I have said, hindsight is a wonderful thing. And even then, we must remember that it is only since World War II that we have broken the genetic code and put together enough primatological, ethological, neurological, paleontological, ethological, endocrinological, ecological, and other such evidence to be even able to begin on the Darwinian science of behavior and society.

There is much more to the 'what happened' story that will have to be told later. Enough to say that the potential Darwinian social science did not get off to a good start despite the rapid success of the Darwinian paradigm within science itself. Both the internal weakness of early Darwinism, the wrong turns that it later took, and above all the entrenched ideological opposition that we have seen goes deep into our intellectual heritage, militated against it. Above all, its early association with dangerous radicalism—when it was seen as another materialist attack on the establishment—was transmuted into an unshakable association with the old enemy of innatism/subjectivism/intuitionism/idealism. This required a twist in thinking that again has not been much explored. Remember that the Lockean attack had been on the doctrine of innate ideas. It did not matter much what men's feelings and sentiments were—even empiricists often had little faith in human nature in this sense—as long as their *ideas* could be changed. This faith in reason—that ideas could impel action—sustained the Enlightenment project to improve mankind through education. But the romantic transformation had given reason some hard knocks, and it was generally agreed—and paradoxically Darwin added to this argument—that feelings and sentiments ruled more than reason in human action. (Schopenhauer—in *The World as Will and Idea* (1819)—was the finest exponent, and Freud was the culmination, of this trend. A whole argument could be made for Schopenhauer as the philosopher most compatible with Darwin—but that is another book.)

Thus, the empiricist agenda had to be extended to include all innate qualities, not just the ideas. Not only were ideas not innate but even our most basic feelings were the products of 'conditioning' or 'socialization' or some such environmental impact. This was the tabula rasa taken to extremes that not even Locke envisaged (but it was there in Helvétius). In Durkheim, then, when the source of the categories of thought and the source of moral obligation was put back onto 'society' so was the source of 'sentiments.' We felt not what millions of years of evolution had 'prefigured' us to feel, but what the collective conscience taught us to feel. Exactly how he didn't say, so it was a great relief when Talcott Parsons completed the agenda by showing how Freud's 'socialization' theory filled the gap and, through the development of the superego, somehow got the social sentiments of the collective conscience to become the 'need dispositions' of the individual organism (*The Theory of Social Action*, 1935). But what did the individual organism bring to the situation in the first place? Bergson's question. Nothing, in this scheme, except the capacity to be programmed *anyhow* by the society. The agenda was complete. The way to any exploration of the social instincts—the 'faculties' in Bergson's excellent formulation—was totally blocked. Boas sent Margaret Mead out to Samoa to prove that the traumas of adolescence were culturally rather than biologically caused and she dutifully did so. And so it was to go.

All these noncommunicating elements in the life sciences and the behavioral sciences were themselves nested in the latest, nihilistic developments in thought in the late nineteenth century, intensified after World War I. The deeply entrenched ideas connecting empiricism, science, and progress that we have seen stretching back to the seventeenth century continued to dominate inquiry. There were irrationalist rebellions from romanticism to aestheticism to surrealism to existentialism. But these only served to show up the power of the scientific paradigm. The other major development, which we can dub relativism, although having roots going back to Machiavelli, did not become a major force until after Nietzsche. It had been there in the romantic nationalisms stemming largely from Germany and which, as we saw, were part of the germ of modern anthropology. Thus, each Volk had its Kultur with its characteristic Geist, which was complete and authentic and not to be judged by the standards of others. (Unless you were an Hegelian, when it came somewhere on the ladder of spirit climbing to perfection in the German state.) But Nietzsche carried this to its bitterly logical conclusion. He harried the whole Enlightenment project of 'natural rights'—of the idea of a generalizable morality (à la Kant) which carried any *absolute* standards of conduct. Such standards could not be shown to exist, he insisted, and all that was left of the rationalist project was a complete relativity of values: God (i.e., absolute or universal value) was dead. The 'superman' was simply the individual left to make his own standards in the absence of any objective ones. His will was the only standard. This is why I put Nietzsche as an "individualist-subjectivist-nihilist" in the two-factor table, although it is at best a loose label, since his nihilism was only for the superman who would create his own values from his will to power while the herd would cringe helplessly, trapped by its collective slave morality.

Thus, not only were cultural values relative, but all values were relative, and ultimately the individual made his own. This Nietzschean critique was supplemented by the taking to its logical conclusion of the empiricist position by the Viennese and English empiricists, usually known as Logical Positivists. The earlier empiricists, like the Utilitarians, had always softened the obviously logical nihilism of the position by looking for some rational standards like the 'greatest happiness' principle. But after Nietzsche such softening was simply weakness. There could no longer be any gods or absolutes in a totally relativistic world; all such standards had to go, and the greatest happiness principle was an absolute like any other. Ultimately, there was only the individual judgment, and this was either purely 'emotive' as with the logical positivists, or consisted of an arbitrary 'commitment' as with the secular existentialists, or a 'leap of faith' as with the religious ones. In either case, aided and abetted by the staggering prestige of the theory of relativity in physics, any notion of absolute or universalist standards—the linchpin of the Enlightenment program—was out the window.

What started as a program of moral nihilism—seen, to be fair, by its proponents as a breath of moral fresh air, as a freeing of the mind from absolutist superstitions, and so entirely compatible with the liberal and Tylorian rationalist program—turned eventually into a relativism of knowledge which in turn seems to be turning into an intellectual nihilism of its own. Social scientists have taken the first step in insisting that knowledge is relative to the culture producing it (no absolute standards of truth etc.), but have not seemed to see that what happened in the relativity of morals—the eventual acceptance of the autonomy of the individual judgment—is the next logical step. But to take up this argument, again, is another book and better qualified minds than mine are already battling it out. All I want to establish here is that along with the already entrenched empirical-liberal prejudices there arose this other logical development of the empiricist-individualist paradigm: the relativity of all values and all knowledge.

The social sciences, and especially anthropology, were more affected by the idea of cultural relativity than anything else. All I have been emphasizing here is the general philosophical and intellectual culture in which the idea gained such strength. The cultural-relativity hypothesis took firm hold in anthropology and Durkheimian sociology because, of course, both were committed to a *collectivist* position. In this sense, they are not so open to the idea of individual relativism. If all individual representations, sentiments, ideas, or whatever come from the society/culture then there is an absolute source for the individual judgements. But, and this is the crux, this can never be a universal source common to all men until such time as the world is one culture. (It has been argued that the modern scientific world is in this sense one culture and that therefore, in that world at least, there are absolute standards. A neat argument. But it is one that does not seem to settle the relativism versus absolutism question at all.) Thus, cultural (or social) relativism became the central dogma of the social sciences. It was helped to this position by the negative notion that to admit that there were absolute standards of, for instance, truth and virtue would be to admit that some or other cultures might have them and others not. This had, of course, been the position of social evolutionists and racists in the nineteenth century and was anathema to the good liberalism of the modern social sciences which were seeking to disengage from this embarrassing heritage of their science. Savages were not lower on the scale of development, they were just different.

The inherent moralism of the social sciences, however, could not just leave it at that. Mere statements of difference do not suit the progressivist mode. Thus, a neat shift in thinking took place. Other cultures came to represent examples of alternative possibilities for living, or as we would say today, alternative life-styles. The prize examples were Malinowski's non-oedipal Trobriand Islanders and Margaret Mead's Samoan adolescents with their untraumatic passage to adulthood. To strict relativists these could not be lauded as 'better' than our own lifeways, but they could be pointed to as alternatives from which we could learn if we wished to avoid the terrors of oedipality and adolescent trauma. Since the greatest happiness principle still dominates the liberal-progressive mind, it is obvious that such alternatives are to be preferred. Thus, there is a kind of sideslipping from strict relativism. We cannot assert the superiority of our culture to that of 'savages,' but we can assert their superiority to us; this is perfectly in order. With this side shuffle the return to Rousseau and the Enlightenment program was completed, and the grimmer, Nietzschean consequences of relativism neatly avoided. The racism and ethnocentricism of the social evolutionary scheme were discarded, but the progressivism was retained. Not since Paul saved Christianity by converting the doctrine of the Second Coming into a spiritual event, has such a neat intellectual volte face been achieved.

Again, I do not want to go into the full ramifications of this since not only have I done so elsewhere, but I am only stressing this issue to make my point that it was one more nail in the coffin of the development of a Darwinian, evolutionary, biological

social science. For such a science must surely rest on some doctrine or other of 'universals.' Bergson's 'faculties,' Darwin's 'social instincts,' Jung's 'archetypes,' Lorenz's 'ethogram,' Count's
'biogram,' Chomsky's 'language acquisition device,' Wilson's
'epigenetic rules,' Fox's 'ethosystem'—or whatever. We are one
species; we have inherited our sociality from millenia of natural
selection; it sets not only our behavioral, but in a true Aristotelian sense our moral agenda: our *telos*. It is what we 'ought' to
do. There is no place here for relativism, even if there is a glory
in diversity. But it should not be too hard for the reader, having
read the foregoing, to see that such a plant is struggling in a
very hostile wilderness; and a wilderness all the more hostile because it is confused and divided against itself. It is couched in
the empiricist-individualist-progressivist agenda of the legacy
of Locke: the Enlightenment project. Yet, it has trapped itself
into a collectivist-empiricist-relativist agenda of morals and
truth—the donation of Durkheim—that is self-defeating. That
it rends itself and others with irrational fury when its contradictory premises are assailed is scarcely surprising. But it must
come to see that the only way out of its intellectual dilemmas,
and its moral bankruptcy, is to embrace what nearly three centuries of dominant wisdom have told it is impossible and incompatible with its deepest convictions both scientific and ethical:
the acceptance of an evolutionary theory of innate social capacities as the basis for a universalistic ethic of natural rights and a
cognitive theory of truth. It is like asking flat earthers to accept
the globe. But in the same way that flat earthers cannot navigate
without accepting what they do not believe, so we must come to
such an acceptance if we are to navigate our intellectual and social futures.

To such pleas the social and behavioral scientists usually answer with dogmatic assertions that it 'cannot' be done. To this
my answer is that it is being done and it will be done and that
probably it will eventually pass them by, as I once wrote, like a
train in the night, leaving them playing with their glass beads
and wondering where everyone has gone. But I am not optimistic that it will be done in time to save our species from the
ravages of the Enlightenment project and the legacy of Locke,

even as I recognize that to blame this latter-day event is to ignore that deeper self-destructive 'faculty' that is the curse of living matter endowed with consciousness. One clings, pathetically, to the hope that a realization of our real human dilemmas will help us solve them. The Greeks knew better. But it is all we have to offer, and so we 'ought' to try: however 'world open' and 'undetermined' we may be, we have no choice but to be human.

5

The Disunity of Anthropology and the Unity of Mankind: Introducing the Concept of the Ethosystem

How difficult it is to get something
of the absolute into the frog pond.
Pablo Picasso

I N this chapter I shall take up some of the themes of the last two chapters but with a somewhat different end in view. I am concerned here with the fragmentation of anthropology as a discipline, and try to trace it back to the problems caused by the Durkheimian disjunctions—of the individual and society and of social facts and biological facts—which are the basis of our current confusions. These dichotomies have been echoed in anthropology as the distinction between nature and culture, a distinction erected, as we have seen, into an impassable barrier by generations of theorists. Since any 'universals' of culture are ultimately suspected of being biological, the search for universals, which offered hope for a unification of anthropology, has been abandoned. Here I shall try to make a case for reinstating it by abandoning the concept of culture in turn, and substituting that of the 'ethosystem.' Having demonstrated that social facts and biological facts can only be arbitrarily separated, I try to show how something as non-biological in orientation as Durkheim's theories of ritual and anomie can be made sense of in an evolutionary context, thus anticipating some details of chapter eight. For the moment, however, let us turn to the aforementioned fragmentation of anthropology which gathered speed along with the much heralded expansion of the same discipline.

The expansion of anthropology, I would argue, came at a most unfortunate time. It came at a time when anthropology was sadly fragmented into specializations and stuck in an ideological quagmire. To this unfortunate mix we must add the structure and expectations of American academic life. The individualistic and entrepreneurial nature of the American academy, where success is measured by weight of publications, leads to the expectation of numerous and, God help us, *original* publications by each and every one. The gloomy population theories of Thomas Malthus used to be answered by the assertion that with every hungry mouth God sent an active pair of hands. Unfortunately, in the academic world, with every active mouth God sends but one indifferent brain. Einstein used to maintain, whimsically, that he only ever had *one* original idea. Most of us don't rise to that. This doesn't mean that good work can't be done; it can be and it is. It means that rather than it being consciously done as part of a collective, corporate activity in which it is seen as a small but necessary contributing part, it has to be exalted into an individual 'achievement,' to legitimize promotion and enhance status. The best way to do this, given an indifferent intelligence, is to specialize like crazy. The smaller the intellectual pond, the bigger appears the academic fish.

This sounds harsh, and I am certainly not suggesting anthropology is unique in this respect. But while in some disciplines there might be a positive advantage to the proliferation of specializations, this hit anthropology at a very bad period. The last thing we needed was specialization. For anthropology was not in that state of development where healthy specialization had begun; it was simply fragmented through a failure to coalesce into a unified science. Specialization is only healthy within a science unified by an accepted general theory (or paradigm, as it has become fashionable to call it). The life sciences, unified by the theory of natural selection, can specialize merrily with profit. They can argue about and modify the theory itself without damaging consequences. Anthropology, however, is unified only by a concern with culture, not by a general theory of it. Any disputes about this subject matter, turning as they do on points of definition and ideology, are preludes to even further fragmentation. The affluent hordes of new anthropologists seized on each new fragment and elaborated it.

One of the consequences of this recent history is that most anthropologists have given up the idea of a unified anthropology and have accepted the necessity of fragmentation as a virtue. Anthropology simply becomes an employment convenience—a useful fiction that administrators accept as valid and which provides a suitable cover for intellectual espionage. Departments go on stubbornly appointing the quota of linguistic anthropologists, symbolic anthropologists, physical anthropologists, archaeological anthropologists, mathematical anthropologists, medical anthropologists, applied anthropologists, ecological anthropologists, primatological anthropologists, psychological anthropologists, feminist anthropologists, cognitive anthropologists, structural anthropologists, marxist anthropologists, urban anthropologists, and, in California, paranormal anthropologists. They do this knowing that they are simply housing these people in the same corridor and with no real expectation that they will do more than preach to each other. Their professional organization, which started as a learned society and was one of America's most distinguished, has now become simply a trade union and lobbying operation for all those who call themselves anthropologists and pay their dues. They have nothing left in common, it seems, except the prospect of unemployment. They are a vested academic interest to be protected, not a collegiate body which exists for learned disputation. The ultimate irony is that a group of concerned members have now founded a new society *within* the American Anthropological Association called the "Society for Cultural Anthropology"! It's that bad.

So much for fragmentation and the institutional problems. I have alluded also to the 'ideological quagmire' and this is, of course, a contributor to the fragmentation. I have argued previously and at length on this subject, so I shall merely summarize here.

Anthropology is an heir to the humanist, empiricist, liberal tradition that started with the Renaissance, coalesced in the Enlightenment, and became a serious political force in the nineteenth century. Darwin added fuel to this position; he did not, as is often wrongly assumed, start it for anthropology. It is indeed curious today to see Darwinism so freely associated with reaction, when in its origins it appeared as a revolutionary materialism threatening the whole establishment. But anthropology was ambivalent during its formative period. In England, it split apart on the slavery issue: there was always a reactionary wing. In America, it found itself having to take a stand on eugenics. How quickly we forget our intellectual history. How many anthropologists could give a coherent account of the once powerful eugenics movement and its alliance with the Progressive movement? This presented a dilemma to anthropology. The 'split mind' I have referred to elsewhere began here. Tylor had uncompromisingly declared anthropology 'a reformer's science'—particularly in its role as sweeper away of 'survivals,' as in religion. The Darwinian theory of evolution gave anthropology an uncompromising materialist base. Yet there was much hesitation on this score. Matthew Arnold in fact elaborated the modern concept of 'culture' for the middle classes to fill the gap left by the receding tide of faith. These two notions of culture sat uncomfortably side by side: Tylor's materialistic, reformist view, and Arnold's integrative and uplifting notion of sweetness and light. Strangely, it was a view of culture more like Arnold's that prevailed in social science, although this again has not been recognized, except by George Stocking.

Anthropology had banished faith and raised the spectre of race. It had to accept evolution, and human variation was real. But how could this be reconciled with its liberal, reformist stance? Anthropology temporized. It mitigated the harshness of its potential materialism and banished the eugenicist/racist spectre by elaborating the concept of 'culture' as non-genetic, superorganic, sui generis. Even Huxley had felt driven to make the distinction between 'cosmic evolution' and 'ethical evolution,' and anthropology seized on this distinction to restore the uniqueness of man. In fact anthropology recast itself in the role of defender-of-the-faith in the uniqueness of man, and thus usurped the church, which was still floundering with the concept of the 'soul.'

In America Kroeber elaborated the doctrine of culture as superorganic, and cultural determinism was launched. Boas sweepingly declared genetics irrelevant and invented the implicit formula:

$$\text{genetic} = \text{race} \neq \text{culture}$$

thus preserving culture from contamination and launching cultural relativism. All this happily coincided with the rise of behaviorism and this seemed to clinch the issue.

In Europe, in a related development, but one with different roots, the answer was to follow the explicit formulations of Durkheim on society and social facts. No one knows quite whether to claim Durkheim for liberalism or conservatism, and he was indeed ambivalent. He ended life as a guild socialist and admired Saint-Simon. But he too was torn between his adherence to the scientific, materialist, positivist tradition, and a concern, like Arnold's, for the anarchistic consequences of the failure of traditional institutions like the church. Comte, the father of sociology, solved the problem by founding his own church. Durkheim was more subtle. His answer: society *was* God, and its members constituted a church. But this had to be phrased in positivist terms. Thus 'society' became for him (as 'culture' had become in America) a reality sui generis, to be examined scientifically through the study of social facts. These were (a) exterior to the individual, (b) general in the society, and (c) exercised constraint on the individual through the 'collective conscience.' Thus Durkheim's political concerns, and the supposedly positivistic science of society, ended in a kind of sociological mysticism. Society was reified, and Durkheim, in his eagerness to carve out a piece of reality for his science, consigned psychology and biology to the individual, producing his basic equation:

$$\text{individual} = \text{biological} \neq \text{social}$$

If we put the two formulae together, then we get:

individual/biological/genetic/racial ≠ social/cultural

This became the ideological linchpin of the social sciences. And for sociology it was not so bad. But for anthropology it created the schizophrenic situation to which I have alluded. For anthropology's distinctiveness lay in its grounding in the theory of physical evolution. The ideological formula, however, sundered this from the study of culture/society.

While we are on the concept of culture, it is worth nothing that Boas, Kroeber, Lowie, and Kluckhohn, for example, were particularly influenced by the German formulation of the idea which had its origins in Hegel and the rise of nineteenth-century nationalism. This was clearly more influential than either Tylor or Arnold (although Arnold was not himself uninfluenced by it). Its clearest expression was probably in the work of the German romantic nationalist, Herder. It is ironic then to follow the fortunes of the idea in American anthropology, for one of its major consequences was the doctrine of cultural relativism: each culture was an entity unto itself, understandable on its own terms, judged only by its own standards. This was conceived as a liberal onslaught on the racists and eugenicists. Genetics was not responsible for cultural differences, culture was. Papa Boas trained various attractive young ladies at Columbia to go out and pursue this, and they dutifully did so. With Benedict it was transparent, and that Mead was more influenced by ideology than ethnography has been recently demonstrated by Freeman (although to her credit she acknowledged this herself). Cultural relativism attacked the twin sins of 'ethnocentrism' and 'racism,' and it became another fixed dogma that this was the *only* answer possible. In effect, this 'answer' played right into the hands of the very ethnocentrism it sought to combat. It said that *every* culture had the right to be ethnocentric. What it was attacking was European ethnocentrism, not ethnocentrism as such.

The real answer to the problem they were addressing—as to all problems of the growing social sciences—was of course 'species-centricism,' if we can coin a phrase: Marx and Feuerbach's 'species being'; and the precious store of variation. The tragedy is that anthropology by its very nature as a distinctive science, that is, by its commitment to man's biological being through the study of his evolution, was the perfect science to insist on this. It threw away the chance. The ideological and methodological traps it set itself with the Durkheimian and Boasian formulae led in the opposite direction. The steady, and at times hysterical, attempts to separate the social and the biological have eroded that special position, erected a new dogma, and fragmented a promising science. Cultural anthropology, with its rampant doctrine of cultural relativism, is in fact a bastard child of German romantic nationalism. As such, it is paradoxically closer to the racism and fascism it fears than is a biologically based science, whose basic tenet is Washburn's empirically established position that all human races share 97 percent of their physical traits in common.

That piece of bald assertion makes for a natural break and gives me the opportunity to go from complaint to construction. I have in several places taken on the culturalist paradigm. I have argued that 'categorical thinking' in man does not separate him from the natural order: that his tendency to classify the world and then act on it in terms of this classificatory redefinition is in itself an evolved natural function that is perfectly explicable as such. I tackled this at the heart of the issue—kinship categories. I have also argued that the much vaunted tendency to taboo that which does not fit established categories has also a natural source and a natural function explained by the evolution of the brain. I shall return to the latter point, but let me take on the issue of 'individual vs. social' and 'biological facts vs. social facts' from another angle.

The only real opposition to relativism has come from those anthropologists interested in universals of culture. But the majority of these were themselves cultural determinists. The closest they came to a notion of culture as biology was the doctrine of the 'psychic unity of mankind'—itself developed in opposition to diffusionism. Thus, if similar institutions or traits appeared in all societies, it was because of standard human responses to similar problems. They didn't want to take it further than that, and those like Wissler who insisted that the logic of this was that cross-cultural uniformities were 'in the genome' were politely dismissed as cranks. Much of the weakness of this school lay in the difficulty it had in defining the units by which to measure universals. Very often, as in the case of 'the nuclear family' the question was begged by definition. In other cases the proposed universals were so vague—'a system of social control'—as to be simply part of the definition of social order itself. Almost all attempts concentrated on what linguists came to call 'substantive' universals. And the parallel search by linguists had some important lessons: the search for substantive universals seemed barren; if there were universals they were at the level of *process*.

Geertz has been lauded for having given the death blow to the search for universals. His argument: the 'universal' capacity that distinguishes man is his capacity to learn culture; thus, when we see people displaying the unique behavior of their particular cultures we are in effect witnessing the universal. Thus, we can forget the problem of universals and get down to the real business of examining the particular cultures. A neat argument that slips in relativity by the back door and allows anthropologists to continue business as usual. No wonder they like Geertz.

But while it is the truth and nothing but the truth, it is not the whole truth, because the acquisition of culture is not arbitrary. Geertz's formula does not dispose of the question: Why are cultures acquired in the way they are and not some other way—or infinitely different ways? They may be unique at the level of specific content—like languages—but at the level of the *processes* there are remarkable uniformities—like language again. Geertz wants to confound the varied manifestations of the processes with the processes themselves. Thus, each outcome of a universal process can look very different. But it is nowhere written that universal processes should have identical outcomes; in fact it is in the nature of such processes that they should *not*.

This is true even at the level of plants. It is one aspect of the

difference between genotype aand phenotype and the same
genotypic processes can have widely varying phenotypic outcomes. But—and here I appeal to structuralism, that perfect
scion of the house of Durkheim—if the reality lies at the level
of the process, then we still have a task to perform, discovering
those species-specific universal processes. In linguistics it has
been realized that this is the case, and while disputes abound
concerning the processes of universal grammar, no one seems
seriously to dispute that this is where universal features must be
found.

What then of the nature of the process? This is where I believe the search for universals ties in with the problems presented by the Boas/Durkheim formulae. Let me try it this way:
it was correct to emphasize the reality of the social collectivity as
more than the sum of the individuals and their actions; it was
wrong to insist that this collectivity could not be biological in nature. It was correct to say the collectivity could not be reduced
to the sum of its individuals, but wrong to assign the individual
to the biological sphere and cut off society and culture from
their biological roots. It was a mistake to assume that the biological basis of local variations could only arise directly from genetic, that is racial, sources.

Curiously, what Durkheim's position leaves us with is the opposite of what was intended. His position was resolutely opposed to utilitarian individualism; but in insisting that the
individual had a biological reality that separated it from the social it perpetuated and hardened the distinction it sought to
overcome! The individual (or the organism) had a hard reality
of its own in its biological facts, while society had an insubstan-
tial reality in its social facts.

There had been the possibility of a different, if related, position, but it came from the idealist philosophers who were
anathema to positivist scientists and later, curiously, tainted
with the charge of reaction, militarism, and racism that we have
seen backfire onto the relativists. Bradley in 1876, for example,
argued brilliantly that society was the reality and the individual
an abstraction. Foreshadowing G. H. Mead and even Goffman,
he saw the individual entirely as the product of his social milieu,

as a reflection or refraction of his society. It sounds very Durk-heimian, but with this difference: Bradley did not then make the error of assigning society to a nonbiological sphere. He caught perfectly Darwin's point that society existed in nature: it predated the appearance of man on earth. It was an evolution-ary, biological phenomenon. The social therefore could not be divorced from the biological. (Durkheim's mentor Espinas had made the same point but this was not taken up by the pupil.) Crudely, we can put Bradley's formula:

$$\text{social} = \text{biological} \neq \text{individual}$$

The individual, however, is not assigned to a different sphere as in Durkheim: the individual does not exist; it is an abstrac-tion from the social. Strictly speaking, then, the formula is:

$$[\text{social (individual)}] = \text{biological}$$

(It is true that Durkheim eventually had to declare that the so-cial was 'natural.' But this was to extricate himself from his own logical difficulties, not a premise of his system.)

How does this apply to process and universals? I have argued that the natural heirs of Bradley and Darwin were the eth-ologists since they developed the idea of the evolution of social behavior. The restriction here is that they concentrated almost exclusively on communicative behavior and saw it as expressing states of emotion (following Darwin). Behavior is more com-plex than this, especially in higher animals, and we needed among other things (like cybernetics) the corrective of ecology to supplement the ethological position. The ecologists also have the advantage of being concerned directly with system and pro-cess—particularly feedback systems—and this is where we have to look for universal, systematic processes.

To this we shall return, but first a small footnote, which will lead us onwards. It is objected that ethologists deal with univer-sal social behavior in a species—species-specific behavior. This is 'the social' at the level of the species. Durkheim, however, was speaking of 'the social' at the level of particular societies or cul-tures. If 'the social' is biological, this argument goes, then the only 'local' basis for it is racial; that is, local genetic variation.

Not so. This assumes a very crude kind of genetic determinism to which no geneticist would subscribe. Again, Durkheim was also speaking of general social processes, but even at the local level, as we have seen, societies and cultures can be seen as particular manifestations of general processes. If we add the ecological context to species processes of communication, then there is room for an enormous variety of such manifestations without invoking genetic variation as a basis. Its effects could at best be trivial in any case. The total mix of behavior and ecology needs a name, and 'culture' is too loaded and overworked. Following the ecological usage which describes the object of study as the 'ecosystem,' I propose that we are looking for basic processes in the 'ethosystem': the total feedback system involving general species propensities and ecological subsystems.

Variation in these can arise in many different ways but from the same underlying processes. It is interesting in this respect to turn to Wittgenstein who supposedly solved the problem of universals in philosophy with his doctrine of 'family resemblances.' Thus within a family, like the Churchills for example, there is a definite Churchill face; quite recognizable as in some sense the same, but which on examination reveals no one feature in common to all faces. This was the problem with substantive universals. If one of them failed to turn up in even one society, it failed as a universal. But there is conceivably a *process* at work which could generate a universal and quite predictable *pattern* in which *no one feature appeared in all cases.* The following figure illustrates this.

Figure 1: *Wittgenstein*

	A	B	C	D	E	F
1	x	x	x	x	x	
2	x	x	x	x		x
3	x	x	x		x	x
4	x	x		x	x	x
5	x		x	x	x	x
6		x	x	x	x	x

The numbers are traits or features, the letters societies or cultures. No two societies are the same at the substantive level, but there is clearly a 'family resemblance': a process is at work generating this pattern. I think, for example, that the elusiveness of the nuclear family or the oedipus complex as universals can be dealt with in this way. Taken as substantives they fail, but if one takes the component bonds and a theory of the bonding process, then one can see how the process generates the patterns and this would include a theory to explain why in particular instances certain bonds were *not* activated for certain purposes, hence the gaps. Thus, their absence would not mean an abandoning of universals, quite the contrary: the nature of the process would explain the distribution; it would be the process that was universal. I have described such a process at length elsewhere, so I shall not dwell on it here.

Another pattern could occur on the 'Guttman scale' model. In this there may indeed be common substantial elements, but very few. However, there is a high degree of predictability concerning the presence or absence of related elements. Again, this is because of the nature of a universal process which operates quite predictably but does *not*, by its very nature, produce the same list of substantial elements in all cases. It is illustrated as follows:

Figure 2: *Guttman*

	A	B	C	D	E	F
1	x					
2	x	x				
3	x	x	x			
4	x	x	x	x		
5	x	x	x	x	x	
6	x	x	x	x	x	x

Here, for example, if a society (A) has a trait (1) we can predict it will have traits (2) through (6). If it does not have (1), but has (2), then it will also have (3) through (6), and so on: the standard Guttman pattern. The pattern of distribution of traits in male initiation procedures seems to follow this scheme, with the only common element being seclusion of the boys (6), and the trait (1) being severe genital mutilations. Ritualized avoidance shows a similar pattern, and with the development of multidimensional scaling techniques we are on the way to understanding how such patterns relate to each other in complex ways. What we have lacked have been theories that would tell us what processes generated the patterns. Now that we are no longer cut off from biology, and now that we know that the social is biological, we can proceed in this direction.

If the processes of the ethosystem which generate these patterns are to be understood, we have to overcome the problems posed by the 'individual vs. society' and 'organism vs. environment' dichotomies that are the legacy of Durkheim and cultural determinism. We have to understand that *the reality is the system,* and that 'organism' and 'society' are abstractions from it. Ecology and ethology both discovered this and we should learn from them. For ecology the system is the total feedback relationship involving all the biota and resources of an econiche. For ethology the system is the set of action patterns contained in the gene pool of a species as these are manifested in local situations. In each case there is a concrete collectivity—a biological collectivity—and 'individuals' and 'organisms' represent points in the feedback system. Only for certain analytic purposes should they be invoked. For other analytical purposes they are not relevant.

Thus, we often hear in social psychology of the importance of *context* and how it impinges on the organism. Context should really be regarded as a *state of the system,* which can ignore the individual-social (or any similar) dichotomy. Once the initial state has caused an organism-environment interaction, the distinction rapidly breaks down. Once the system is set up it becomes totally recursive and you can 'start' at any point in the system. The underlying reality then is the process that generates the system, not the analytically separable points of the system. Thus, the organism has an output which modifies the environment; the organism-modified-environment then reacts back on the organism; the resultant organism-modified-by-the-organism-modified-environment reacts back on the organism-modified-environment . . . and so on. Reduced to a formula this is easier to see:

$$O > E(OmE) > O(OmEmO) > OmE(OmEmOmE) >$$
$$OmEmO(OmEmOmOmEmOmE) > . . .$$

The simplest process that illustrates this is the interaction of resources, digestion, and growth. But if we include the *social* environment, then the same recursive model becomes true for social behavior. Intelligent action by an organism is easily enough assimilated. With the evolution of a large prefrontal cortex concerned with future plans and strategies, and with increased memory storage, input from the environment (memory) has itself been selectively scanning the environment for further such input. Again, after a hypothetically necessary initial state, the distinction becomes for most purposes irrelevant. This is the outcome Durkheim wanted, in a way, but not by this route. It would certainly suit Bradley's model, however. (See addendum.)

Let us take an example from ecology that will illustrate one way in which a Durkheimian definition of social facts can apply perfectly to a sturdy biological fact—the biomass. This is the total amount of organic material in a population and can be simply expressed by weight. Thus, a human population on a small island could weigh, say, a total of 10,000 pounds. For certain analytical purposes, for instance analyzing the carrying capacity of the island econiche (its ability to support its population) this is the operative measure. It does not matter how it is composed. And it has real consequences. If the biomass exceeds the carrying capacity then starvation results and this can radically redistribute the units of the biomass (people). The biomass is a stern regulator. It is 'exterior' to the individuals, in Durkheim's sense that it was not created voluntarily from individual wills. It is certainly 'general in the society' since it includes everyone, and it exercises a savage constraint. But most dramatically it is *independent of the nature of the individuals*. It could be made up of one hundred 100-pound adults. It could be ten 300-pound males, twenty 200-pound females, and sixty 50-pound juveniles. Or any such combination. It doesn't matter. The social fact of the biomass is independent of these differences, but the lives of the individuals and the structure of their social order are heavily constrained by it, and their destinies influenced by processes involving it and the resources in a recursive relationship of the kind we have explored.

Take another striking example from the theory of kin selection. Too much has been claimed for the principle of inclusive fitness as a total form of evolutionary explanation. But
as Tiger and I discussed (for the social sciences) in 1969, the
work of Hamilton on the evolution of altruism filled an otherwise awkward gap in natural selection theory that Darwin had
recognized as such. In this area at least it remains a powerful
explanatory device. But for 'altruism' to evolve, as we know, behavior has to be selected that will result in maximizing inclusive
fitness—the fitness not only of the individual altruist but of a
critical minimum of genes identical by descent with his. If the
altruistic strategy succeeds, then the genes of the altruist will
spread in the population. They will, however, always be open to
victimization by cheaters, and cheating strategies could also
spread. There exists an equilibrium point between these two
sets of genetic strategies since clearly cheaters cannot over-
whelmingly outnumber altruists. The balance is known as an
'evolutionarily stable strategy' or ESS. It is arrived at by a process of kin selection. Once arrived at, the individual organisms
will act in accordance with the demand to maximize their inclusive fitness either as altruists or cheaters. Even in this oversimplified model, we can see again that the ESS is a true social
fact with all the characteristics Durkheim ascribed. Again, individuals are only analytical units for some purposes. Various
collectivities—the groups of genes related by descent, the population or gene pool (local), the species itself—are the real elements in the process. A whole population can here be seen as a
collection of genes, and the 'units' for kin selection purposes
are bundles of related genes which cut across other units like
organisms.

Consider one more example: the relation between hormonal
states and social relationships. This has been confused by simple-
minded cause-and-effect thinking resulting from the bugaboo
of 'determinism.' Again we must think in system terms. The
ethosystem here consists of an interplay, for initial analytical
purposes, between organism and *social* environment, that is
the other organisms with which it must interact. But if we are
looking at hormonal states, we can abstract out the individual

organisms and see the system as a constant distribution and redistribution within the biomass of whole-blood serotonin, testosterone, adrenalin, norepinephrine, and so forth. These can be seen as shifting around in certain concentrations and combinations. If we concentrate on certain 'point' combinations, that is individual organisms, we can see that these vary with behavioral states. If we stop the system at any one time, we can see, for example, that the distribution of dominance, aggression, copulation, submission, escape, and so on are correlated with hormonal states, and that these constantly shift. Thus, as one organism becomes more dominant, forcing another to submission, another to aggression, another to escape, and another to copulation, the previous balance of hormones shifts and has a different distribution. This different distribution in turn shifts the balance of social forces which in turn shifts the balance of hormones—and so on in the completely recursive manner already described. This is one way in which the biology of behavioral systems works. It is exactly like an ecological system with the society being the environment. And that is why I think the term 'ethosystem' is appropriate if one includes the ecological component. But it is a bio-behavioral system. And I must stress *system*. Testosterone does not *cause* dominance or aggression, but it is necessarily implicated in the ethosystem of which these are processes. At the risk of being boring I add again that the 'reality' is not the elements of the system but the processes that integrate them into a system.

One could add many other illustrative examples, like the synchronization of menstrual cycles in closely associated females that has been demonstrated in nonhuman primate groups, female prisons, women's dorms, and hunting bands. Such processes are social facts and biological facts; collective facts and products of evolution. They do not recognize the individual-social distinction as an absolute; it is relative to analytical purposes. For most purposes the distinction is not useful. This approach has little use for the concept of race, which is not a category well enough defined to be useful in analyzing ethosystems. Our approach puts the emphasis back on species-specific behavioral and cognitive processes, but looks at these in ecological perspective. This perspective over short runs is of course an 'historical perspective,' and, as we have seen, once genetic modifications have occurred over longer runs, an evolutionary perspective. Thus, the analysis of ethosystems is structural, historical, and evolutionary. With its knowledge of the long-run universal processes produced by evolution, it is perfectly capable of analyzing the short-run local differences produced by history. So that particularly silly debate is circumvented. It can perfectly well handle the role of intelligent, conscious behavior in the ethosystem, and it does not therefore, thank God, require the concept of culture at all—which is as well since we cannot seem to agree on its definition.

I said I would return to the brain since I believe that many issues in anthropology can be settled eventually through a study of its mechanisms. I have elsewhere explained why I think a study of the memory mechanisms of the brain will help us understand anthropological quandaries over taboo and pollution. I can only summarize here. Douglas and Leach have argued persuasively that we regard as polluting and tend to taboo those things that offend our systems of categorical thinking. What they do not explain is *why*. I followed Winson in showing that ever more complex studies of the memory system—including the role of slow-wave sleep and REM sleep (dreaming)—have established a three-year period during which long-term memories are laid down. During this period items assembled in the prefrontal cortex are constantly 'rehearsed' by being passed through the limbic system, which is also the center of emotional facilitation and control. The upshot of this is that nothing gets lodged in the long-term memory unless it has had a three-year vetting by the emotional system. In Ojemann's graphic phrase, this 'stamps in' the memories. The remarkable conclusion is that there is nothing in the long-term memory, including our most 'rational' of categories and systems of classification, that has not undergone a three-year testing and validation. The categories of social classification are established on a strong emotional basis. And this basis is *physical*—actual changes in the size and functions of the synapses occur, triggered by the cell DNA, after a critical point of 'rehearsal' has been passed. That is why it takes three years. It is small wonder that we react with extreme anxiety (again physically measurable) when this established category system is challenged by ambiguous items.

This has tremendous implications for our understanding of the relation between systems of classification from kinship terms through to totemism up to vast religious schemes. It makes immediate sense of Durkheim's theory of social solidarity. In traditional societies where everyone went through much the same experiences, the collective consciousness could be very strong because the *same* systems of emotion-laden categories would exist, *physically*, in everyone. The collective representations and the individual representations would be the same. Once society became more differentiated, then different groups would have different, or only partially overlapping, systems, and these must be in conflict. What disgusts or pollutes or even only upsets one group is not the same as in another. In a society like our own, where individuation and differentiation has reached its height, we are almost at the stage where every individual has a different physically based set of categories and anxieties. This is Durkheim's anomie, and it is real, physical, measurable.

The decline of social solidarity, the increase in individualistic suicide, social anomie, and the weakening of the collective conscience all follow. The role of ritual, as Durkheim saw, must change accordingly. When the experiences were uniform, the physical category systems were the same for everyone and the anxieties associated with them consequently 'general in the society.' Thus *collective* rituals could work, because they were therapeutic bastions against totally collective anxieties. As the process became more and more specific to the individual, the therapies had to be so tailored, until in the end each person is having a highly particularized ritual performed, or is taking drugs which specifically modify those synaptic connections we have spoken of, thus bringing temporary and artificial relief. The difference then between different states of social solidarity and the collective conscience, and the basis for our reactions of pollution and taboo, lies in the mechanisms of the brain, themselves the product of an evolution that makes sense of it all by explaining these, not as social pathologies, but as adaptational outcomes of quite understandable selection pressures—in this case of social and sexual selection pressures that have understandable social and reproductive results, lodged in the brain.

I speak here as though this approach was an accomplished fact, as Jane Austen would have said, 'universally to be acknowledged.' That is my little fantasy. Alas it is not, and I seriously doubt that it will be accomplished by the reform of anthropology. The ideological stubbornness and vested academic interests are too strong, and people by and large too intellectually lazy, for this to happen. Their synapses are too enlarged by now. But happen it will, even if not in anthropology. The sheer weight of evidence from the natural sciences will swamp the simple-minded ideology of social science. Soon it will be obvious even to the most recalcitrant cultural determinist that Durkheim and Boas—right as they were about many things— were essentially prescientific, and that their formulae were political adaptations fully understandable at the time but no longer binding on a better-informed generation. By that time, however, a new social science will have arisen, probably directly from natural science itself.

ADDENDUM

When looking for a simple illustration of the positive feedback loop involved in one type of ethosystem, I invoked the relation between resources, digestion, and growth. This was intended simply to illustrate the point that a process was involved here in which 'organism' and 'environment' were only analytically distinguishable, since part of the 'environment' was constantly being converted into 'organism'—and with the production of bio-degradable excreta, vice versa. But this simple resource → digestion → growth model can be expanded to include *social* variables if certain digestive conditions hold. I am thinking here of the work of Richard Wrangham (some unpublished, but see "An Ecological Model of Female-bonded Primate Groups," *Behavior*, 75:262–300, 1980). He has demonstrated that primate species differ in certain crucial features of their digestive systems, notably the ability to detoxify unripe fruits, seeds, grasses, or young leaves high in tannin and alkaloids. A specific liver enzyme—urate oxidase—is responsible for this digestive ability. Wrangham argues (although I can only give a simplified version here) that these differential digestive abilities facilitate different optimal feeding strategies for secondary food sources. In particular, for those species with the enzyme, it encourages the classic maternal extended families, or female kin coalitions, that primatologists have described in such detail. I myself noted that these seemed to be associated with particular species, but did not know why this should be ("Primate Kin and Human Kinship" in R. Fox ed., *Biosocial Anthropology*, New York: Halsted Press, 1975). This is a beautiful example because it shows that while there are 'genetic,' 'social,' and 'ecological' *components*, again *the reality is the process itself*—the system/feedback-loop—and not any simple unidirectional causal relation between components. If the animals are put into an environment where these secondary food sources (the resources) are not available, then the feeding strategy will change and hence the social grouping, for example. We can envision it thus:

Figure 3

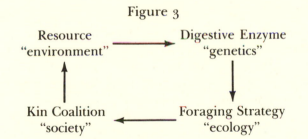

Therefore we can see that not only the growth of the organisms (which we could include in the loop under 'metabolism' or some such) but an important component of their social structure is part of the continuing—and continually readjusting—feedback process. If they lack either the enzyme or the resources, primates are forced into other strategies, other maximizations, other social structures. For what it is worth, *Homo sapiens sapiens*, like its cousins the great apes, lacks this enzyme. But that is another story.

6

The Violent Imagination

The women of the Triple City wept from lotus eyes
as Śambhu's arrow-flame embraced them;
but still, though shaken off, the fire caught their hands,
though struck, did pluck their garments' hem,
denied, it seized their hair, and scorned
like lover who has lately loved another, lay before their feet.
May this same fire burn away your sins.
    Bāṇa (A.D. 600–651), from Vidyākara's *Subhāṣitaratnakoṣa*

The satisfaction in destroying seems to me peculiarly human, or, more exactly put, devilish in a way animals can never be. We sense it always in the Mephistopholean cry that all created things deserve to be destroyed. Sometimes there is no more concrete motive for destroying than this one, just as there is no expressible motive for creating.
    J. Glenn Gray, *The Warriors* (A.D. 1959)

W E hear a great deal today about the problem of violence, but if man has a problem of violence, it is a problem only because he makes it so. Nature knows no such problems. In nature violence is commonplace; aggression is commonplace. Both are undoubtedly necessary. The lion knows no problem. The lion knows when to be violent; when to assert itself; when to kill; when to run. It knows these things in a sense that perhaps no human being knows. Its knowledge is the same as the body's knowledge of digestion and movement, flight and sleep. For man there is a problem of violence in much the same way as there is a problem of eating, of sleeping, of making love, of worshipping the gods. There is a problem because man imbues violence with *meaning*. Without meaning there is no problem; with meaning there are a host of problems, problems that are largely symbolic, organizational, semantic, comprehensible, and avoidable—but problems none the less.

In the same way, no animal has a problem about eating. The animal knows what it eats: if it is a hunting animal it kills its prey and devours it; if it is a scavenging animal it follows the killer to the prey and eats the leavings. With man, in the earliest years of his truly human existence, there was also no problem: he ate what it was his destiny to eat; he killed what he knew he should kill; he asserted himself against that which he knew he should overcome.

The problem arises not out of the desire to kill, any more than out of the desire to eat. The desire to kill is certainly different from the desire to eat, and this is something we must examine. But it is as real as the desire to eat; as natural as the desire to eat; as unavoidable as the desire to eat. If one considers that the desire to kill is in itself a problem, it is a little like saying that the desire to eat or the desire to copulate is a problem. In what sense is it a problem? There is no problem for the lion: it is certainly no problem for the theory of natural selection that the lion should desire to kill, in the same way that it should desire to eat or copulate. The same is true for man. Only if one wishfully decides that there should be no killing does the very existence of the desire to kill become a problem. In and of itself, the desire (and the killing) is neutral. It is a problem only if one chooses to make it so. For many animals killing is reasonable within the framework of their experience and their need to survive. It makes as much sense to say that killing per se is a problem as it does to say that the herbivore's desire to eat grass is a problem because it destroys the grass: it is a problem not for the herbivore, but only for those who can imbue behavior with meaning. The herbivore and the carnivore do not do this: omnivorous man does. And the problem exists because he is the animal that creates problems, not because he is the animal that kills, or eats, or copulates.

Since man evolved as a hunting, omnivorous species, it follows that he will destroy animals, plants, and even other members of his species who threaten him. He is right to do so. All these things are totally natural, totally within a comprehensible scheme of evolution. They are not problems. That man is on occasion both aggressive and violent presents no more of a

problem, in a scientific sense, than the violence of the lion: it is
the same. Many herbivores, even, can be aggressive and violent,
although they kill only rarely and accidentally. They were
mostly created for flight, not fight. But even then, their violence against their predators is natural and explicable. It is the
other side of the coin of altruism. The most pacific of animals
will be furious, for example, in the defense of their young, or in
the battle for mates. And this is totally comprehensible within
the explanatory theory of natural selection. The animals protect their genes; protect their reproductive efficiency; protect
their fitness—in Darwinian terms. To do this, they must alter-
nate between altruism and aggression. This is explicable, natural, and unproblematic.

There is really no point and no future in trying to prove that
man is *not* an aggressive or a violent animal. It makes as much
sense as trying to prove that he is not an altruistic, kind, and
self-sacrificing animal. Even if he is all these things, he is an animal. And when he lived on a scale that was the same as that of
other animals, there was no problem. He defended his territo-
ries; he hunted his prey; he devastated the vegetable environment; he killed his enemies. In this he differed not a bit from
other similar animals, for example, wolves, lions, hunting dogs,
or even the occasionally predatory baboons or chimpanzees, his
closest relatives. There was no problem. He killed his fellows;
so do lions. He killed his prey; so do baboons. He defended his
territory; so do wolves. He fought his fellows for status and
the right to reproductive success; so do other animals. There
was no problem. There would have been a problem for some
tender-minded god who preferred a system in which there was
no killing, in which there was no aggression, in which there was
no status, in which there was no struggle for reproductive success; in the absence of such a tender-minded deity no problem
existed, any more than it exists now for the lion and the ele-
phant, for the walrus, for the dolphin, for the giraffe, or for
the baboon. All animals have difficulties, but they do not have
problems.

It is not even enough to say that the problems stem from
man's consciousness of his own existence. Consciousness was a

necessary but not a sufficient cause of the problems. In the stage of his existence when he lived in much the same kind of balance with nature as his fellow hunting animals, exploiting much the same kind of territory as the wolf pack, for example, and employing much the same means of hunting as the wild dog, he was as conscious of his existence as he is now, and it is highly likely that as a consequence he created certain problems for himself. But these were not problems that were out of scale with his mode of existence. They did not in any real sense interfere with it; they did not prevent him from successfully attacking and competing with his fellows—they may even have helped him to do so.

But man began to believe that his own unaided efforts were not enough. Unlike his fellow hunting animals, he was aware of the vagaries of nature. His memory storage and his conceptual ability had made him understand that the seasons differed vastly from each other; that nature was not instantly bountiful; that hunts might not succeed; and that there were forces beyond his comprehension and immediate control. So he created systems of magic and religion to aid him in controlling this probabilistic universe. He created systems of artistic endeavor to enable him to comprehend it as a whole rather than piecemeal; and, of course, he always had language in which to cache all his doubts and all his approaches to magical certainty. There was no real problem—no real intellectual problem—about the nature of what he was doing. He was surviving. He was competing with other animals, with other groups of his own species and, in a sense, with the total environment. And in this gamble he used such means as were at hand. There would have been no future in doubts, questions, and concerns about the very mechanisms that his magical and religious systems supported and expanded. He did not use magic and religion to *question* the very nature of violence, or to ask whether it was necessary, but merely to supplement it and help it, and also to comprehend it in a sense very different from that which we mean today. He meant to comprehend violence as a potentiality; as something to help him survive; as something he knew was both natural and necessary—as natural and necessary as sex and

eating, artistic expression and language. It was not therefore to
him a problem, any more than sleeping, waking, walking, hunting, and singing were problems. He knew why he did these
things, knew it immediately, in a way that we cannot know today, simply because they are not in the same way necessary for
survival. We can comprehend the possibility of living without
violence. We have even, in certain of our communities, and in
many personal lives, evolved ways of living without reproductive sex. We certainly live without hunting. And we certainly, in
most cases, live without an immediate fear of the vagaries of the
universe. We are cushioned against all these things.

But in a paradoxical sense, it is because we are cut off from
the roots of violence—from the roots of the reproductive
struggle—that we make these things into problems. It is true
that the lion, cut off from all these things, as for example when
caged in a zoo, does not in the same sense make them into problems, because it lacks consciousness. What it does is to ritualize
its behavior in much the same way as the inmates of lunatic asylums, who have also cut themselves off, even from such rudiments of their natural existence as civilization leaves them. But
man's self-consciousness, his awareness of his own existence,
does not in and of itself create the problems unless he is placed
in a position where that self-consciousness is not being employed directly as an adjunct to those natural propensities to
violence and copulatory success.

It is not then the self-consciousness in and of itself that creates the problem, but the context in which the self-consciousness
has to operate. And the major context in which it has operated
has been that of 'early man': 99 percent of our existence as a
distinct genus. (It is really an absurd term—we should rather
refer to ourselves as 'late man,' since so-called 'early man' is the
true representative of the species; civilized man is a mere after-
thought.) Early man utilized his self-consciousness largely to
deal with difficulties rather than create and solve problems. For
example, his self-awareness led him to understand that the end
result of violence could be death. (It is possible in some sense
that some animals understand this, but certainly not in the
same way that man does.) But this very knowledge is a diffi-

culty; because the knowledge that in, for example, tackling an enemy or large prey the possible outcome might be death may very well cause fear, cowardice, and failure. In magic and religion, therefore, the strength of group sentiment and a whole host of rituals could be employed to bolster individual males against the possible consequences of their own fragility. This was not a case of attempting to understand the problem of violence, but of understanding the difficulty that might arise from individual weakness or failure of nerve. There was never any question that violence was both necessary and useful, and in a very positive sense good—as good as eating, copulating, singing. Only obviously it created more difficulties, because the possible outcome was the loss of an individual life—which is clearly a difficulty for the individual—and the loss of a member, which was a difficulty for the group. But when I say this was not a problem, I meant it was not an intellectual problem. If one likes one can say it was a practical problem. I prefer simply to call it a difficulty. One tried to overcome practical difficulties; one did not try to solve intellectual problems.

Again, I am not saying that early man never tried to solve intellectual problems. I am merely saying that, unquestionably, he did not create unnecessary intellectual problems where they did not exist. There was for him no *intellectual* problem of violence; there was for him no intellectual problem of sex. These are later inventions of human self-consciousness, not a necessary consequence of human self-consciousness.

What I am arguing is that in a sense—in some natural and nonteleological sense—there is an intended balance of nature in which even man's self-consciousness is in harmony with the environment because it is being *used* by him as part of his struggle for existence, as part of the adaptational process. It is being used in a very positive sense to advance the reproductive interest of the individual and, as a necessary by-product, the reproductive success of the population and ultimately of the species—even if, paradoxically, this involves a great deal of killing between members of the species, and between the species and its prey.

These things are not at all incompatible, however unpleasant they may appear to the tender-hearted god that we have posited as the original problem maker in this otherwise happily Darwinian universe. In this stage of human existence, where men lived in small hunting groups scattered over the face of the earth with plenty of room in which to move, plenty of space for maneuver in the chase and in the skirmishing that in those days passed for warfare—in this stage of existence there was no problem of violence, no problem of aggression. There *was* aggression, and there *was* violence. Both had consequences. But they were not problems. There was eating, and there was copulation. Each equally had consequences. Each equally was not a problem. There were many difficulties (indeed, it may have been a precarious time for the species), and if the difficulties had not been adequately handled, and if those attributes of consciousness—language, art, religion, science, conceptual and classificatory ability, and the like—had not been brought freely into play, we would not be here to create problems. True, if all that apparatus had been devoted to problem solving, we might not here to solve any more problems; instead, it was devoted to overcoming adaptational difficulties.

The problems arise, therefore, not because of man's self-consciousness; not because of the relationship between that self-consciousness—that thinking, concentrating, classifying aspect of cerebral activity—and the lower brain with its emotional demands; not in conflicts between superego, ego, and id; not in any real evolutionary disjunction between different aspects of man's personality, or between the forebrain and the nervous system. They arise simply from the rapid and bewildering change of context that occurred as a result of the neolithic revolution: the invention of agriculture, the expansion of population, the growth of dense communities, the beginnings of coercive economies, the origination of social classes, the founding of nations, and the advent of industrial society. Nothing in man's nature changed, and nothing in man's nature is basically at fault—contrary to what many contemporary thinkers would have us believe. There is no war between the higher sensibilities and mental capacities and the basic aggressive, instinctive violent perturbations of some unwanted reptilian preexistence. When we lived in small hunting groups, there was a perfect harmony between all these aspects of consciousness and the higher brain: between art, religion, science, and conceptual and mathematical thinking on the one hand, and hunting, killing, and the pursuit of men and animals on the other. All these higher attributes enabled this curiously successful beast to be more and more successful. And of course therein lies a paradox. The very nature of its success meant that it would overreach itself; and in so doing rapidly destroy, recreate, change—change utterly— the whole environment for which its violence, its aggression, its copulation, its eating, its art, science, technology and religion had been adapted.

Neither its violence nor its most exalted religious thought had developed in order to enable man to live with cities, armies, industries, and social classes. They had been intended for face-to-face status competition, for rapid skirmishing between small groups, and for all the intimate, ebullient complexities of the small-scale tribal existence. The brain that painted the caves of Altamira was quite good enough to invent moon rockets; it has not changed in the meantime. The violence in man that drove herds of horses and ungulates over cliffs by the hundreds, or fought for diminishing hunting grounds during the glacial periods, was also quite good enough to win the battle of Waterloo or conduct World War II. That brain could have invented the hydrogen bomb, and that capacity for violence could have used it. What presents the problem here is neither the brain nor the capacity for violence, which when dealing with other small groups of human beings, and even with herds of mammoths, was acting within its evolutionary range: what creates the problem is the atom bomb and the armies and the industrial technology, which are outside this evolutionary range. Because if the Upper Paleolithic hunters that we are continue to behave as though huge armies are skirmishing bands, as though atom bombs are stone arrowheads, and as though the destruction of three-quarters of mankind is a raiding expedition against the next tribe, then we have problems.

But it is not our very nature that is the problem, for that is totally unproblematical. It is not violence that is the problem, for this is part of the unproblematical nature. It is not aggressiveness or killing that are the problem, for these are as natural as copulation and eating. It is the *new context* in which these totally natural activities have to operate that is the problem. The problem is not violence, but warfare; the problem is not aggression, but the stratified societies in which aggression is manifested; the problem is not weapons, but the very scale of the weapons, which if used will destroy even the user. The problem is not even man's capacity for illusion, or his greater capacity for evil; for, again, in the small-scale context both of these are explicable, understandable, useful. It is the scale on which they must operate that makes the illusions dangerous and the evil cruelly destructive instead of merely exciting.

Above all it must be understood, and the need for this understanding is rather desperate, that the problem is not in any way one of violence, but one of human imagination. The human imagination can create incredible systems of symbols because it can imbue natural processes with meaning. It can, for example, create extraordinary gastronomic schemes and rules and rituals of food usage, because it can take a natural activity and out of it create symbolic meaning. Similarly with sex: rules, interdictions, magical incantations, art (or pornography, as we call it), and elaborate beliefs and practices can make the simple process of reproductive success into a vast system of meaning. In either, it can create both problems and difficulties for the individuals enmeshed in these systems. By and large, these do not have wholly disastrous consequences, unless the systems get out of hand and, for example, eating or sex is totally forbidden. After all, whatever the systems of meanings, as long as people copulate and eat the species will survive. Similarly, when it comes to the sheer business of making symbols, the human imagination can weave symbolic systems out of symbolic systems. A great deal of religion must be understood as precisely this. In the same way as food and sex can be woven into systems of meaning, so can symbols themselves, because symbol making is as much a human attribute, and in a curious sense more so, than sex or eating.

But what is perhaps most difficult to grasp is that exactly the same reasoning applies to violence. Like sex, eating or symbol making, violence is natural and explicable. But the human imagination can take violence in all its natural aspects and, using it like the colors from a painter's palette, create from it elaborate systems of understanding—systems as complex as the sexual intricacies of the Kamasutra, the sexual complexities of Protestantism; systems sometimes as baffling as the most intricate philosophy or religious rituals; systems maybe even as beautiful as those of art, music, or dance; systems that, indeed, employ all these others, but culminate in a consummatory act of violence on a scale and magnificence that exceeds anything in any other sphere because it is more terrible, and more profound.

The problem for the species is not violence itself. The fascination of violence is as real and as profound as the fascination with sex, with food, with the supernatural, and with knowledge, exploration, and discovery. And its satisfactions are of much the same kind. The problem lies with the capacity of the human imagination to create its encompassing, consummatory systems with violence as their focus and purpose. We call these systems battles, wars, pogroms, feuds, conquests, revolutions, or whatever, and therefore what we must understand is that the problem is not violence, but war; the problem is not aggression, but genocide; the problem is not killing, but battle. And into the organization of war, of battle, of genocide, goes far more by way of imaginative energy than physical violence. Indeed, if one were to do an inventory of the energy expended in a war, the actual physical violence would probably amount to very little. And with modern war this is even more striking. Modern war is almost better understood as an aspect of complex bureaucracy on the one hand and artistic capacity on the other. A quartermaster is as important as a general. A quartermaster—the logistics man—is the super-bureaucrat. He must insure that the battle equipment, and all the men, are in the right place at the right time. Without this the relatively little violence involved would be useless. The general often never sees the field of battle and spends most of his time with maps and communiqués. He is perhaps best likened to a conductor of a vast orchestra of a rather modern piece, in which the tune is hinted at and the orchestration only partially developed, and in which a great deal is left to the conductor himself. (Maybe an even better analogy would be that of a chef who knows roughly what dish he is going to prepare, and so invents a stroganoff as he goes along, and in the end produces something the like of which has never been seen before, mistakes and all.)

The problem here is not violence. The problem here is the use to which violence is put. The problem with Puritanism is not sex, but the uses to which sex is put in the control of people. The problem for Orthodox Jews is not eating, but the imaginative restructuring of the conditions of eating that the religion demands. The problem is not our violent nature, or even the nature of violence, but our violent imaginations, and our imaginative use of violence: an imaginative use that no longer bears any close relation to the evolved conditions of violence—the conditions in which violence is a contained, normal, explicable, and unproblematical aspect of our adaptational history as a species.

In thus recreating violence in another image, we are at our most magnificent, most terrible, most inventive, and most destructive. We are using at one and the same time the highest intellectual and the highest imaginative capacities. We are also utilizing our deepest resources of compassion, cooperation, courage, love, and self-sacrifice, along with our capacities for destruction, hatred, xenophobia, sadism, and revenge. But it is the canvas on which these are painted, their orchestration and reorganization, the use to which they are put, the scale on which they operate, the context in which they are organized that is the problem. Violence and compassion are not problems, in and of themselves. When they become caught in the great symphony of war, and large-scale corporate conflict generally; when they become built into the code of the Mafia, or written into the Geneva Convention, or woven into the elaborate framework of the rules of warfare of the eighteenth century, then they may become a problem in their own right. This problem cannot be understood by a simple reference to the roots of human nature, to the desire of man to dominate and kill other men, to simple human evil, to innate aggressivity, or to any other such inborn tendencies, sure as it is that these exist. For 99 percent of our existence there was and has been a context in which all these could operate and without problems, because their orchestration was preordained, and their imaginative use was therefore constrained. It is only within the last few thousand years that they have become problematical and have caused man to regret his own nature. And, after all, this is an extremely foolish thing to do. Man's nature is all that he has. The lion does not sit about regretting his nature, nor did self-conscious and aware man for 99 percent of his existence. He may have bewailed his difficulties, but he saw these not as stemming from his own nature as much as from problems he had in struggling with the total environment, which included, of course, his fellow men.

This bewailing of our own nature is the true alienation of modern man; and by 'modern man' I mean man since the Neolithic revolution, and probably even later than that—probably man since the advent of cities and conquest; man particularly since the advent of literacy and class society. For all these are in a very profound sense unnatural to man. Status, hierarchy, aggression, killing—these are in no sense unnatural to him. Armies, warfare, classes, exploitation, alienation—these are all unnatural, in a sense that we must explore more fully. This is not to say that the natural attributes of animals, like the weight of the dinosaur, might not often get them into extreme difficulties. Had such an animal been endowed with self-consciousness, the dinosaur might have bewailed its fate. And there may indeed be a lesson in that. For we have done for ourselves what nature did for the dinosaur: we have created our own weight problem—literally, since it is sheer weight of numbers that is at the root of all our problems and present difficulties. The dinosaur evolved a huge bulk but could not adapt to changing conditions. We have evolved a huge population which is in danger of not being able to do the same. We have evolved along with it a weight of armaments and of ideas that are as dangerous to our survival as the bulk of the dinosaur. That is what our capacity for self-consciousness has managed to do with our natural resources.

This argument does create something of a paradox, because if it is in our nature to be imaginative then we can argue that, in using our imagination to create unnatural conditions, we are only acting in accordance with our nature. This is something like the Cretan liar paradox. I am not too sure how it can be resolved, but in saying that it is not our nature that is at fault, what I am saying is that conditions can be imagined—and, indeed, for that precious 99 percent of our existence, did exist—in which this nature could operate without problems. Then it was comprehensible and adaptive, and within the natural scheme of things. But because, paradoxically, of one aspect of that nature, we have changed that context for ourselves, and we have added the bulk and weight that threaten to drag us down, that cause our present troubles, and that give rise to the so-called problem of violence. Possibly I will have to admit that our nature is at fault. But it need not have happened. It was certainly not inevitable. We existed for long enough without this albatross around the species's neck.

To return to the crux of my argument, even if we are to blame and bewail our nature, what we should blame and bewail is not the violence per se, not aggression per se, or hatred, or evil, or sadism per se, but man's violent imagination, which enables us to use these in unprecedented, unforeseen and unintended ways—unintended, in the sense that they are not ways appropriate to the small-scale hunting existence for which we were evolved. The flaw in the scheme, then (if we are to look for a flaw, and it seems that, like the Greek dramatists, this is what we are to do)—the Achilles' heel—is our violent imagination. Again, I insist that, in and of itself, this can operate within a context where it is constructive: the orchestration of a paleolithic hunt or a Red Indian raiding party did not threaten any species. But of course the potential was there—the potential for organizing this entirely constructive violence on a scale that threatened not only the species itself, but all the other species as well.

We often hear about the problem of violence in the modern world, about the problem of violence in cities, in the ghetto, in schools; about the problem of seemingly endemic violence in such places as the Middle East and Northern Ireland; about the problem of the apparently ever greater willingness to resort to violence. But, this is not a problem of violence: it is a problem of ghettos, of xenophobia, of capitalism, of economic exploitation, of racial prejudice, and of a whole host of other things. *These* are the problems. (There is really no problem involved if, when, for example, a person is standing on my foot and refuses, despite all my exhortations, to move, I push him off. After all, I'm faced with only two alternatives: I can either grin and bear it or I can knock him off. If I choose the latter there is no problem involved.) A problem is created when, in our infinite capacity for problem making, we insist that those who resort to violence to redress grievances have no right to do so because, for example, there are many other channels open to them to right their wrongs.

This argument, of course, can be used endlessly to bolster exploitation. It was an argument used against the followers of George Washington and Padraig Pearse. It is an argument used today against ghetto blacks and Palestinian guerrillas. I am not saying that in all these cases violence is in any abstract sense wholly justified—I am not interested in justification. This is part of the elaborate symbol system. To some people violence is never justified. But this is nothing to do with violence. This is to do with schemes of abstract ideas. The point that I am trying to make is that in none of these cases does the violence itself present the problem. The violence is a perfectly natural and useful response. One is at liberty not to like the response; one is at liberty to prefer some other response; but one is not at liberty to say that the problem is the violence as such. In many cases this is simply a way of dodging the real issues, or dodging the issues to which the violence was a response.

The violence can be a response in two ways. As a rational, calculated response it is simply one alternative among others, and sometimes the only effective one for achieving whatever an individual or a group wants. We have to consider this rational aspect of violence. Too often, to hide from the problems, we look only at the purely expressive side of violence. That is another kind of response: not a rational attempt to gain power or to

force a solution on an opponent, but simply an expression of a
state of frustrated oppression. Even here there is no problem of
violence. It is perfectly reasonable in some evolutionary and
natural sense for a cornered animal to strike. To those who deplore this, one can only quote the French:

> Cet animal est très méchant
> Quand on l'attaque, il se défend.

To the retort that in many cases these people have not been
physically attacked, one can always say that there are attacks
and attacks. Constant humiliation, constant psychological cas-
tration, constant denial of basic rights and needs are as much
an attack as a smack in the face; insolence is as much an attack
as a jab with a cattle prod.

This may appear to sound like something along the lines of
the aggression-frustration hypothesis, and it is something like
that. But frustration is not the only thing that provokes violence. Violence itself begets violence, and in perfectly unfrus-
trated people. The example of violence is easily imitated. We
also know how easily violence can become endemic—can become a cult. This business of routinization can apply to almost
any human emotion or activity. Under such circumstances one
does not need to be in any way frustrated in order to be attracted by violent activity. The problem lies not with violence
but with the human capacity to create cults, and with the context in which these cults must operate. Our dispersed, primitive
tribes were not particularly frustrated, but their males—at least
a considerable number of their males—certainly enjoyed going
on the warpath, and they made of this an elaborate cult activity,
connected, as we know, with status within the group. As a consequence of this routinization, this transformation of a natural
activity into a symbolic one, young men are enormously
attracted to these violent escapades because they expect considerable rewards; because the activity is itself rewarding and pleasurable. It has to do with excitement, the sense of danger, the
sense of achievement. As I have emphasized, within its proper
context this is, as far as the species is concerned—or even as far
as considerable populations of the species that are involved are

concerned—a perfectly harmless activity. If some males get killed, it will not affect the breeding potential of the group very much, if at all. In fact, the net effect may be to increase the sexual activity, the spread of genes, and the fertility of the groups concerned. It may even be part of the process of selection within populations which improves their general stock, intelligence, strength, and all-around ability.

Again, it is only when this cult activity of violence, which has nothing whatsoever to do with frustration, is taken totally out of context and placed in, for example, the supposedly orderly, rational, law-abiding framework of a modern city that it has the disruptive effect of a Mafia gang or a street mob. In the absence of police, city hall, school systems, welfare services and all the other paraphernalia of a modern, bureaucratic, industrial city, street gangs rapidly reach accommodation with each other, and their system of cultic violence achieves some sort of equilibrium and steady state. Again, it is not the violence. The context of articulation, the new orchestration—the gun, the city block, the police, the politician, the alcohol merchants, the dope pushers—rather than the violence itself, is the real problem. And I am talking now about a problem of understanding, not what I have previously dubbed a 'difficulty.' Certainly, all this violence is a 'difficulty,' but it is not in the intellectual sense a problem, whether it be the response in various forms—crude or sophisticated—to frustration and exploitation; whether it is expressive or rational; or whether it is cultic organization of violence which seems self-rewarding and exciting on the one hand, and rationally rewarding in terms of status on the other. It is all perfectly understandable, and presents no problem. It is what men do. If you take a group of men and oppose them in some way to another group of men, the likelihood of their coming up with a violent way of distinguishing themselves the one from the other, and of organizing themselves internally, is very high. This is not to say that in many cases groups do not exist that have other than violent solutions: we are talking here about probabilities, and the probabilities are extremely high. If a violent solution is not sought, it is usually because of a threat of even greater violence from some other source. Then again, throughout, the problem is not one of violence, and to pose it as such is to avoid asking the real questions.

And this leads us on to a further consideration, since I have been talking repeatedly about *provoking,* or calling forth, violence: the extent to which violence is an appetite, like hunger or sex. First we must consider whether hunger and sex are even comparable. We must remember that all these three activities are located in the same circuit of the brain and, indeed, the sparking off of one of these three often leads to the arousal of another. But with sex and hunger we have a problem; for, as far as the individual organism is concerned, whereas it can do without sex and still survive, it cannot, clearly, do without food. Sex could perhaps be considered as an appetite like hunger if we consider the species, rather than the individual: the species will not survive unless it reproduces itself, and in this sense, the individual must reproduce to survive in the same way that he must eat to live.

If one is deprived of food for long enough, a great need for it is aroused, much stronger than the need for it if one is being regularly fed. Similarly with sex. This will be disputed, and, of course, individual capacities differ enormously. Sex may be desperately necessary to some people and not necessary at all to others, with the vast majority lying somewhere in between. Of course, sex must differ in some profound way from hunger since it is possible, as Freud pointed out so brilliantly, to sublimate sexuality; that is, to substitute other activities for sex, which would be difficult to do for very long in the case of food. But we can see that, although unlike hunger sex does not impose a constant daily demand on the individual, the individual must be motivated to want to reproduce in order for the species to survive.

A well-fed individual can be aroused by the thought of a delicious meal, or the sight of a particularly tasty dish. Similarly with sex: even in the absence of any craving or frustration, an individual can be aroused by fairly straightforward erotic stimuli. On the other hand, if systematically frustrated and subjected to erotic stimuli, an individual is likely to burst out in rather violent sexual activity. It seems to me that there is really no harm, and a good deal of common sense, in regarding violence similarly. To some extent, the individual has to be capable of, and easily aroused to, violence in order to survive. But this is more like sex than like hunger: one does not need it all day and every day, but on the occasions that one does need it, it has to be easily facilitated. Both sexual desire and the lust for combat, as it were, have to lie somewhere near the surface.

These basic motivations can be tampered with and deeply interfered with, since there is nothing rigid or instinctive, in the old sense, about them. They are highly malleable drives. They can be reflected, suppressed, sublimated and subjected to all the other manipulations psychologists describe so well. But they cannot be eradicated. With sufficient punishment, or with sufficient bribery, one can suppress them, but one could do so in the long run only with great damage to the integration and stability of the rest of the organism's behavior. To use the modern slang expression that is extremely expressive, we can say that the human animal is very easily 'turned on' to sex and violence. And while not every human animal is exactly the same in this respect, it would be very rare human beings indeed who had *no* propensity to violence and *no* attraction to sexual activity. Critics to this point of view are very fond of pointing out that the wickedness of its proponents is subtly visited upon the whole species: because, for example, my friends and I are easily turned on by violence, we assume the rest of the world is the same. I have a great many friends who are not all that easily turned on by violence, but none who are not turned on at all, although such people must exist; I have some friends who are extremely timid about sex, but none who would maintain that they are not turned on somewhat by the appropriate erotic stimuli. But then, no one suggests that sex drives and sex needs do not exist, as a great many people wish to do with violent drives and violent needs. (I am always very curious about the lives of these loquacious pacifists who, certainly in print and very often in their personal behavior, are most extraordinarily violent people.)

The human capacity for illusion, the human imagination, the human conceptual schemes certainly allow us to arrange communities of people who deplore violence, and maybe even deny its reality, and certainly outlaw it. Similar communities have existed that have outlawed sex, and it is obvious that they cannot survive by the normal processes of reproduction. They tend, in fact, not to survive as viable communities. But we recognize the absurdity of hoping to produce any kind of organic community (as opposed for example to some kind of association like a monastery) by outlawing sex. It is probably equally self-evident, if we really look it in the face, that it is very difficult for communities to exist that totally outlaw violence, and indeed, the very fact that they need these elaborate precautions suggests, as do the elaborate precautions that surround any attempts to suppress sexual activity, that what is being dealt with and denied is real and persistent.

This way of looking at violence, as very similar in some respects to sex, gives us a hope for dealing with it. For if we see it as something with appetitive elements, but which basically requires 'turning on' for full arousal, then it is open to us to engineer a low-key system of arousal. Thus, in any ongoing community we can expect a certain amount of sexual activity, because people enjoy it and, even if not particularly stimulated, will still want it. We also know that cultures that bombard members with erotic stimuli will produce high levels of sexual activity, far beyond what is necessary for pleasure or reproduction. Similarly, we can expect that in any normal ongoing organic community there will be a certain level of violence, both among the members of the community and towards others. We can also recognize communities that have effected the institutionalization of violence, its elevation to a cult status, its glorification, its frequent representation in symbolic forms and artistic performances, its constant evocation, and its justification at the highest religious and philosophical levels. In such a community, because its members as a result of their evolutionary history must be easily turned on to violence, we would indeed find many times the normal level of violent activity.

Thus, to insist that violence is normal, natural, and unproblematical when seen in its proper evolutionary perspective is not to say that extremely high levels of destructive, pointless, irrational, emotive, cruel, and barbaric violence are normal, necessary, or in any sense desirable any more than to say that, since sex is a normal, explicable, and unproblematical evolutionary activity, constant orgies and elaborate but nonreproductive perversions are also normal, or to be expected in every organic community of humans. Man needs sex, not orgies; in the same way man needs violence, but not the massacre of innocents. Therefore, to accept the nature of violence in the way I am suggesting it should be accepted is not at all to accept the inevitability of certain extreme forms of violence. Which brings us to the queston of the control and the regulation of violence, the rules of violence—perhaps what one might even call the *inherent* rules of violence.

In much the same way as violence itself is a natural attribute, so the regulation of violence is an equally natural attribute. Again, the analogy with sex may be argued. The propensity for sexual activity is of course natural, but so is the propensity to regulate it. There is a long evolutionary argument behind this argument which states, briefly, that it is a major characteristic of man that he will formulate rules about the things which most concern him. Food, sex, and violence are of course high on this list. But it may go deeper than this; for it may be that the conscious and even elaborate rules that men make are not something that self-conscious and aware culture imposes on a crude and vicious nature, but are themselves a product of that nature. These rules and regulations, in other words, are the labels that speaking men use for the kinds of behavior that nonlanguage men would have indulged in anyway. Roughly, the issue is that even nonlanguage men did not fight without rules, any more than they copulated without codes. These may not have been explicit, but they existed; and when he came to speak and to symbolize man gave them expression. In other words, the rules of fighting are as natural as the fighting itself. Given symbolic capacity, men can play elaborate games with these rules, in a way that a nonsymbolizing animal could not. But the fact that he is moved as strongly to regulate as he is to fight is another intriguing source of hope. Because man is as turned on by rules and regulations, even when he opposes them, as he is by sex, food, and the joy of combat. Left to his own devices, in other words, man would regulate his sex and violence with as much relish as he copulates and fights.

I have said that this goes deeper than cultural and symbolic activity, and indeed it is perhaps one of the greatest contributions of the ethologists to show us how animals 'ritualize' their violent behavior. They can perhaps be criticized for overemphasizing this ritualization and for ignoring the real violence that does occur; but what they have pointed out is that within a species there are strong tendencies to turn potentially sanguinary and death-dealing combat into a ritualized game. It does not always work, but the tendency is there and it is strong, and the more violent and better armed the species, the greater the tendency. It all works within limits—real violence is still prevalent—but the limits are interesting. The fact that they should exist is hopeful. For in man also, by nature a creature easily aroused to violence and obviously gaining enormous satisfactions from its expression, the same tendency exists, and exists strongly. And what is perhaps amazing about this violent species of ours is not that we kill so many, but that, given our potential, we kill so few and so infrequently. And this is not because we are not violent, or because we can easily substitute passivity for violent activity, but because we inherently develop ritualized means to regulate violence. And we perhaps now should ask how this operates. We should address ourselves, in other words, not to the question of violence, the so-called 'problem of violence' which we understand really very well, but to the question of the *regulation* of violence—equally basic, and equally natural. The real question for research is: why, if this regulation is so basic and so natural, do we seem to find such difficulty with it?

We must then ask about the conditions for the ritualization of violence; that is, about any processes that serve to minimize the sanguinary outcome of violent conflict. Under many circumstances this reaches almost absurd heights, whereby the conflict, even involving hundreds of thousands of people, has virtually no sanguinary outcome whatsoever, despite all the panoply of war, and the seemingly savage intentions of the participants. At the other extreme, there seem to be no regulations whatsoever, and the outcome is mayhem, massacre, and the slaughter of millions. Which, we might ask, is nearer to that 'normal' state which is always at the back of our discussion? I think there is no doubt that a relatively highly regulated state is a normal one. It is a state in which violence and killing occur, but in which the degree of regulation is high, and the sanguinary outcome relatively minor. I must repeat that this is not to deny the violent nature of man, but to add this extraordinarily important qualification: that in his natural setting he'll eat his violent cake and have it. He will have all the benefits of violence without excessive mortuary consequences—all the excitement, the danger, the exploration, the comradeship, the compassion, the daring, the beauty, and the glory, but as little as possible of the death. Even so, the reality of death must always be present, for this is never a mere game, much as it may often approach one. (That is why, whatever its popularity, football can never have the religious fascination of bullfighting.)

What then are the conditions of successful ritualization? This is always relative. When we say that the outcome is only a 'minor' amount of killing, this depends on the scale involved. When two armies of 100,000 are facing each other, and after the supposed battle is over 2,000 or 3,000 are left dead, one must suppose this to be a relatively small number in terms of what might have been the case. But it is not usually upon such a scale that violence operates, but rather upon a very small scale—a scale, in fact, on which we evolved. Within any small community, there cannot be too much sanguinary conflict without draining the population of its resources and its manpower, and eventually effectively injuring its chances of survival as a community. Therefore, within community boundaries there is a strong immediate urge to regulate the violence that is bound to occur.

There is always the tendency to regulate, even though it does not always work. No one would want to claim that these regulatory activities were all successful. But there is a persistent tendency for them to operate. In all communities there are some standard ways of engaging in relatively violent conflict, while limiting its incidence and modifying its outcome. The duel and single combat are the prototypes. In some communities, like the Pueblo Indian, where these forms of ritualized violence are not allowed—where the regulatory attempt is a blanket prohibition of violent activity—the result is a high level of personal, expressive violence, which, from its very unregulated nature, can be very dangerous. Also, there are often extremely high levels of communal violence, as in the persecution and beating to death of witches. The Pueblos might turn out to be excellent examples not of the perfectly harmonious pacifist communities they are often taken to be, but of precisely how *not* to deal with violence. We should look rather to those many examples of communities in which fighting of one sort or another occurs but within an explicitly or implicitly defined and often sanctified set of rules and regulations that allow the combatants all they need by way of expressive violent activity. When does this work, and when does it break down?

Moving from the small to the large scale, we can reinterpret the history and current state of warfare to try to understand the ratio of negotiation to combat, and the conditions under which the elaborate regulation and restriction of warfare evolves. This approach would not so much look for the 'causes' of war—it would assume that wars occur for many reasons—but would concentrate on searching out the factors that lead to the regulation and restriction and ultimately containment of war. Its assumption would be perhaps a variation of Clausewitz's dictum: it would assume that war is diplomacy's way of creating more diplomacy, since men love the treaties and negotiations at least as much and probably more than they love the combat. To this end, wars cannot be allowed to get out of hand, or diplomacy would suffer.

I venture a rough-hewn hypothesis: where 'pure dominance' is involved—a simple matter of who is top nation, tribe or kingdom—the rules, negotiations and displays proliferate; where 'real interests' (territory, population, women) are involved, the rules break down and we approach mayhem. The basic hypothesis behind this one—that men are as attached to the rules as to the killing, and that other things being equal they will minimize the killing in favor of the display—is precariously hopeful. Other things are equal more often than we imagine; it could be much worse; and, given the awesome possibilities, we may be living in something close to the best of all possible worlds.

7

The Inherent Rules
of Violence

> The comparison between species with less and those with
> more ritualized fights, and the study of the developmental
> stages leading in the life of the individual, from the young
> fish fighting without rules to the 'fair' Jack Dempsey, give
> us definite clues as to how ritual fights have evolved.
>
> Konrad Lorenz, *On Aggression*

> The two worthies, after a brief bandying of words, seized
> each other's throats leisurely, so as to give the spectators
> time and encouragement to interfere.
>
> Sir Richard Burton, *Personal Narrative of a*
> *Pilgrimage to El Medinah and Meccah*

I N this chapter I want to ask something about the very nature
of social rules as exemplified in fighting, about what might be
called the 'rules of violence.' Unfortunately, once we begin to
talk about violence and aggression we get into all sorts of semantic problems. But I will not be concerned here with those.
Instead I will focus on fighting, as in punchups, when people
actually engage in physical combat with each other. We don't
have any definitional problems here; we all know what fighting
is. Thinking about fighting and having, in the course of my own
field work, had to watch and extricate myself from, and generally be concerned with, fighting, I consider that it raises certain
problems about the very nature of social rules which are ger-
mane to anthropological debate. So I shall begin with a few remarks on the issue of rules and behavior in order to show why I
am interested in fighting in this respect.

There seem to be two issues that one can pin down: one is the
anthropological-sociological position that rules as such repre-

sent 'culture' as opposed to 'nature.' You get this notion in all kinds of guises. Rules are seen as—to use Lévi-Strauss's (1969) expression—an 'intrusion into nature'; they are an aspect of the superorganic, the nongenetic heritage of men. Basically, the fact that we order our lives according to rules is what divides us from nature. Nature, we are told, may have regularities but it does not have rules. So human behavior is primarily different from animal behavior because it is rule-governed. Now in a sense this is obviously true if one thinks of rules in the sense of edicts or laws, because animals don't have language and self-consciousness and they don't make laws. This is therefore almost a trivial sort of truth. It is a characteristic of this particular species, *Homo sapiens,* that one aspect of its species-specific behavior, if you like, is that it makes rules. But then, I think, we need to ask, what is the significance of this as the basis of a nature-culture distinction? Lévi-Strauss, for example, takes incest. Animals have incest, we have rules against incest, and this he makes the great dividing line between nature and culture. Actually, when we look at animals, they have about as much incest as we do, by and large, if we look at what we *do* as opposed to what we *say* we do. If you simply compare human behavior with animal behavior you find that in nearly all species of animals there are quite elaborate mechanisms preventing incestuous inbreeding, or at least two-thirds of it. They will exclude mother and daughter, and brother and sister, and leave in father and daughter, or something to that effect. But most of the 'weight' of inbreeding, as it were, gets taken out by some mechanism or another. In our case it is much the same; we remove the bulk of incest but we leave in some. So the question then becomes, what is the significance of these rules if, as far as actual behavior is concerned, there is no firm distinction between animals and man?

What are these rules doing, these incestuous rules? Are they really intrusions into nature, are they really attempts, as Lévi-Strauss suggests, to say 'No' to nature, or are they simply, as I think they are in many cases, labellings of natural tendencies? That is, do we simply put into words and formulate into rules things that we would do anyway in the absence of language or self-consciousness? I am not saying they are or they are not, I am just saying that it seems to me to be an open question as to whether or not in many cases rules are simply labellings of natural tendencies and therefore not in any sense antinature or an intrusion into nature. The sort of work I've been doing on kinship systems comes to a similar conclusion. Roughly speaking, I think we can carefully put together all kinds of evidence which suggests, again, that in the absence of language and self-consciousness, we as a species would probably have kinship systems that were recognizable in terms of very regular patterns of discriminatory behavior towards kin. That is, we would probably have lineages and alliances and all the things that we find in human kinship systems. What we do with human kinship systems is to label all these things. Once you label them you then get a feedback effect and you begin to play games with the labels and the whole symbolism of kinship systems emerges. A great deal of the time what we are doing is labelling 'natural' tendencies, not in any sense intruding into nature. I think that Lévi-Strauss has this mistaken notion in that he confuses rules with order: we have rules, animals do not, therefore animal life is unordered. Animals mate promiscuously and are incestuous, we mate selectively and are not incestuous, and that's because of rules. Well, the answer is that animal life is not so chaotic; it's incredibly ordered, and if you're going to make that kind of mistake you are back to the old 'law of nature' and 'law as edict' confusion again. Certainly, coming from a Frenchman, this idea that human mating is not promiscuous and disordered is rather curious!

I raise these various problems very briefly in order to ask, if you like, 'What price rules'? Now, one can find various cases in which it's fairly clear that rules *are* intrusive, that is they do say 'No' to nature, and that they do somehow formulate a kind of behavior that is wholly peculiar to man. I think we could probably winkle out some systems of that kind. But a lot of the time I think that rules are what I call simply labelling devices for things that would happen anyway.

This takes me on to the second and related question. This is the question which, I suppose, lies behind all anthropology and social psychology, and that is the question of social order—what I prefer here to phrase as the 'Hobbes-versus-Aristotle' issue. For Hobbes, the state of nature is a 'war of all against all.' We are told that life is 'poor, nasty, brutish and short,' so that in order to attain a state of culture, or a state of civil society if you like, you have to have a social contract, which is the first rule. Basically, a social contract involves the instigation of rules in order to bring order to a previously disordered state of nature, in which every man's hand is turned against that of every other man. I think Hume (1739) was the first critic, in this sense the first really acute social psychologist to point out that most of human behavior is of course not ordered by explicit rules, contracts, agreements or the like, but, as he put it, is ordered by 'conventions.' He gives the example of two oarsmen in a boat who have no specific contract or agreement as to how they will row, but who nevertheless end up rowing perfectly in time and pulling the boat. This is his model for most social conventions. We all end up somehow pulling the boat in the same direction without ever having agreed that we will do it in any particular way. Again, at the bottom of this whole contract theory is the notion that rules order nature; if you did not have rules, agreements, conventions or whatever, you would have disorder.

This Hobbesian notion appears to have stuck with us. It is basic to most of the empiricists' and environmentalists' views that, in the absence of rules that are established through material interest, there would be disorder. Against this there is the Aristotelian tradition, which says that man is *by nature* a social animal (I think it's Tiger who keeps pointing out how curious it is that whenever this gets quoted people leave out 'by nature'). This tradition holds that society precedes culture, that society is part of nature and that it is perfectly natural for men to live in a rule-governed situation. In so doing they are not somehow imposing themselves on nature, they are not making a radical change. They are *expressing* their nature. They are social animals and they will therefore live in a civil state. You get this tradition warring rather weakly against the Hobbesian tradition in the nineteenth century, in people like Espinas, who was Durkheim's teacher but whose book, *Des Sociétés Animales* (1877) was, as far as I know, never translated into English. In Bradley (1876) we find the first social psychologist to anticipate theories of status and role. And of course in Darwin (1871) we find implicit this same notion which Bradley advances, namely the idea that rules are an inherent part of the nature of the creature, and not something imposed upon the nature of the creature. Bergson (1935) had this same idea in his notion of the evolution of the two kinds of life processes, intelligence and instinct. He pointed out how intelligent animals have to re-create out of their intelligence, almost quasi-instinctual societies, because you cannot stop and think about every move. Here he is back to Hume's conventions again: you need to have a whole set of hidden understandings, according to which everybody will work, and you end up behaving as though you were driven by instincts, even though in fact you are not. This Hobbes-versus-Aristotle issue, this question of social order, is linked, I think, with the anthropological-sociological notion of rules as an imposition on nature. Lévi-Strauss takes incest as his perfect example of the institution of a rule. The incest taboo, he thinks, is a perfect example because it partakes of both nature and culture. It is at the fulcrum between nature and culture, it is universal, it occurs everywhere. Hence, he suggests, it is part of nature, but it is also rule-governed and hence part of culture, so it is *the rule,* the essential rule that gets all culture going. But as I said before, I think he is wrong here, because we would have incest avoidance even if we did not have taboos and rules.

Now I want to look at the same issue as regards fighting. If you take fighting you can assume that, as in the promiscuous incestuous state that Lévi-Strauss and no doubt Hobbes have imagined to be the natural state of man, you would have disordered Hobbesian mayhem. You have it in promiscuous incestuous mating, you have it in fighting—a very similar thing. When you are down to the fisticuffs and the adrenalin is surging through the body, and all those hormonal changes are occurring, and the blood is up and so on, you would imagine that you had somehow returned to a precultural level. Here you somehow abandon the world of rules, the world of culture, the world of order, of reason, of categories, of cognition, of self-consciousness—all those wonderful things that make us men. When we begin a punch-up, we are somehow back to the 'natural' animal state. However, the more closely I look at fighting, from the individual pub brawl up to some of the most intricate organized warfare, the more obvious it becomes that fighting is heavily rule-governed; it is rule-governed in the same way that language is rule-governed, where none of us are aware of the rules of language but where nevertheless we speak according to them. In other words, it is very rare to find fighting that is random, disorderly, totally unstructured. Therefore, what I'm asking about fighting is, is there something going on here that is the same as occurs in incest or kinship or anything else, namely that there are certain *inherent* rules of violence? Is there something 'inherent' about the very structuring of fighting, and if so, then what is it? Furthermore, are many of the rules—the explicit rules, the Queensbury rules, the Geneva Conventions, the elaborate rules that we weave around fighting—attempts at social contracts, attempts to impose rules on this mayhem of natural bloodletting, or are they labelling devices? Are they merely elaborate cultural expressions of what would happen even in the absence of explicit rules, consciousness, and so forth?

Well, that is my idea and there is really not much more to say except to describe some aspects of fighting as I have observed it on Tory Island. The name Tory is derived from the Gaelic word for 'robber' or 'brigand' which was the basis of the insult that was thrown by the Whigs at the King's Party in the eighteenth century. People ask me if it is an island for retired Conservative MPs, but it isn't. It's a small island, three miles long, widest a mile wide, with nearly 300 people living on it. They are all Gaelic speakers, all Roman Catholics, and living a life that is relatively removed from what goes on on the mainland. The islanders kicked the landlord's bailiff out in 1861, after which nobody really gained much control over them. A gunboat was sent to try to collect their rents and rates but the gunboat sank and fifty men were killed. The Admiralty said it was a navigational error, but the islanders all know that it was the king in fact who turned the cursing stones on the boat and sank it. There is no

point in my going into a long description of the island, except
to say that it's nine miles off the shore, very remote and very
difficult to get to. It's one of the last really archaic bits of Celtic
twilight left to us. So you can imagine this little island, with its
tiny harbor, its cluster of houses and, of course, a church.

It would be wrong to give the impression that Tory islanders
spend most of their time fighting. But on those infrequent occasions when fights do occur, they become matters of intense
interest, and the cleavages and tensions of the whole community are brought resoundingly to the surface.

I will leave aside the question of why the Irish have a reputation for bellicosity, as well as the question of why they are so
bellicose. Certainly communities differ, and so may national
characters, in the amount of violence they tolerate or encourage. There are several ways they can handle violence. They can
forbid it altogether and punish those who resort to it, which is
really a matter of reserving 'legitimate' violence for the gover-
nors of the community or the state. They can bring up their
children to avoid violence except as a last resort. Or they can
allow violence only under certain restricted conditions—such
as in sports, or in 'legal' manhunts. But there is no one way of
dealing with the potentially disruptive effects of violence. It is
sometimes said that there are communities that are totally nonviolent, but this can easily be refuted. Pueblo Indians, Eskimos,
Bushmen, have all been cited as examples of nonviolent people,
and all turn out to have high rates of personal violence. The
Bushmen of the Kalahari Desert, it turns out, have a higher
homicide rate than Chicago's! A book was written about them
called *The Harmless People*, which only goes to show that while
anthropologists might be nice folk who like to think well of
their fellow men, they can be poor guides to reality.

Violence can be channelled, suppressed, repressed, and variously kept in corners, where it can fester largely unobserved by
those not looking for it or not wanting to see it. But it is a rare
community of human beings that does not have its quota of violent activity. It is interesting not to try to explain this away
somehow but to see how it is handled. Another fact must be
faced: violence is pleasurable. We have to face up to the fact

that violence generates tremendous excitement, either in participation or in observation, and this seems to be a universal and deep-seated facet of our behavior, so that it's very easy to teach us to enjoy violence. In other words, we may not by nature be aggressive killers, but it is terribly easy to turn us into them. It is in fact so easy that it suggests that the animal must be rather ready to learn this pattern of behavior in the same way as it is ready to learn language.

I do not think that Tory men are 'by nature' more violent than other men. In most of their dealings they are gentle and considerate. But they have a threshold of anger and, once it is reached, they are quick to respond with aggressive acts—always, however, in defense of what they perceive as their legitimate interests. The tensions that can occur on a densely populated little island with few resources are without number. There is no authority other than the priest—and how much influence he has is open to question.[1]

When alcohol is brought to the island, as it is from time to time, and rapidly consumed, there is a consequent lowering of inhibitions. Quarrels at the verbal level are rare, and antagonists will usually just avoid each other. A visitor to the island will be surprised when, suddenly, a fight starts for seemingly no reason and with few preliminaries. At first sight, it seems to be an unstructured scuffle. But this is the main point I want to make about Tory fights: they are never unstructured. This may seem strange, for it appears that fighting is something below the level of culture and rules; that it takes men back to something primeval, to a state of nature that is red in tooth and claw. Perhaps. But equally primeval is the principle of ritualization, and I think that this is the clue to the islanders' ability to manage their aggression. The principle of ritualization can be stated in a general form: in any community of animals there usually exist forms of combat that allow antagonists to settle their differences with violent exertion and yet with a minimum of serious damage. Sometimes the exertion itself can become ritualized—as when an exchange of shots at a distance in a duel or the drawing of blood in a fencing match satisfies the honor of the antagonists. And honor is very important on the island. The ideal outcome of an agonistic encounter is one in which the parties feel that honor has been satisfied.

In this respect the Irish attitude is quite Mediterranean. What is usually considered to be at stake when one man challenges another is honor or reputation or pride. (The whole thing is a peculiarly male affair. Women fight, but not over honor; their fighting is fierce and destructive, and almost inevitably ends in serious hurt to one of the partners. There may be a moral in this.) When a man makes a challenge he puts his pride on the line. He cannot back down without suffering a wounding hurt to his pride and a loss of reputation. It is an old story, perhaps older than history. It seems to tap something deep in men, something to do with the old interplay of dominance and virility that we see so effectively at work in nature. It is the stuff of literature, the story line of many movies. It is something the sociologically unsophisticated respond to with immediate empathy and excitement. But then the sociologist has been defined—along with the psychologist—as the man who goes to the striptease show to watch the audience. The obvious is the last thing he tends to see.

How is this universal theme treated on Tory? I have recorded details of some thirty fights on the island, and four off the island involving Tory men. I have details of fights from other parts of Ireland and between Irishmen in London. While they have some things in common with the Tory pattern, there are differences. On Tory there is rarely an obvious cause for a fight. The principals are usually traditional antagonists in that often they have inherited the antagonism. The fight may go back to someone's grandfather—no one knows why these two particular people fight, and they may not be very clear about it themselves. Sometimes there is a rambling story about some insult or piece of chicanery in the distant past. But for the most part no one cares. "He's doing it to show he's a man," they'll say. Sometimes, however, there *is* a recognizable cause—a dispute over a girlfriend, usually, or a wife or a sister, and for the usual reasons.

Here is a fight sequence. The setting is the parish hall late at night where a dance is being held. The band is playing traditional Irish dances. The old ladies on the benches along the walls look on and tap their feet. The young people are dancing a reel and getting very excited. Then the young men go to one end of the hall, near the door, where some of the older men have gathered to watch (This segregation of the sexes is important. It occurs in church, in dancing and, as we shall see, it occurs in fighting). In the ensuing lull, some of the men slip out to get bottles of Guinness, which they drink outside in the dark because after all it is illegal and the priest wouldn't like it. The priest is at the dance. He usually comes to watch for a while and, as his singing voice is much admired, is often asked to give a song. He once made an attempt to stop the dances from going on all night. He said it was bad for the children and told the hall committee to stop the dances at one o'clock at the latest. They said the people would not stand for it, that it 'was against the custom of the island.' Several lads got drunk and went and threw bottles at the priest's house. Next day they apologized and cleared up the mess. After that, the priest just left the dances at midnight and said nothing. The point of this is that there is no external authority here to interpose itself if a fight starts and the priest simply takes no notice of it.

This night, however, he did not go home at the accustomed time. There was a noise outside the hall during the lull. Shouting, curses. People rushed through the narrow door to see what was happening. A door off the stage at the other end of the hall was opened and people poured out, knocking over instruments in the rush. But it was all over by the time they got there. Old Paddy had been shouting imprecations at Wee Johnny. But Paddy had come into the hall before Wee Johnny could do anything but shout back. The crowd drifted back inside and the band struck up again. Paddy sat at the side, muttering. Suddenly, as the dance was about over, he jumped up on the stage and started to shout and kick the big drum. Several people tried to restrain him. He yelled that he would surely do some killing before the night was out. They tried to calm him but he pushed his way outside again. Wee Johnny was out there drinking with his cronies and as the doors opened a flood of light from both ends of the hall hit the dark roadway. Paddy, swinging wildly at Wee Johnny, caught him by surprise and grazed his mouth. As both men were more than a little drunk, it is unlikely that either of them could have focused well enough on the other to make an accurate hit; but Paddy's glancing blow enraged Johnny, who roared and made for his assailant. He was grabbed and held back by several hands. By now both men were rather dazed. For a while they just looked at one another—each firmly held by his supporters—and presently they began shouting insults again. Over and over Paddy repeated— my translation from the Gaelic is very rough—"You don't need to hold me, I wouldn't dirty my hands with him." Johnny replied that Paddy's hands were so dirty to start with they couldn't get any worse.

The priest came out and told everyone to go home. No one listened and soon, still protesting, he was brushed aside. The hall had emptied and most of the old ladies were now lining the roadside. At one end was Johnny's party—all men—milling about and arguing with him. At the other end was Paddy's group. Scattered between them were various groups of men not attached to either party; all around milled little boys imitating their elders, cursing, bluffing, swaggering, threatening. It was particularly fascinating to see how the children learned the whole sequence of behavior. Anything that the men did, they would imitate, shouting the same things, strutting and swaggering. Most of the little girls stood some way off with their mothers, who had banded together to deplore the episode—quietly. So we have an arena here, the two groups of men with the principals, as it were, holding them on either side of rather amorphous groups of other men not principally attached to either group. Old ladies on either side of the road were watching, and the mothers and daughters were standing, while the little boys were running all around mimicking.

The noise from Paddy's group was getting louder. Paddy was setting off down the road. The bastard, he was shouting, was going to get it this time. He'd been asking for it long enough. Several of the men on the way tried to reason with him until the main body of his supporters caught up with him and began restraining him again. They were close to Johnny's group now—

about three or four yards away. Johnny moved forward and was restrained again by his men. "Hold me back or I'll kill him for sure!" Johnny shouted again and again. The two crowds came close and even intermingled, and some minor scuffling went on. Two of Johnny's supporters began to argue and immediately attention passed to them. This seemed to annoy the principals, who began shouting again, louder now, and clawing their way through the mob to get at each other. They were pulled back, dusted down, showered with nonstop advice, and implored to cool down and go home.

Once the antagonists were separated, some of the nonpartisan older men moved about between the two, waving pipes and either talking quietly or shouting. (This is another instance of the old Irish principle of the intermediary. You get it when they're selling cows, arranging marriages, or almost anything else.)

There was a lull in the movement during which both principals again came forward yelling at each other. The insults rose in pitch and complexity until Johnny, provoked beyond words, tore off his coat and threw it on the ground. Now this is a serious matter on Tory. "I'll take off me coat"—this is an invitation to a real fight. As long as the coat stays on, serious fighting is not intended. But even the act of peeling back the sleeves is a drastic escalation.[2]

The coat was immediately retrieved by his group and desperate attempts were made to get it back on him again. At this point, a newcomer could have been forgiven for thinking the fight was between Johnny and those who had his coat, for he was inflicting more damage on them than he would ever get to inflict on Paddy. The coat stayed off. Now Paddy began to disrobe.

By that time everyone was sobering up, and the dash and fury of the early part of the fight were over. There was a last flurry; again the principals were pulled back; and now someone was bringing Wee Johnny's weeping mother forward; the crowd parted for the old lady. With prayers and admonitions she pleaded with Wee Johnny to come home and not disgrace her like this in front of her friends and neighbors. Saints were liberally invoked and the Blessed Virgin implored often. People

hung their heads. Johnny, looking dazed, told her to quiet herself—she didn't—and hurled himself at Paddy and his group:
"I'd have had yer blood if me mother hadn't come. Ye can thank
her that you're not in pieces on the road, ye scum." Paddy spat
and said nothing, and Johnny and a few of his crowd went off
to his house, turning occasionally to shout back something in-
distinct. "Well," said one of the old men turning to me with
a chuckle, "and wasn't that the great fight, for sure?" "Right
enough," I said.

The great fight was the subject of discussion for days after-
wards. The priest said that he would ban dances if this kind of
thing ever happened again, but he was told that the hall was
built by Tory men and that they would settle their affairs in
their own way, according to 'the custom of the island.' The details of the fight were discussed endlessly, and various positions
were taken according to how one was related to the combatants.
Either Johnny was justified and Paddy a troublemaker or vice
versa, or they were both troublemakers. But the excitement
and interest, despite the clucking and disapproval in some
quarters, was very real. When either of the principals walked
through the village, everyone stopped to look respectfully. Each
of them had a little more swagger than before, talked a little
more aggressively; each had shown that he was a man; each had
been the center of attention. "A man when he has the great
anger on him is a wonderful thing, is he not?" I was asked. "He
was surely," I said, "but weren't people disturbed by this kind
of thing?" "A nine-day wonder," I was told; "it never comes
to anything, anyway." The women were particularly sceptical,
passing many a sharp comment about men who were quick
enough to fight but ran at the sight of hard work. And one
young woman laughed, "Oh, those lads—always heroes when
there's a crowd."

The significance of this remark, and of the whole episode,
was brought home to me by an extraordinary occurrence a few
days later. I was up on the hillside outside the town taking
photographs when I saw Johnny walking down the road alone.
From the opposite direction came Paddy, also alone. Waiting
for the clash, I wondered how neutral I could be, and whether

I should intervene or, more likely, run for help. But Paddy passed on one side of the road, looking out to sea, and Johnny on the other, looking at the hills. Neither acknowledged my presence or the other's and each went his own way without a word.

This was my first fight and I had no reason to think that it was anything but a random affair. But some fifteen fights later, I was beginning to get bored with the predictability of the performance. There was always this stereotyped sequence of events, the insults, the rushes. There were certain conditions under which a fight would start. There had to be enough close kin of each principal on the one hand and enough related to both on the other. The close kin of each were the 'holders-back,' whilst the kin of both were the 'negotiators.' This was something I learned after photographing, getting to know everybody who was in the fighting, and watching their various roles. The more closely you were related to the principal, the more you were obliged to 'hold him'; and the more distantly related—if you were related to both—the more you were obliged to try to stop the fight by negotiating. Always the 'hold me back or I'll kill him' pattern predominated; often to the extent that even when the supporters had become bored, the antagonist would go around begging to be held back. The characteristic removal of the coats, the attempts to calm the men down, the pushing and scuffling, all fell into a predictable pattern. And when she was available, the mother of one of the parties was paraded, with her lines well rehearsed (or so it seemed), to bring the fight to an end. If it was not a mother, a sister might be brought on, or else a crowd of female relatives. (Again one is reminded, I suppose, of the monkeys who when they are being pursued by another male monkey will pick up an infant and hold it, and this 'cuts off' the male monkey's attack.)

The participation was always intense, as though this were the first time a fight had occurred, and after each fight the same discussions would rage. But after a while they took on for me, the punch-drunk anthropologist, the air of a ritual ballet; it was all choreographed, seemingly rehearsed, stereotyped. The language was always the same. The insults that at first had seemed so rich in their inventiveness turned up again. It began to dawn on this over-trained anthropologist that it was not mayhem and chaos, but ritual in the simplest sense. It was entirely rule-governed, even though no one could have told me what the rules were. If you sit down and ask people, "Will you explain to me how a fight goes, what happens?" it's simply regarded as an absurd question: "Sure you have a fight, anybody gets in there and fights, and everybody fights to hit everybody else." The idea that there was any sequence to this, that it had in any sense a set of conventions, was quite foreign to them. Yet it was entirely rule-governed—in the same way that language is rule-governed, although only grammarians know what the rules are. And in the same way that we know when the rules are broken even if we don't know what they are, so we all knew (and deplored the fact) when the rules of the fight game were broken, as they sometimes were. For example, it was unthinkable for a group of men to set on a lone antagonist who had no kin with him, or for two lone men on a road to start a fight with no audience around. When these things did happen, there was universal condemnation. A 'proper fight' was a different matter. Two men with a quarrel—never mind what—had stood up to each other and had it out. They had shown that they were men and were willing to fight, but the situation was so structured that they seldom got hurt.

Nobody ever got more than a bloody nose out of it. No matter. Honor was salvaged by the mother's intervention; a man could not refuse a mother's prayerful pleas and obviously his opponent could not hit the old lady. Failing this, exhaustion and the pressure of kin would make each give way. But if a man actually fled, or flinched from the ordeal in any way, he lost face. Sometimes, if there were few people around, the antagonists might actually come to blows. But if the fight were managed properly, everything would eventually come out even—although each side would declare itself the winner and claim that it was the other side that had backed down, run away, or called for help. Outside the community, fights are a different matter. The fights involving Tory men that I have witnessed in Glasgow or London have been very nasty: broken bottles, boots, and gore.

After one such episode, an islander ended up in the hospital with nine stitches in his scalp. But then that was in a Glasgow dance hall. Only the police there were neutral; that is, they hit everybody just as hard, without regard to national or local origins.

I am reminded of ritual fights—or as the ethologists call them, 'agnostic encounters'—of animals. It seems that men, in- *agonistic* cluding Tory men, try to ritualize combat between members of the same community, much as animals do. As Lorenz has pointed out, many animals that are equipped to kill have powerful inhibitions against killing their own kind. Very often combats are reduced to exhausting wrestling or butting matches, or even to simple displays of threat and counterthreat. The stags who compete for harems at rutting time lock antlers and wrestle. Stallions, playing the same game, nip each other on the neck, instead of slashing each other with their hoofs. Some animals, like the fiddler crab with his great, exaggerated right claw or the marine iguana with his horny crest, have evolved special organs for this purpose. Man has not evolved special organs. Instead he has that remarkable organ, culture, to do this ritual work for him. Perhaps this is an example of culture building on nature, rather than as is usually assumed, running counter to it. As I said earlier, one could regard fighting as a relapse to the precultural, the prerule, state of nature. But nature has its way of coping with fighting among conspecifics: the fighting is ritualized so that status competition can take place without anyone getting too badly hurt (although with animals, as with humans, it doesn't always work). It might well be, then, that culturally patterned, ritualized fighting is something 'in our nature'; that men, left to themselves, will, within and even between the small communities that are their natural environment, manage to come up with elaborate bluff and threat displays that satisfy pride while doing a minimum of damage. After all, the elaborate single combat of the Greeks and Trojans cut down the killing considerably.

However, I do not want us to run away with the idea of ritualization. It isn't all quite as simple as it has been made to be. Ritualization is, after all, only one aspect of real conflict; fights and killings amongst conspecifics do commonly occur in nature. Schaller has that lovely phrase where he says that when one lion strays on to the territory of another lion pride, the only ritualization available to it is to run like hell, otherwise it will be torn to pieces. It is all a matter of degree, and it seems to me that ritualization tends to work once it is clear within the community that violence does not work, or where violence fixes the order of things anyway. In other words, if two animals find that they are so evenly matched that it would have been a fight to the death if they really tried to decide it, then they will ritualize the process between them. It would become a matter of threat, bluff, and so on.

I'm reminded here of another curious institution in the west of Ireland known as the 'pub-fighter.' Very often the pub-fighter will be pointed out to you if you go into one of the bars. He has a special stool at the end of the bar which you are not to take. You see it as you come in. And the pub-fighter sits at the end with his back to the wall looking out, with his pint of stout in his left hand, and his right hand ready. I have never ever seen a pub-fighter fight, nor have I met anybody who has actually seen a pub-fighter fight. There are stories of his past fights, but that is all in the mythological past, in the time of the previous pub owner, when he beat up six men while still drinking. The pub-fighter is of course incredibly deferred to; no one would dream of starting a fight with the pub-fighter. He is treated with awe, as 'the Pub-Fighter.' So this is the kind of situation where the ritualization has been carried to its extreme. What I am really getting at here, I suppose, is that there is a tendency to ritualize in any sort of 'steady state' situation, in any situation where animals or men have to live together as a group and where the group has to live with its neighbors. The group does not necessarily forgo violence. On the contrary, it may engage in a great deal of fighting, so that we find again this curious paradox, that there are societies in which the whole way of life is geared to fighting and violence of one sort or another, and yet there is order. They don't wipe each other out; there isn't a terrible breakdown of the social system and there aren't any of the terrible consequences one might expect entertaining a Hobbesian view of it all.

What I've described here is, I think, something that's interesting because there are no *explicit* rules. If two Tory men have a quarrel they don't go and appeal to the duelling master. What happens seems to be spontaneous. There are no written sets of rules and yet it falls into this pattern of fighting which everybody enjoys thoroughly, and through which the men can make their point without effecting too much damage. That is at one level. The next level up, I suppose, is where you do get fights between communities which are so highly ritualized that it's almost as though the business of preparing for the fight and celebrating the victory or mourning the loss is an end in itself, because the fight amounts to very little at all. I am thinking of the so-called warfare between Plains Indians, and of the fights between villages in New Guinea. The film, *Dead Birds,* shows the fighting between villages in New Guinea, where they actually prepare the battleground by levelling the ground and engaging in other elaborate preparations. (See Gardiner and Heider 1968) When someone from a village has been ambushed and either wounded or killed, or sorcery has been practiced by another village, they set out to stage a fight. Prior to the fight, all the men dress up in fantastic rigs of headgear, bones through their noses, penis sheaths, and then, carrying elaborate spears, they all meet on the battleground. There's a great deal of throwing of spears, but the spears are very big and it's very difficult to throw them accurately over a long distance, so you get fairly close, throw the spear and the young blood has to come out and dodge the spear as it comes towards him; and that's the big thing. He dodges the spear and sooner or later somebody gets hit, and as soon as somebody is hit (usually just wounded), the fight is over and everybody goes back. There is a terrific feast among the victors, and condolence and mourning among the vanquished, and then they prepare for the next one. The whole male culture here is really devoted to fighting. They have this elaborate war-cult, much the same as with the Plains Indians.

One imagines from all the movies that Plains Indians were for ever engaged in scalp taking and battles. This was not the case. Most of the fighting that took place was hit-and-run, sneaky stuff in which the aim was to catch an enemy horse or to count coup on an enemy—a perfect example of ritualization taken to the absurd. The young brave would ride towards the other group of warriors, who would fire arrows at him; he would dodge in, touch one of the enemies, and ride back; and that was the highest honor he could possibly achieve. Within both of these communities fighting between antagonists would again be highly ritualized; the fighting would be with clubs or sticks, so that damage could be inflicted without too great a likelihood of any killing.

We can also look at what happens when there is bound to be killing. Again, in a steady state relationship, there is a tendency to ritualize combat almost out of recognition. It is true even of huge combats that took place. For example, in the Mogul Wars in India, you would get as many as two hundred thousand combatants, with sixty elephants on each side and cavalry and bands and kettle-drums, and the whole panoply of war. Yet it was only when things really went badly wrong that very many people got killed. You had to have two princes of equal status before you could have a war. If the other side couldn't produce a prince of equal status to yours, you wouldn't fight, the excuse being that you couldn't surrender; if your prince was defeated you could only surrender to someone of equal rank. So the two princes had to be present and since it seems that on most of these occasions the two princes had not the slightest intention of getting killed, when the battle started very quickly one of them would turn round and bolt, and of course if the prince wasn't on the battlefield the whole thing would collapse and everybody would run off home and the other side would declare itself the winner. Now people would of course get killed. You can't have two hundred thousand combatants and all these horses and arrows and guns without somebody getting killed. I think on one occasion they reckoned fifteen hundred people were killed, still a very small proportion of the mayhem that could have occurred (Hansen 1972).

Again one is reminded of medieval warfare and that great reformer, Joan of Arc, who quite spoilt the whole thing. If you remember Shaw's *St. Joan* at any rate, you recall that she explains to the French generals why they are not winning the wars and expects them to be grateful for this information, instead of which they hand her over to be burned, because she was going to spoil all the fun. She explains that they were not fighting their wars to win, but that they were fighting their enemies to knock them off their horses and take them for ransom; to which the French general replied that that was what wars were about. War was not about killing all those peasants—one could do that any time—war was about knights. The lances that they used were ridiculous. As people who set up tournaments and try to use them know, it was terribly difficult to maneuver a lance, to do anything but simply knock someone off his horse. It was terribly hard to do any damage to somebody protected by a ton of armor around him, and of course when he fell he could not move and so was easily captured. The whole thing was almost absurdly designed to this end. As soon as people began to take war really seriously, they had to abandon all that armor and those lances so that they could be mobile and actually kill people.

Even in eighteenth-century warfare there was this tendency to ritualize. Was it not at Malplaquet that the French general strolled over to the English side and said, "Tirez le premier, Monsieur l'Anglais," and then strolled back again? So the English accepted the offer, fired first and decimated his army. Wars became incredible polite set pieces, fought between professional armies, with fantastically elaborate rules of honor and warfare to do with captives and the conduct of war. They had almost nothing to do with the people for whom the wars were fought and on whose territory they were being fought.

What I am saying in all of this is that there is this one tendency that as long as you have a 'steady state,' in which nobody particularly wants, or has any reason, to change things very much, there will be violence, and it will be ritualized. This does not mean that nobody gets killed; it merely means that killing is reduced to a minimum. The question then becomes: when doesn't this work? In effect, I am really reversing the whole question about war and peace. It is not a matter of how terrible war is, wouldn't it be better to have peace? My question is, if you're going to have war anyway, what's the best kind of war to have? When it doesn't work is, I think, a matter for empirical research, and a lot of people are in fact working on this. It doesn't work when you get conquest, when you get huge population explosions, when people spill over from one territory into another; it doesn't work when you get displacements of people, or when the weapons of war outstrip the ritualization of it.

So I want to conclude, I suppose, by saying that if we can't have peace, which is probably impossible, then perhaps the state to aim for is the state of contained or ritualized fighting, because this allows men to maximize those grandiose vainglorious and combative status-striving motives that they seem to like, and to minimize the damage that is brought about. If contemporary political leaders could count coup on each other, indulge in arm wrestling, or play a game of tiddlywinks, then we would be back in a human state, as it were, where conflicts and even violence could be organized and coped with, where—to get desperately back to my title—we could tap those inherent rules that are part of the nature of the beast, of the nature of fighting, rules that tend to make it an organized and structured aspect of human behavior.

8

The Passionate Mind: Brain, Dreams, Memory, Evolution, and Social Categories

> Are concepts disembodied abstractions? Or do they exist only by virtue of being embodied in a being who uses them in thinking?
>
> G. Lakoff, *Women, Fire, and Dangerous Things*

ONE of the briefs offered to participants in the 1984 Star Island Conference of the Institute on Religion in an Age of Science was to examine the findings of Claude Lévi-Strauss and the structuralists in light of the findings of neuroscience. I shall attempt to do this, but my attempt is not primarily directed at questions of myth and ritual; it seeks rather to understand the neurological base of what lies behind a good deal of myth and ritual, namely, social categories. By extension, it must deal with categories per se, but since the stress in anthropology since Emile Durkheim has been on the social origins of categories and since this stress is what has inspired the anthropological study of myth and ritual, I here concentrate on social categories by way of illustration of the thesis. And the thesis is really very simple: if one may paraphrase John Locke, there is nothing in the memory that was not first in the emotions.

At first glance this may not seem so startling, but it runs quite counter to the assumptions and indeed the overt statements of the structuralists. Victor Turner, in whose honor the conference was held, had come to realize this late in his anthropological career and was about to launch on an ambitious program of rethinking to right the record. His tragic death robbed us not only of a good friend and a great anthropologist, but also of a chance to see where he would go from his promising start on the relations between the structure of the triune brain and some aspects of ritual (Turner 1983). I am approaching from a slightly different angle, but we cover a lot of similar ground. A great deal of the material I draw on was not available to Turner since it comes from the latest research of Jonathan Winson, and not all of this was published (Winson 1985). Also, it would not necessarily have been obvious from what was published that there was an immediate relevance to the subject in hand. I shall try to make the connection as best I can.

CATEGORIES, DREAMS, AND THE EMOTIONAL BRAIN

I first made the point in chapter 7 of *The Red Lamp of Incest: An Inquiry into the Origins of Mind and Society* (1983), but I had not at that juncture got the Winson argument quite right.[1] I shall attempt to make good the deficiency here. I was trying to make a connection between evolution, memory, dreams, and social categories. My starting point was the structuralist assertion that we do not view the world, or act upon it, directly in the way animals do; rather, we act upon it through the medium of social categories which define for us what falls into one class and what into another, and how to act towards each set of 'objects' so classified. The structuralists were not the first by any means to make this observation, and it has a venerable history in philosophy— and a strong modern influence through Ludwig Wittgenstein— as well as a firm place in the history of anthropology through the influence of Benjamin Lee Whorf and his followers. But it is a point central to the arguments of the structuralists whom we have been asked to consider. Lévi-Strauss, for example, seems to accept that there is a basic, appetitive drive to classify (Lévi-Strauss 1963), but he regards the act of classifying and the consequent behavior as purely acts of the 'intellect'; indeed he pours scorn on those who would hold an 'emotive' view of, say, totemism and urges us, in the title of the penultimate chapter of his book on that subject, "Vers l'Intellect" (Lévi-Strauss 1962, chap. 4). This, I believe, is one of the many Cartesian-type dichotomies in social theory that bedevil us and that neuroscience may help to eliminate. For an 'intellect versus emotions' dichotomy can only be translated into a 'prefrontal cortex versus limbic system' dichotomy, and, as I hope to show, this simply does not jibe with what we know of the role of these parts of the brain in the creation of categories.

Let me first of all insist, however, that I totally accept the structuralist premise that we view and act on the world through our acquired categories. This is not what is at issue. Where I part company is when this fact is used to remove us from the process of evolution and the state of nature. It does neither. It is an evolutionary development like any other—a very powerful one from the point of view of adaptation. Clearly any discussion of it belongs in the general discussion of the evolution of language. This is not because acting in terms of categories is unique to a language-using animal. Any long-term observation of chimpanzees, for example, would leave one in no doubt that they act upon such categories as opposed to acting 'directly' upon reality. But even if the difference is one of degree, the degree is so great as to be rightly regarded as another level of action with truly emergent properties. When linguistic labelling enters, the whole picture changes. But I do not want to linger on this point since it would get into a long discussion of whether we can be said to be acting on the basis of social classifications even if we do not have words for them ('unconsciously') and that is not part of my problem. Whether we need the labels or not, we must enter the categories into long-term memory. It is here it seems to me that neuroscience can come into the picture and, while accepting that action in terms of coded social categories is a defining human characteristic, can explain the mechanisms by which this is made possible and suggest the probable evolutionary origins.

The structuralist argument is in line with the general theory of the social determinants of perception.[2] The categories by which we classify the world and through which we act upon it are socially derived and hence differ from society to society (or culture to culture, whichever you prefer). I have always been at the center of this debate since, as an expert in 'kinship systems,' I have been constantly faced with the argument that kinship

has nothing to do with biology because kinship terms—the classifying categories of the kinship universe—do not designate
true genetic relationships but indicate socially determined roles
and statuses. This is true, but it does not follow that such systems have nothing to do with biology unless one defines *biology*
narrowly as meaning 'designating true genetic relatedness.'
Since it is indeed a wise child that knows its own father it would
be rather remarkable if kinship terms did do this. What they in
fact more probably designate are categories of prohibited and
preferential mates—and that has a lot to do with biology (Fox
1979)! But it is certainly true that we act towards individual kin
according to the category designation and not directly. If a total
stranger to whom we had been quite indifferent were to be revealed as a 'brother,' our attitude would certainly undergo a
significant change as he was shifted from the one category to
the other. As Durkheim saw, these categories cannot stray too
far from objective reality (or 'nature') without serious consequences (Durkheim 1915, 18–19). Thus, what foods will be defined as polluting will differ from group to group, but no group
can define *all* foods as polluting without starving to death. This
was not Durkheim's example (he did not give any), but I think it
illustrates what he meant. And it is not a bad place to start since
pollution and totemism—both central to many theories of religion—have been prime examples of the structuralist point.
Thus, Mary Douglas uses different classifications of 'pollutants'
to show how society indeed determines what people will find
'dirty' and what not. Her famous dictum that dirt is "matter in
the wrong place" beautifully sums this up (Douglas 1969; 1973;
see also Leach 1964). After numerous discussions with neighbors who are passionate gardeners and hence horrified with my
survival-of-the-fittest approach to plants, I have come to define
a 'weed' as a 'flower in the wrong place.' But note that passions
are here aroused.

  This brings me to the first sense of disquiet with structuralism
in its approach to categories. Edmund Leach has expressed the
same disquiet, although he too holds firmly to the Durkheimian
doctrine. In questioning Lévi-Strauss's self-avowed 'intellectual-

ist' approach to totems, Leach notes that, while it is true that the universal function of totemism (the naming of social groups after animals and things in nature) may well be simply intellectual (part of a desire to 'order out the universe' as E. B. Tylor [1899] put it), nevertheless, people do get very emotional about the things they categorize. The question, says Leach, is why is the totem so often taboo (Leach 1964; 1970)? Why should the categories evoke such passionate responses? The answer that he and Douglas give to this question was implicit in my anecdote of the weeds. People become upset when their established category systems are disturbed. Polluting things, obscene things, dirty things, suspicious and evil things, uneatable things, and so on, are all things that disturb the established category system—the socially derived system of classifying the world. But then the question still remains: if the classifying function is purely intellectual—simply part of a desire for order—why the powerful reactions of disgust, horror, unthinkableness, and even homicide, when faced with what should be simply an intellectual disruption? One can imagine perhaps minor irritation and even some anxiety over a disruption of an established category system; but accusations of witchcraft and beating to death? I think one can be forgiven for believing that something else is going on here that is only uncomfortably accommodated within the category 'intellectual.' Lévi-Strauss is willing to go as far as 'anxiety,' and in a little-read passage in *Mythologiques: L'homme nu* he actually looks for a physiological basis for this anxiety (lactic acid) (Lévi-Strauss 1971, 588). But reactions range from mild anxiety to homicidal passion, and this is still puzzling if the original intellectualist premise holds. That Lévi-Strauss should invoke a physiological mechanism at all is interesting, because it suggests a wired-in mechanism to deal with category disruptions. If this is so, what does it suggest about the creation of the categories in the first place?

It is here that we must turn to neuroscience, and we must turn also to an area of neuroscience that has been neglected because a simple connection has not been made. The category systems of which we speak—the vast and complicated systems of social classification—'exist' in the mind, of course, but more particularly they have to have been entered, as we saw, into the long-term memory storage which is indispensable to the mind's functioning. Naturally, not only linguistically coded social categories enter this storage system but, if something is true of *whatever* enters it, then it will be true also of such categories and hence may give us a clue to the question in hand: Why the heavy emotional loading in a supposedly unemotional and purely intellectual system?

Let us then examine the long-term memory process in as simple a way as is possible given its obvious technical complexity. To this end, a simplified diagram may help. Diagram 1 shows, topologically, the relationships between the areas of the brain that are involved in memory processing. It is based on one designed by Vernon H. Mark and Frank Ervin who note that all the areas so associated are also those associated with emotion: the so-called limbic areas or limbic system. The crucial organ which makes the connection is the hippocampus. The hippocampus, like the other structures of the limbic system, does not receive direct sensory information, but rather a higher level of abstracted and processed information from various areas of the cortex—the thin (one-tenth of an inch), convoluted tissue which surrounds the limbic area. This 'acquired' information is gathered in the cingulate cortex or cingulate gyrus and transferred, via the cingulum, to the hippocampus. It then passes via the fornix to the hypothalamus, thence to the thalamus and back to the frontal lobe of the neocortex. When, how, and why does it make this journey? Let us start at the beginning.[3]

One major function of the hippocampus is short-term memory processing. People with hippocampal lesions literally cannot remember anything from one moment to the next. They live in an eternal present. But for our purposes, more significant is the role of the hippocampus and the rest of the limbic system in long-term memory. Those with hippocampal lesions, while unable to remember any recent experiences, repeatedly show that they can remember events that occurred three or more years ago. Thus it has been shown that it takes three years for experiences to enter long-term memory. Once entered they

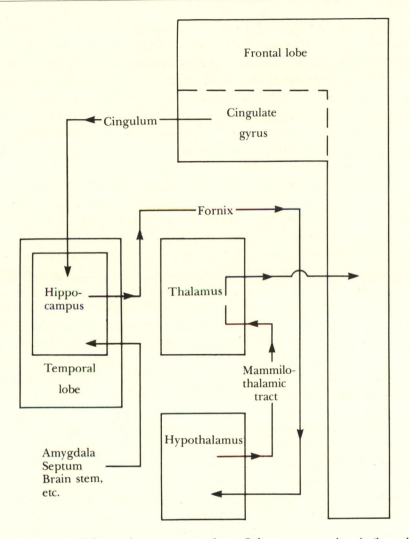

DIAGRAM 1.—Schematic representation of the memory circuit (based on Mark & Ervin 1970, 142).

are very resistant to loss (as experiments with electroconvulsive therapy have proved), but we still do not know why some are resistant to conscious recall. Nor, for that matter, are we certain how they are stored. But of the processing of input for storage we now know a great deal.

It turns out that the hippocampus is as important here as in short-term memory. This was first discovered in animals in the following way. During the waking state, and when performing species-specific behaviors of crucial importance to the species' ethogram (burrowing in rabbits, exploring in rats, pouncing in cats, etc.), the animal exhibited certain highly distinguishable brain rhythms (EEGs) that were designated theta rhythms. This was interesting enough, but it was then found that during REM sleep these same theta rhythms reappeared. Now REM sleep (rapid eye movement sleep), as we have all come to know, is what we commonly call dreaming. In an average eight-hour sleep period there are usually four such intervals during which the eyes move rapidly although there is no other body movement. All brain centers are active at this time, and this conjunction of total body immobility and totally active brain caused the French researchers of the phenomenon to coin the delightful term *sommeil paradoxal* or paradoxical sleep. There is no body movement (although there may be minor twitches and 'intention' movements that you can easily observe in your sleeping pet) because the brain stem effectively shuts off during this period thus preventing the translation of the cortical activity into motor activity. (Sleepwalkers may have some minor deficiency of this mechanism.)

What is going on here? Well, dreaming of course, but what is this process? Why in animals are the theta rhythms reappearing during dreaming? Winson discovered a remarkable process he terms *neuronal gating* (Winson 1985, chap. 8). It is too complex to discuss in detail, but again it takes place in the hippocampus. During the waking state, neural gates in the hippocampus remain closed, but once sleep begins they begin to open, letting chemical material circulate around the lamellae (the disc-like components of the hippocampus) and out to various parts of the limbic system. At the deepest point of sleep, REM sleep, the last gate opens and the theta rhythms appear. This is repeated roughly four times per night. Human subjects, too, report dreaming only during the REM period, although dreamlike states can precede and follow it. Humans, however, do not show theta—a point to which we must return; but for the moment let us stay with the animals. Repeated experiments have again shown that animals deprived of REM sleep fail to remember tasks from one day to the next. We can at this point even jump to the theta-less humans since they show the same results: memory deficits resulting from REM sleep deprivation. So one conclusion is obvious: whatever else dreams are doing, they are serving as a processing system for memory; and this processing system is located in the hippocampus and its limbic connections. The hippocampus can handle short-term memory, but for anything to enter long-term memory it has to be processed (i.e., dreamed) for at least three years in some form or other. Experiments have shown that during this process the synapses—connections between neurons that carry the 'information'—actually grow and harden into habitual pathways thus facilitating the rapid processing of memory.

But this processing is taking place, as we have seen, during dreaming when in animals the distinctive theta rhythms occur. We can only speculate here, but it does seem that what is happening in REM sleep for animals at least is that current information, blocked from the hippocampus and the limbic circuit during waking, is allowed in there during sleep to be 'matched' against those wired-in survival behaviors that are the species' ethogram—its record, if you like, of successful adaptive behavior. If they are 'passed' as being relevant, then they are shunted on through the rest of the limbic circuit to be, in the graphic words of G. A. Ojemann, 'stamped in' to the long-term memory, and eventually stored in the neocortex (Ojemann 1966). Without this information the neocortex could not perform its essential function of assessing experience in order to make plans and goals for future action.

And here may be the clue. There is no way in which the neocortex could store *all* the information it receives without becoming so large that, as Winson says, we would need a wheelbarrow to carry it around in. Also most of the current information is not relevant to survival functions. In humans who suffer certain deficiencies (I suspect in the neural gating mechanism), the tendency to remember everything proves totally debilitating and self-defeating: they cannot function. And, if Sigmund Freud called schizophrenics 'waking dreamers,' he may have been uncannily near the truth since it could be that their neural gates are not working either (being perhaps deficient in a necessary inhibitor from the brain stem during the waking state) and that a process is going on with them continually that should only take place during REM sleep. But that is to speculate beyond my brief. In any case, we have a dramatic discovery here. Let us put it this way: memories must be dreamed to be retained; this involves their vetting or appraisal by the brain's emotional system; only certain material will be passed into memory; the process takes three years to complete—three years of intensely emotional dreaming.

EVOLUTION, LANGUAGE, AND REPRESENTABILITY

Winson's point about brain size and memory storage has an equally dramatic illustration in the brain of the echidna or spiny anteater. Along with the duckbill platypus this is the last of the surviving monotremes: the egg-laying, warm-blooded creatures that emerged from the reptiles more than 60 million years before true marsupials and mammals. Reptiles have no REM sleep and precious little by way of brain; their brain stem carries in it enough information for most of their needs. Mammals do have REM sleep and the combination of limbic system and cortex that we have discussed. As we go up the phylogenetic scale the brain-body ratio goes up accordingly, and the size of the neocortex increases reaching its highest ratio in *Homo sapiens*. But there is a remarkable fact discovered as long ago as 1902 by Grafton Elliot Smith who was rightly puzzled by it: the small echidna has a neocortex as large as ours (Winson 1985, 56, 257n)! It is a primitive pre-mammal, only a move from the reptiles (in evolutionary terms) yet with an enormous neocortex. (To be exact, we are talking of a particularly large, prefrontal cortex.) It would have remained a mystery without the discovery of one vital fact: the echidna has no REM sleep; it does not dream.

The pieces fall startlingly into place. The growth of the neo-cortex and limbic systems was essential to 'mammalian' evolution—the step beyond the reptiles. Paul D. MacLean describes the reptile as 'doing what it has to do,' while the mammal can in varying degrees 'do what it plans to do' (Turner 1983, 244 n. 16). To achieve this it needs an efficient memory, and the neo-cortex is obviously the repository of memory since the echidna, in its behavior, is not that much different from a low-level mammal. But obviously there came an evolutionary point beyond which the neocortex could not simply go on growing indefinitely in order to store memory, and the amount it could store at the echidna level was limited. Evolution could have stopped there (and probably did for many millions of years) until the incredible breakthrough of REM sleep, or dreaming. What evolved was a *selective processing device* that enabled recent memories to be evaluated against the 'phyletic' memories of the species, and giving them time in which to be so processed and evaluated. They would be passed through the limbic (emotional) circuit while the animal was immobilized, then 'tagged' and passed on into memory storage which was thence not burdened with the necessity of containing everything from current memory but only the most 'emotionally' significant (i.e., that with survival value).

What about the lack of reappearance of theta in human dreams? This may well extend down into the primates—it has certainly not been reliably reported in higher primates—and may therefore represent an equally significant new departure in that evolutionary line culminating in the remarkable abilities of humans. Again this is speculative, but what seems to have happened is that dreaming in the higher primates has been freed from the tie to the phyletic past to some degree. While human dreams obviously reflect many features deep in our phylogenetic experience (archetypes?) and are subject to the same emotional 'loading' process as other mammals, we may be freer to mix recent memories with old experiences in a process of evaluation not as open to lower mammals. These older experiences, for reasons I will go on to explain, may be primarily related to the period of brain growth from conception to completion, that is, prenatal experience and childhood. This 'uncoupling' of memory from too close a tie to species-specific experience may be the most crucial of breakthroughs since the invention of REM sleep itself.

To summarize then, let us repeat the maxim we invoked at the beginning: There is nothing in long-term memory that was not first in the emotions. And in a very particular way: via dreaming. Social categories, for example, totems or kin terms, are stored in long-term memory. Very often societies use a particular process we commonly call 'initiation' to 'educate' young people in the more explicit social categories of the group. While initiations serve many functions, this educative element with its often graphic and traumatic teaching mechanisms is obviously important; and it may represent one way in which the social wisdom is transmitted by evoking dramatic images and instilling them by repetition and often quite frightening rituals. The dreams and nightmares thus produced, often over a period of years, will do their work of lodging the social categories pretty well.

But, it might be objected, when it comes to it, these explicit social categories are words and these are what are remembered. It is not that clear. Of course the words are remembered because words are sounds and sounds are remembered. But memory existed long before speech, and dreams are always visual scenes. When speech came along to be remembered, Winson postulates, then what Freud called the 'need for representability' in dreams arose: the speech had to be translated first into a visual image before the memory process could work on it. Hear Winson:

> This may be a direct result of the phylogenetic origin of the brain mechanism I have postulated. Language, and abstract concepts derived therefrom, played no part in the lower mammalian brain. The limbic-frontal cortical system governing interpretation of experience and planning operated solely as the basis of action and this remains the case in man. Thus, abstract concepts arising with language, which are a large part of our experience, can only be integrated into our unconscious brain mechanism by translation into visual scenes and actions—giving rise to the

witty, fascinating and difficult to translate components of dreams
Freud identified as transformed by the need for representability.
(personal communication)

The implications of this fact are mind boggling. For example,
if categories have to be 're-represented' as images, then how
much more economical and powerful if they are couched in im-
agery to start with? This theory would make totemic categories
far more intelligible than any of the theories Lévi-Strauss dis-
misses, but also more intelligible than his own 'intellectual' version. Yet it would tie in. Totems are not simply as in his formula
'good to think' because they are metaphors (should we say
metonyms?) drawn from the natural world to classify the social
world, but because they are 'good to remember.' They have
presented to the hippocampus and the limbic circuitry a graphic
image on which to work in REM sleep, not simply a word or
abstract concept. They have contributed from the start—as
kangaroo, emu, snake, or eaglehawk—to the need for representability; and as such they have been open to the emotional
vetting system which has, during three years of activity, stamped
them in. Is it any wonder then that they have a heavy loading of
emotion and that a disturbance of the conceptual system so set
up will cause a strong emotional reaction? To understand how
the concepts got into long-term memory is to accept their 'intellectual' function, but it is also to understand how this cannot be
dissociated from their 'emotional' function. Indeed it makes the
distinction an analytical one rather than anything in the real
world. Categories are 'good to think' because they are 'good to
remember,' and they are good to remember because the emotional brain has been able to represent them in REM sleep—to
dream them into memory. Totems, according to the Australian
aborigines, were laid down in the 'dreaming'—the period in
which the world and people were originally created. Their own
formulation may then turn out to be nearer the truth than the
tortuous analyses of the anthropologists. (Obviously, some categories are remembered better than others, and some evoke
more emotion; and this needs investigation. I would suggest
that those categories that are laid down in early childhood, and

those that are taught either consciously or unconsciously by those methods of initiation involving traumatic but ultimately triumphant—becoming a full adult—processes, will have the most emotional loading and will evoke the strongest responses. But to spell this out would be another chapter.)

METAPHOR, LANGUAGE, AND MEMORY

We have seen then why, to answer Leach's question, the totem is so often taboo (although not always, because sometimes the totemic categories are not laid down in the severe manner described above), but what about less dramatic categories like 'time' for example? The position of the structuralists and the Whorfians is much alike on this in that they demonstrate the relativity of notions of time, showing how these are socially derived (i.e., characteristic of a culture, not innate or invented by an individual) and how they vary so that no two cultures seem to view time in quite the same way (Whorf 1956, Durkheim and Mauss 1963). What is more, again, people can become quite upset when confronted with a disruption of their time categories—by people from another culture, for example. But let us consider: How do we eventually integrate such seemingly abstract notions into our long-term memory? It has to be through representability, and indeed the whole language of time that a child learns is not one of abstract concepts but of vivid metaphors. Lewis Carroll used this to great comic effect with time being 'beaten,' 'wasted,' and so on. But this is exactly how we talk of it. Time 'marches on'; like the tide it waits for no man; time 'flies'; we 'run out of' time and we have 'time outs'; time is an 'old father'; there can be a vital 'nick' of time; time 'presses'; time is 'short'—one could go on almost endlessly. But what is this presenting to the emotional circuitry—an abstract, intellectual concept? Not at all. It is a series again of graphic metaphors, a 'prepackaging' if you like of representability for the hippocampus to seize upon and turn into graphic material for dreams. Thus a growing child will develop not an abstract and bloodless category of the intellect but a many-layered emotional notion of time rich in metaphor and associations and loaded with emotional content in its three-year journey through the circuitry. Again, this needs to be explored further, and I can do no more here than suggest the possibilities. But it is an interesting point where cultural anthropology, linguistics, and neuroscience can meet amicably for once and not waste time on time-consuming disputes.

The implications of this approach go deep into the nature of language itself, and that would be going too far perhaps. But I cannot help thinking that the despised theories of language of the first great cultural anthropologist (Ibn Khaldun was perhaps the first great sociologist) might be seen in a different light. Giambattista Vico (1668 to 1744) was totally neglected in his day; and although he has had something of a revival recently, his theory that the original speech of man was poetry is still smiled at. Yet what he was saying, as Isaiah Berlin lucidly points out, was that what we call metaphorical speech was the original speech of the human race, and as late as the *Iliad* this was still the case. "Ploughs actually appeared to have teeth, rivers, which for them were semi-animate, had mouths; land was endowed with necks and tongues, metals and minerals with veins, the earth had bowels, oaks had hearts, skies smiled and frowned, winds raged, the whole of nature was alive and active" (Berlin 1980, 97–98). Thus, they thought in pictures, and like the Neanderthals in William Golding's *The Inheritors* they translated their images into rudimentary expressions conveying the images. What this could be is not the famed 'primitive mentality' of totally mythopoeic thought, nor the right hemisphere of the brain giving orders to the left, but simply a necessary phase through which early language had to pass since it intruded into a neural world where it had not been; and in order to be remembered, without which it could not function, it had to pass through the ancient mammalian memory circuit which demanded visual representability. What 'early language' then would be, would be a language of metaphor that was intimately close to the process of memory. Again I suggest this for the possibilities of exploration—particularly of preliterate languages. But, as we have seen with 'time,' our own is not immune from the early influences. Of course, the hippocampus will provide the representability even if we do not appeal directly to it with metaphor, but it is tempting to think that before the curse of literacy we were more in tune with our unconscious processes, as the poets still are (we suppose).

MEMORY, MISMATCH, AND EMOTION

Let me clear up a couple of technical points before either going further astray or concluding. I have said that with the 'uncoupling' from theta, human dreaming could function by referring present information to past experiences rather than directly to ancient phyletic memories. In this way ontogenetic learning could become stored and built upon with an efficiency not known to other mammals (except, but to a lesser degree, our primate cousins). In this context early learning becomes especially significant because it takes place during critical periods when the very structure of the brain is being laid down. One of these periods, that between six months and fifteen months, seems to be especially crucial since it involves the coincidence of two processes: the dramatic 'fear of strangers' and 'fear of separation' response in behavior, and myelination of the fiber bundles which are the essential 'pathways' of the limbic circuit, which is both the emotional and memory circuit, as we have seen.

Let us back up for a moment and come into this by another route which will return us eventually to our original question of the emotional disturbance felt over the disruption of intellectual categories. In a series of brilliant experiments, various ethologists and animal behaviorists worked out what has come to be known as the 'mismatch' theory of fear responses in very young animals (Eibl-Eibesfeldt 1982, chap. 10). Thus, it was noted that chicks ran fearfully to their mothers when they saw the shadow of a hawk on the ground. At first it was thought that the shape of the hawk was a 'releaser' of innate fear responses, but later experiments showed that what the chicks in fact responded to was not specific shapes but any major *discrepancy* in shape that they encountered. If one habituated them to the hawk shape, they showed a fear reaction when a goose shape was introduced. The

Canadian psychologist Donald Hebb had advanced the same theory in a famous paper describing the behavior of young chimpanzees (Konner 1982, chap. 10). He suggested that it was not the intrinsic nature of the objects that caused the fear re-action, but the degree of discrepancy between them and other similar objects with which the infants were familiar. He argued that the brain was somehow designed to generate fear as a result of such a 'cognitive mismatch.' But *how* is the brain so designed, and what is the neural source of the fear? (Minor discrepancies, by the way, only arouse 'alert' behavior: the major ones provoke fear.) We now know from human (and primate) infants that there is a definite developmental stage at which this 'mismatch fear response' occurs: it is between six and fifteen months and seems to be at its peak at about twelve months. This 'fear curve,' Melvin Konner reports, coincides with the period during which the major fiber tracts of the limbic (emotional/memory) system are receiving depositions of myelin, which 'sheath' them and al-low them to work with maximum efficiency. Up to this point they have been growing, and the infant has no discrepancy mecha-nism. After this point (six months) they become rapidly 'fixed' and the fear reactions can begin to work (Konner 1982, 225).

The tracts involved are the fornix, connecting the hippo-campus with the hypothalamus; the mammilothalamic tract, connecting the hypothalamus with the anterior nucleus of the thalamus, and thence with the cerebral cortex; and the cingulum bundle, connecting the cortex with the hippocampus. If the readers will refer again to diagram 1 they will see that these are indeed the major connecting pathways of the limbic circuit.

That fear of discrepancy or mismatch should set in when the myelination process is at its height is extremely suggestive. What it suggests to me is that this may be one of those crucial early experiences that lays down the basis for the extremes of mismatch phobia that we are discussing under the heading of emotive reactions to the disruption of (social) categories. The dream-memory process in future years will have a major refer-ence back to this established fear base—as opposed to the ap-parently automatic reference back to theta-associated behaviors in the nonprimate dreaming mammals. Konner, who reports all this, was not concerned with our problem and knew nothing of Winson's hypothesis. But hear him on infant mismatch:

> From several lines of evidence it is now fairly clear that the hippocampus . . . is involved in the process of comparing newly presented perceptual configurations with those already stored in memory. The report of a mismatch to the arousal-fear mechanisms of the hypothalamus would thus almost have to involve the hippocampus and its major fiber bundle, the fornix. Thus the ability of human infants to respond to perceptual discrepancy from an established schema, known to increase as the brain grows during the first year, may be in part dependent on the myelination of the fornix. One can visualize, for example, that the approach of a stranger to the infant at twelve months of age might occasion a rapid "filing through" of the faces stored in the infant's memory (a process that would involve the hippocampus and fornix) followed by the reporting out of a mismatch (Konner 1982, 225).[4]

He goes on to observe that the cingulum bundle is what neurosurgeons lesion in cases of severe phobia. We can, on the basis of what we know of the preservation of information in long-term memory, extrapolate forward from this to the dreaming, memorizing, and categorizing adults, whose fiber tracts in the limbic system are completely intact and who have therefore a complete phobic mismatch arsenal at their disposal.

CONCLUSION

This, as I said, brings us round full circle to our original question addressed to the structuralist intellectual theory of social categories. Insofar as these are a function of memory and especially of long-term memory, then they cannot escape a heavy 'emotive' content. Indeed the distinction ceases to be very real; it only makes analytical sense to distinguish between certain mental processes such as getting angry on the one hand and deciding that two and two equals four on the other. This is a reasonable enough distinction perhaps, but it becomes dangerous when we foist it on to the real world—like associated distinctions of nature and nurture, mind and body, or individual and social. If anyone still doubts that this is so, then perform this little experiment. Insist, calmly and rationally, to another calm and rational person that two plus two does not make four, and persist, with smiling reasonableness, that this is the case in the face of all rational objections. But I would advise not persisting for too long, for I confidently predict that your companion will become quite emotional in one way or another about your refusal to accept the 'obvious.' Why should it matter? Because even such a seemingly pure intellectual statement like 'two plus two equals four' is so heavily loaded in our category system with feelings of 'rightness,' of 'truth,' of 'proof,' of 'logic' and 'reasonableness' that any persistent denial will cause a severe emotional reaction. A 'logical,' 'sane,' 'reasonable' person cannot deny this established categorical system of mathematical certainty so rooted in our notions of how the world is ordered. It was the genius of George Orwell (and I am writing this in 1984 after all) that saw that the *ultimate* test of Winston Smith's total mental surrender to Big Brother did not lie in his betrayal of his lover. The rats and the betrayal were a means to the end of having him finally accept, without any mental or emotional reservations, that two plus two equaled five.

9

Kinship Categories as Natural Categories

> Imagine a scientist who is unencumbered by the ideological baggage that forms part of our intellectual tradition and is thus prepared to study humans as organisms in the natural world.
>
> Noam Chomsky, *Reflections on Language*

OUR starting point must be the accepted universality of kinship classification. This is as universal as language itself, and more universal than, for example, a nuclear-family incest taboo. There exists no known society which does not have classification of kin: it must therefore be accepted as a universal human attribute in the same way as language, of which, of course, it is a part. It is also a function of another attribute which Lévi-Strauss (1962) has claimed to be universal, namely the tendency to classify for its own sake. Although both classification itself, and its subset kin classification, are dependent on language, they do not follow logically from it. One can imagine a species that evolved language, but that neither classified nor named categories of kin. Especially with the latter, there has to be some reason—or perhaps we should say some function, some survival value—for so doing, independently of the capacities to speak and classify themselves. It is not simply *that* we classify, but *what* we classify that matters; and universally we classify kin.

It is commonly stated in anthropology that this very fact makes us totally different from the rest of animal nature, and hence it is not amenable to the same form of analysis that might be applied, say, to a universal feature of the behavior of some animal species. This is because we act *in terms of* these classifications, not in terms of genes or whatever is assumed to motivate animals. We imbue nature with cultural meanings and act in terms of these meanings rather than of nature itself. Kinship categories are, in this sense, 'cultural' categories and hence outside the realm of 'natural' explanation.

I have already argued (1971) that this general position is based on an untenable distinction between nature and culture, and here I wish to pursue this argument into the heartland of the culturalist position: meanings and categories, and in particular kinship classifications. To accept the position of those who, like Lévi-Strauss (1949), at least in his earlier version[1], wish to make the nature-culture division the pivot of analysis, is to end up with some odd logical difficulties. Let us take his argument on the incest taboo: it is universal, therefore biological (a natural feature of the species), yet at the same time a rule and very variable, therefore cultural. This he describes as a situation that is theoretically scandalous, and one he seeks to resolve by making the taboo the fulcrum that tips the balance between nature and culture, 'partaking' of both.

The same argument can be applied to kinship classification: it is universal therefore biological, but involves rules which are variable and hence is cultural, and so forth. Of the incest taboo, I have argued (1975) that what is cultural is only the rule, not the avoiding of incest—which is common to most sexually reproducing species and certainly all mammals (cf. also Bischof 1975). To say the rule is cultural, then, and hence unique, is not to say much, because we are, by definition, the only animal that makes rules since we are the only animal that has language in which to couch them. Thus, our uniqueness lies in the use of language, not in any incest-related behavior.

Similarly with kinship classification: our uniqueness lies not in having, recognizing, and behaving differentially to different kin (this happens throughout nature), it lies in giving this process names and rules of naming; in the classification not the kinship.

Incest avoidance does not make us unique: the rule does.

Kinship grouping and kin-derived behavior do not make us unique: the naming of kin does. In each case a universal, hence biological, feature is associated with a 'cultural' practice.

But by the same logic, the cultural practice—ruling and naming, that is, classification—if universal, must also be biological.

Hence one set of biological features—the propensity to classify and regulate—comes into conjunction with two others: the propensities to outbreed and to behave differentially toward kin. All this is possible through the mediation of language.

The latter, however, being universal, is also biological, and hence, the unifying feature of the other two biological features is itself biological.

Ergo, there is no nature-culture distinction, everything is natural-biological. Hence, the argument that we cannot use analyses developed for nature to interpret culture fails since by its own logic the supposedly unique cultural features turn out to be natural.

This tedious demonstration fortunately leads us easily, and without having to bother with most culturalist arguments, to ask some simple questions of evolutionary biology about language, rules, and naming systems, whatever these apply to.

The argument with the incest taboo is simple: the propensity to avoid incest exists; what the taboo does, literally, is to give voice to this propensity via rules couched in language.

The argument then with kin classification is the same: the propensity to discriminate among kin exists, and what the kin-term systems do is to give voice to this via systems of linguistic classification which operate according to certain rules.

This is not a cultural 'intrusion' (Lévi-Strauss) into nature in either case, but a set of naturally occurring phenomena for this species.

The outbreeding propensity requires different degrees of flexibility under different circumstances in nature. There is no absolute requirement. It is all relative to group size, rates of mutation, adaptational requirements, and so forth. Degrees of outbreeding and inbreeding, in other words, differ according to adaptational circumstances. Both different species, and populations within species, exhibit different patterns.

For the species *Homo sapiens,* the consequence of this trajectory of evolution that included the origination of language, classification, and rule obedience, was the rapid migration of populations into numerous very varied niches. Therefore, adaptational circumstances changing as rapidly as they did in space and time, *H. sapiens* required a mechanism for regulating degrees of outbreeding more flexible, say, than mere recognition of individuals.

The feedback between these processes—linguistic and mental advance making more rapid adaptive movement possible and in turn requiring greater linguistic and mental advance . . . and so on—selected for creatures that could define and redefine outbreeding/inbreeding boundaries to suit the differing circumstances. That is, it selected for speaking, classifying, and rule-making creatures *who could apply these talents directly to the breeding system.*

Differing human systems of incest prohibition, exogamy, and endogamy are therefore to be understood as products of natural selection.

By extension, the same reasoning applies to the concomitant evolution of the classification of kin and its development into systems of kin categories. The kin-discriminating tendency requires flexibility in its handling in nonhumans; in the rapidly evolving hominids, this requirement was many times compounded. Therefore selection was in favor of creatures who could define and redefine degrees and kinds of kin relationships according to changing circumstances.

Again, the processes that enabled this greater complexity to evolve—language, categories, and rules—in turn were redemanded by the more complex creatures they helped to provoke. Once more the feedback process selected for creatures that could utilize these procedures better in the business of kin definition.

The flexible use of categories of kin, then, by *Homo sapiens,* is to be considered a natural product of natural selection.

The current complexity and variability of systems of kinship classification cannot be used as an argument for not treating human kinship systems as natural phenomena amenable to sociobiological explanation—in the widest sense. Language, as we have seen, must be considered a naturally evolved propensity itself. The complexity of natural languages does not argue against this. In the light of the work of transformational grammarians, we see that a few basic components, and the rules for their transformation, can account for endless complexity. The whole issue of 'variability' is in fact a red herring. That universal features do not, under varying conditions, produce uniform responses, is a well-enough established fact for all natural phenomena. Variables—which is what we are concerned with— vary: by definition.

With systems of kinship classification, whatever method of componential analysis (widely understood) one chooses, one finds a system of few elements with rigorous rules for the generation of any set of terms. The number of elements and rules is small and well within human mental capacity. The generation of complex systems requires nothing more complicated than the following of half a dozen rules of logical application. The results can be quite complex; the procedures are basically simple.

Tax (1955), for example, following the example of Kroeber and Lowie, lists a 'set of rules that seem to be fairly universally followed.' They number twelve, and some are not necessary to an understanding of terms per se: they apply to customary behaviors and even then are suspect. The true list is probably nearer six items (like Kroeber's). Needham (1971) comes up with six 'elementary modes' of descent, and, I think, two basic dimensions of terminology (linear/non-linear; symmetric/asymmetric). Murdock (1949) finds four types of parental-generation terms and six types of cousin terminology. Complexity is easy to achieve in this latter case since by combination, ninety-four types are possible. Surprisingly few actually occur. One could go on citing examples, but the moral is the same: few elements, many combinations. (The minimum 'elements' seem to be: generation, sex, affinity, collaterality, bifurcation, and polarity.)

Given a small set of elements and combinatorial principles, *Homo sapiens* was able, via naming and simple logical processes, to produce flexible and adjustable systems of classification. The nature of the classification would depend on the types of discrimination demanded by different circumstances. These would determine who should be (a) classed as kin versus non-kin, (b) classed as marriageable or unmarriageable, (c) classed as close or distant, and so forth. What is remarkable is that there are in fact, as Morgan (1870) realized, so *few* types that emerge when such a finite but huge variety is possible. There is after all no logical reason why each society should not be totally different.

Having established that the classification of kin is a specific, naturally evolved propensity (like language itself), requiring names and rules of application to make discriminations, we should try to establish in a preliminary way the basic principles for a naturalistic analysis of these systems. How are they to be understood in terms of evolutionary biology?

We shall be concerned with classification. As far as behavior is concerned, the analysis is easier and is in any case proceeding. With institutions, customs, and the like we can go forward immediately. I have chosen here to attack 'meanings' directly, since it is these that are, as we have seen, offered as the bulwark of human cultural uniqueness.

We must start again with the very universality of kinship classification. This reflects the universal, hence biological, fact of kin selection,[2] rooted in the evolutionary processes characteristic of all sexually reproducing species. With animals, as far as kin discrimination is concerned, certain rules of thumb seem to apply: "those animals around you—that you grew up with, that are close to your mother, etc.—are likely to be kin." (Nature only needs probabilities, not certainties, to operate kin selection adequately. The same is true of incest avoidance.) With *Homo sapiens,* once exogamy is invented, more specificity is required.

Exogamy requires not just random outbreeding but specified and bounded exchanges. Therefore, to arrange the breeding systems of human populations, specifications of marriageable and unmarriageable are required. This is ultimately the basic classification: the alliance theorists are correct. In whom should one invest—parentally—becomes an issue for more than just individuals. *Categories* of 'invest in' and 'not invest in' become necessary, and are invented.

Thus, kin classifications and outbreeding principles are 'run together' in human kinship systems. To repeat the crucial point: the biological propensity to (a) classify and (b) regulate, embraces, through the biological feature of (c) language, the two biological tendencies to (d) outbreed via exchanges (exogamy) and to (e) behave differentially toward kin.

Kinship systems then, can be seen as assortative mating systems (in one of their aspects), and kin classification as a flexible means of adjusting the categories of marriageable and unmarriageable kin. At its most extreme it can define simply 'kin' versus 'non-kin' and specify 'marry non-kin.' Mostly, however, it either (a) specifies "degrees of kinship" from Ego and varies the restricted degrees, or (b) it specifies the kind and composition of descent groups and varies the details of their exogamic relationships, or (c) it categorizes kin and specifies categories of marriageable and unmarriageable.

On the surface these might appear very different; in practice they can have similar effects. The first is best known in the so-called Eskimo and Hawaiian systems where various forms of reckoning—by degrees, stocks, and so forth—decide where the circle of 'non-marriageable' ends: first cousins, fourth degree, and so on. The second can vary from a simple injunction not to marry into one's own clan, for example, to an injunction not to marry into some or all related clans, through a positive injunction to marry into certain clans other than one's own. The third method includes all those systems of preferential (or prescriptive) marriage where types of categories of kin like mother's brother's daughter (MBD) or mother's mother's brother's daughter's daughter (MMBDD) or father's father's sister's daughter's daughter (FFZDD), for instance, are specified as marriage partners. (This can encompass some of the second category, but one must allow for the cases where such specifications are made but where unilateral descent groups do not exist.)

The similar effects, in small populations, can be seen by comparing three possible examples of the above three variations. In (1) we could have a prohibition on marriage with kin up to first cousins—second cousins and beyond can be married. In (2) we could have a ban on marriage into one's own clan (assume this to be matrilineal) and one's father's clan (mother's mother's and father's mother's clans), but a positive injunction to marry into mother's father's and/or father's father's clans. This is common in many 'Crow' systems (e.g., Cherokee). In (3) we could have a positive rule to marry MFZDD or FFZDD, or, more commonly, MMBDD (irrespective of the existence or type of unilineal groupings). All of these are quite common and standard examples in kinship analysis.

In effect, in each case, in a relatively small community (500–1000)—our typical human breeding pool for evolutionary purposes—the effect for the individual investor might look much the same. In each case, for example, the children of brother and sister could not marry (first cousins), but some of their grandchildren could, and in a small community, even without positive injunctions, they would likely have to. This possibility increases further as the 'degrees' are pushed out (to second and third cousins, for example), or the categories made more stringent.

This can be viewed schematically from the point of view of the descendants of a brother and sister (see Figure 1).

Taking the simple case of a 'first-cousin' marriage rule (common in western Europe), we can see that any of the 'second cousins' from group A can marry any of those from group B. But in a small breeding pool, if this is pushed to a 'second-cousin rule,' it is going to be hard to find anyone to marry who is *not* a third cousin anyway. This has a similar effect, then, to a

Figure 5–1   Descendants of a Brother and Sister

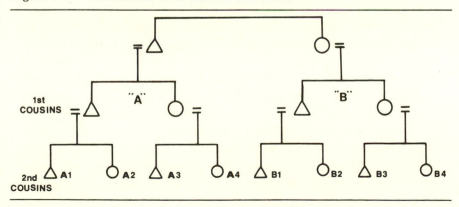

'positive' third-cousin rule de facto. But note that, if this were a matrilineal system with our previously noted injunction to avoid mother's mother's and father's mother's clans, but to marry into mother's father's or father's father's, then A3 would have to marry B4, and similarly A1 would have to marry B4's sister. If this were variation 3, then in the case of a MMBDD rule, B3 would marry A4, and with a FFZDD rule, A1 would marry B4. (All the combinations cannot be shown since for simplicity we have not shown the offspring of the siblings of the spouses of the original brother and sister.)

These various systems of classifying kin (by degrees, by descent group, by category) can then be seen as various ways of combining an outbreeding tendency with a closely endogamous tendency: to avoid sibling, and often first-cousin marriages, but to encourage, or render inevitable, second and other cousin marriage. The 'range of marriageability' can be narrowed or widened by simple devices such as extending prohibited degrees (as the church did in the Middle Ages to profit from the sale of dispensations), changing the specification of marriageable and unmarriageable clans (see next paragraph), or changing the specification of category from MBD to MMBDD and so on as happens, for example, in the geometric progressions from 'two-class' up to 'eight-class' systems in Australia; or by combining two or more of these principles for somewhat more hair-raising effects. Marriageable and unmarriageable groups can also be differently aligned by creating asymmetric rules, for example, and banning one set of cousins while prescribing another, thus potentially widening the range while controlling the 'flow' and containing it. The examples are familiar, as is the demographic argument that suggests an inbuilt tendency to asymmetric flows (Fox 1965).

This possibility of easily redefining the categories of marriageable versus unmarriageable, can be seen in the variations of 'Crow' systems. It is for this reason that I would argue, following Lévi-Strauss (1949), that such systems as 'Crow' or 'Omaha' should be regarded as descriptive of tendencies, not as static types. These matrilineal systems with 'lineal' classifications can work in three basic ways. (1) There can be a simple rule against marriage into one's own matriclan (mother's clan); (2) there can be a rule banning not only one's own clan but that of one's father (i.e., father's mother's clan), and one's mother's father (the two clans, incidentally, to which Ego's clan has 'given' women matrilineally related to him); (3) a rule banning two clans (mother's mother's and father's mother's) but enjoining marriage (or at least preferring it) with father's and mother's father's clans. This easily can be seen schematically in figure 2:

Figure 5–2

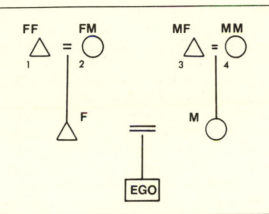

Under rule (1) Ego is simply banned from clan 4, his own. Under rule (2) he is banned from 2, 3, and 4. Under (3) he is banned from 4 and 2, but should marry into 1 and/or 3. Thus, in the first case Ego can technically marry into any other clan in the tribe (although, interestingly, all parallel cousins are usually banned); in the second he is banned from 'wife-taking' clans, and must look beyond this linked series, his nearest possibility being his father's father's clan (this all has a decidedly 'asymmetrical' appearance); in the last case he is banned from the two 'closest' but enjoined to marry the *next* two closest (they are all, of course, genetically as close—but thereby hangs a tale). In effect, in the third type, he is well into the classic 'second-cousin marriage' pattern typical of his counterparts in a 'four-section' system.

I have not been able to go into all the complexities here, but the essential point is that the system of 'lineal classification' makes such switches from simple exogamy, through asymmetric flow, to second-cousin direct exchange, very simple—however complicated it may seem in analysis. The reasons why such switches and changes might have been made are not our immediate concern (nor are they all known) and neither is the question of their possible developmental sequence (which is still conjectural). All we are establishing is that they have an inbuilt flexibility that allows for simple but dramatically effective changes in the specification of marriageable and unmarriageable; changes that can alter significantly the range and type of spouses 'at risk of marriage' to any person in the breeding pool. The next step in analysis should be the examination of the various payoffs of the various systems under different circumstances.

The classification systems, then, give human breeding groups the degree of specificity and flexibility they obviously need to combine kin selection, outbreeding, and boundary maintenance. They put the assortative mating system under the possibility of simple conscious control. This may not always seem to be exercised, and indeed changes may often occur without conscious intervention (just by the gradual dropping of a rule, for instance); but as Lévi-Strauss points out, someone has to initiate the changes even though once established they are regarded as having existed from time immemorial. Whether the switches are conscious or not, however, they are easily made and readily available in the logic of the classificatory systems.

The evolutionary function, then, in this interpretation, of something as simple as 'lineal terminology,' is that it allows (like 'classification by degrees,' etc.) for an easy manipulation of breeding units to meet changing circumstances. Other functions can of course accrue. As we have seen, in small groups (our evolutionary context after all) different devices may have similar 'breeding effects,' despite apparently large 'cultural' differences in style. But a small change—for example, in population size from 1000 to 5000 or more—can have far-reaching effects, and give an adaptational advantage to certain systems over others. Again, the point is that whatever the specifics of such changes, the potential for making them is latent in the system of classification.

Thus, we can see that the objection that 'social' rather than 'genetic' classifications are used by man and hence render his kinship systems outside the realm of sociobiological analysis is wrong if it merely means that persons genetically equivalent are classed differently. If the classification is seen as a breeding classification, then its biological significance may be even more far-reaching than would a simple one-to-one 'genetic' classification. The latter might be, for assortative mating purposes, largely irrelevant anyway. Most of the argument within anthropology on this point has therefore been equally irrelevant up to now.[3] But the sociobiologists are in danger, paradoxically, of making exactly the same mistake.

Thus, it appears from the growing amount of work in this area (largely unpublished) that sociobiologists of the 'kin-selection' persuasion often wish to oppose 'what people do' (i.e., maximize their inclusive fitness) to 'what the system says they should do' (i.e., act in terms of social categories). What they 'really' do, the implication is, is the former, whatever the rules might be about categories: they will act nepotistically or altruistically toward close relatives genetically and symmetrically defined whatever the categories say. Similarly, their opponents, when they find that there are cases when human beings do not so act, reckon to have disproved the 'kin-selection hypothesis.'

There is a double confusion here. For a start, according to kin-selection theory, the formula for action is $k > l/r$. To assume, either pro or con kin-selection hypotheses, that all behavior, or all institutions, can be predicted from 'r' alone is erroneous: this is to ignore 'k'. Some behavior can be predicted from 'r' undoubtedly, when people know their exact genealogical relationships. But a lot cannot. There are undoubtedly cases where 'r' will predict behavior. But there are plenty of cases where it will not, while 'cultural r' will. This is clearest in the case of marriage proscriptions and prescriptions. Here marriage choice is governed by category, that is, by 'cultural r.' (People of course break the rules: no one is suggesting they act like machines.) My point is, however, that in acting exogamically according to 'culturally redefined r,' people are *not* doing the opposite of acting according to 'real r.' This is the nub of the argument: the propensity to redefine 'r' for purposes of assortative mating is as entrenched in the selection process as the propensity to act according to real 'r.' In a very profound sense it is just as real, and part of the same process.

The second confusion is this: while both proponents and critics of kin-selection theory are concerned with the prediction of actual behavior, that is not the issue here. The nearest we can get to a prediction is that "people are likely to choose mates from the approved categories and not from the disapproved"— not much of a prediction about specific behavior, although not a trivial statement about the species. And this is the point: We are concerned here with the evolutionary (teleonomic) functions of kin categories, not with the prediction of fitness-maximizing behavior, connected as the two may be. We are asking, in other words, why certain institutional arrangements exist at all. Any 'prediction' then—and I would not go further than suggesting some covariation—would be at the institutional level.

We should be careful, therefore, to distinguish the level or explanation that is involved. As far as social (kinship) categories are concerned, in this view, they are largely to do with the definition of exogamy. Other functions—definition of inheritance, succession, and so forth—are accruals. Most of the things sociobiologists wish to 'predict' have to do with actual interaction— who favors whom, and the like. At best, here, we can only say that categories provide a reservoir of potential recipients of discriminatory behavior, in the same way that categories of 'potential spouse' provide a reservoir of actual mates. Which actual relatives will be nepotistically or altruistically favored is another matter.

There is nothing really very strange in the human propensity to act, for some purposes, in terms of categories. Even animals do not act symmetrically toward genetically related other animals, since all these relatives may not, physically, be available. Animals act according to the rules of thumb we have already noted—largely in terms of proximity. Human systems of kinship classification are the equivalent of the differential behavior of animals, only they are more precise. With animals, some physical mechanism puts one 'category' literally closer than another. Kinship classification does the same thing definitionally, conceptually, as is the human way. But the end result is similar, differing in the degree of precision with which categories can be defined. We can do two things more precisely: we can trace and remember actual genealogical connections, thus allowing us to override category in favor of genealogy; we can classify together genetically disparate relatives, thus allowing category to override genealogy. But these are two sides of the same coin and it would be a terrible pity if sociobiologists should through misunderstanding of the true evolutionary significance of categorization re-erect the false dichotomy that their opponents favor.

The above was written before the advent of Sahlins' (1976) critique, but my response to him will be obvious without further comment since his basic misunderstandings are answered by the whole argument of this chapter—as are those of the people he is criticising. I am also, on the basis of this argument, forced to support a modified notion of 'group selection' against the 'individual selection' attacks. Thus, it is possible that gene frequencies change within a population as a result of individual selection, itself a result of maximization of inclusive fitness. But the individuals do this—particularly in the human case—within the framework of a system that itself has adaptive properties. (This is another reason we cannot separate out 'individual' from 'system.') Thus an individual's 'success' in such maximization may result from his pursuit of a strategy that in fact maximizes the benefits that the system itself—as a successful adaptive device—makes possible for him. There is, in other words, selection at the system (i.e., group) level, as well as at the individual. The two need not, but could, be incompatible. This is an empirical matter.

It will be obvious that, from the point of view of the 'natural' analysis of systems of kin classification (as products, that is, of natural selection), we should favor the 'categorical' approach rather than the 'extensionist.' The latter is too close to our own ethnocentric notion of 'real' relationship. Also, an 'alliance' approach is preferable to its rivals overall, since it concentrates on kin units as breeding units—although its proponents might not see it quite that way. It also, by the central position it gives reciprocity, opens the way for an analysis of human kinship systems as systems of reciprocal altruism—where calculations of real relatedness are not needed. Thus, we have come the full circle to Lévi-Strauss, classification, exchange, and alliance, but fully within the neo-Darwinian mandate and without the obfuscations of the nature-culture distinction. The aim has been simply to demonstrate that a fact like the classification of 'father's sister's daughter' with 'father's sister' in some systems, with 'sister' in others, and with 'grandmother' in yet others, is a fact of the same order and open to the same analysis in principle, as the sterility of certain relatives of the queen bee, the regurgitation of food by canid predators, or the gamble with death of the cleaner fish. Now the task begins.

10

Consciousness Out of Context: Evolution, History, Progress, and the Post-Post-Industrial Society

> What is your opinion of Progress? Does it, for example
> Exist? Is there ever progression without retrogression?
> Therefore is it not true that mankind
> Can more justly be said increasingly to Gress?
>> Christopher Fry, *A Phoenix Too Frequent*

> —History, Stephen said, is a nightmare from which I am trying to awake.
> > James Joyce, *Ulysses*

> A trout is only as smart as he has to be: a fisherman is twice as smart as he needs to be.
> > Old fly-fishing proverb

YES, Virginia, this is yet another 'commentary on the human condition.' Despite the ponderous overtones, this really is a serious tradition and one I am glad to belong to. But the conditions under which we now have to write such commentaries have drastically changed. Two things have altered our sense of ourselves radically: the daily prospect of total annihilation for our species, and our very recent awareness of our ancientness as a species, with all the implications this has for an understanding of ourselves.

It is a sad irony that the latter crucial knowledge, which promises to transform our ideas of what we are and what we can hope for in the future, has been acquired at exactly the time when we are threatening to make that future impossible. We are like someone who has been handed a great fortune along with instructions to commit suicide.

206

Reason, imagination, and violence today coexist in a way we
can only try to analyze or express. But the two cultures of reason and imagination—the wrong basis for the antagonism between the humanities and the sciences—do not exist out there
in the world; they only exist in our categorical reconstruction of
it. Before Plato they were not sundered, but before Plato there
was no science either. Yet Plato wanted the poets and artists out
of the republic because, as Eric Havelock (*Preface to Plato*)
rightly observes, they laid claim to a rival truth—not just to a
superior capacity for entertainment. So Plato argues for their
banishment:

> Οὐκοῦν δικαίως ἂν αὐτοῦ ἤδη ἐπιλαμβανοίμεθα, καὶ τιθεῖμεν
> ἀντίστροφον αὐτὸν τῷ ζωγράφῳ· καὶ γὰρ τῷ φαῦλα ποιεῖν πρὸς
> ἀλήθειαν ἔοικεν αὐτῷ, καὶ τῷ πρὸς ἕτερον τοιοῦτον ὁμιλεῖν τῆς
> ψυχῆς ἀλλὰ μὴ πρὸς τὸ βέλτιστον, καὶ ταύτῃ ὡμοίωται. καὶ οὕτως
> ἤδη ἂν ἐν δίκῃ οὐ παραδεχοίμεθα εἰς μέλλουσαν εὐνομεῖσθαι
> πόλιν, ὅτι τοῦτο ἐγείρει τῆς ψυχῆς καὶ τρέφει καὶ ἰσχυρὸν ποιῶν
> ἀπόλλυσι τὸ λογιστικόν, ὥσπερ ἐν πόλει ὅταν τις μοχθηροὺς
> ἐγκρατεῖς ποιῶν παραδιδῷ τὴν πόλιν, τοὺς δὲ χαριεστέρους
> φθείρῃ· ταὐτὸν καὶ τὸν μιμητικὸν ποιητὴν φήσομεν κακὴν πολι-
> τείαν ἰδίᾳ ἑκάστου τῇ ψυχῇ ἐμποιεῖν, τῷ ἀνοήτῳ αὐτῆς χα-
> ριζόμενον καὶ οὔτε τὰ μείζω οὔτε τὰ ἐλάττω διαγιγνώσκοντι,
> ἀλλὰ τὰ αὐτὰ τοτὲ μὲν μεγάλα ἡγουμένῳ, τοτὲ δὲ σμικρά,
> εἴδωλα εἰδωλοποιοῦντα, τοῦ δὲ ἀληθοῦς πόρρω πάνυ ἀφεστῶτα.
> *Republic*, book 10

This perhaps necessary divorce, however, like so much of the
Platonic heritage, may yet cost us dearly. It may yet cost us
everything. As Voltaire, in 1770, passionately declaimed:

> "O Platon tant admiré, j'ai peur que vous ne vous ayez conté
> que des fables, et que vous n'ayez jamais parlé qu'en sophismes.
> O Platon! vous avez fait bien plus de mal que vous ne croyez.
> Comment cela? me demandera-t-on: je ne le dirai pas." *Diction-
> naire Philosophique*

Why wouldn't he say what the damage was? Perhaps because
at that time it had not been fully assessed. Perhaps because
Voltaire sensed the dangerous fragmentation that Plato had
wrought, but had not seen its full effects. If that is the case,

Voltaire was truly prophetic. And again there is a real irony, because when Plato wanted to express the great truth of truths, in the *Timaeus,* he resorted to the language of myth and poetry, and obviously meant us to take him seriously. (Which leads me to wonder if the mass of the Socratic dialogues are not perhaps some kind of send up—a vast satire on the misuse of reason.)

But the reintegration that our condition cries out for cannot be on a pre-Platonic basis: a tribal, heroic, oral basis. Our capacity for literate communication and self-annihilation has outrun that possibility. Yet, we do not seem able to make the necessary imaginative/rational leap into the state of consciousness needed to handle this monstrous situation that we have ourselves created out of the debris of the Platonic sundering of reason and imagination.

Where must we start in trying to re-understand ourselves? It will be a basic contention here that we must condemn as deficient any commentary on the human condition that fails to take into account the ancientness of the species and the more than five-million years of natural selection that have molded the questionable end product that includes the commentators and their commentaries. That is to say, anything but an evolutionary view of modern man is going to be insufficient if its purpose is to calculate the possibilities of human survival. This rules out most of the governing paradigms of informed commentary, scientific, literary, political, and religious. In particular it rules out most of social theory as it now stands. To see why, let us look at one of the best examples of modern social theory; for what the author of this theory finds hard to handle, given its assumptions, turns out to be the cornerstone of an evolutionary understanding.

FOR WHOM THE BELL TOLLS

I would recommend anyone to read Daniel Bell's brilliant analysis of trends in the contemporary world, *The Coming of Post Industrial Society.* I marvel at the skill with which he analyzes the complexities of industrial society and its transformations. In particular, he makes a good case for taking the 'disjunction between culture and social structure' as the major agent of change. Roughly speaking, this means that ideas, values, and knowledge get out of kilter with established social institutions, and when this gets disjunctive enough, a readjustment has to take place. Contemporary culture developed in an industrial society that was labor intensive, but already that culture is changing to one based on knowledge, information, and communication, and this demands a change to a service-intensive economy that will be the chief characteristic of the postindustrial society.

This is all wonderful and convincing. But at the same time I am faced with the old question, which Bell never systematically takes a pace back from the detail of his material to ask, namely: Can the creature sustain all this complexity, these numbers, this intricacy of organization? Can this kind of creature sustain it? For there is a hidden assumption in the work of Bell and all like him—that the creature can, in effect, do anything. The limitations of the creature, therefore, do not need to be taken into account. Indeed, they do not exist. Paul Goodman in 1960 castigated this kind of thinking as "the final result of the recent social-scientific attitude that culture is added onto a featureless animal, rather than being the invention-and-discovery of human powers." (*Growing Up Absurd*) At about the same time Clifford Geertz had the same insight:

> Man is to be defined neither by his innate capacities alone, as the Enlightenment sought to do, nor by his actual behaviors alone, as much of contemporary social science seeks to do, but rather by the link between them, by the way in which the first is transformed into the second, his generic potentialities focussed into his specific performances. (*The Interpretation of Cultures:* 52)

I am going to argue that Bell doesn't really believe his own ideology—that there is a built-in ambivalence; that like me he in fact accepts that 'capitalist/industrial' society is only made possible by the grasping hand, binocular vision, and hand-eye coordination shaped by seventy million years in the trees; by the solidly planted foot and muscular power developed by at least six million years on the savannas; by the 'storage and re-trieval' and 'planning and foresight' capacities of the neocortex developed by systematic hunting. In saying that we are shifting from a labor-intensive to a service-intensive system—or what-ever—we are saying that we are shifting from emphasis on one part of the human primate repertoire to another. But the brain, with its mechanical adjuncts (to which we are turning more and more desperately) is still the primate brain retooled by preda-tion. And it is not an organ of cool rationality: it is a surg-ing field of electrochemical activity replete with emotion and geared for a particular range of adaptive responses. Force it to try to work outside that range for long enough, and it will re-act—it will rebel. It will regress to those pristine behaviors (in-cluding the very necessary aggressive ones) surrounding its primary functions, survival and reproduction.

The sociologists—including Bell when he is on his guard—write as though none of this matters because the institutions themselves are what are at issue, and they are somehow 'au-tonomous'—detached from the grasping hand, the striding walk, and the self-deceiving brain. All this 'organic' stuff can be left out of the equations. Thus, giant bureaucracy will fail, per-haps, because of internal structural conflicts or conflicts with other institutions, not because this animal—this *Homo sapiens*—will only put up with it for so long before it subordinates it in some ways: sabotage, 'inefficiency,' absenteeism, alcoholism, 'work-related stress diseases,' nepotism, 'issueless' strikes, burn-out, and straight rebellion. Why, if indeed we can 'add culture to a featureless organism,' shouldn't we be able simply to 'train' people to enjoy large-scale bureaucracy, to 'adjust their work habits and attitudes'? Shortly before he died so tragically early, Victor Turner, the arch-priest of 'symbolic' social science, wrote poignantly, in *Zygon:*

> The present essay is for me one of the most difficult I have ever attempted. This is because I am having to submit to ques-tion some of the axioms anthropologists of my generation—and several subsequent generations—were taught to hallow. These axioms express the belief that all human behavior is the result of social conditioning. Clearly a very great deal of it is, but gradually

it has been borne home to me that *there are inherent resistances to conditioning.* (My italics)

There are flickers of understanding of this in Bell when he lets his guard drop. For example, on page 163 (1976 edition) he discusses why things have 'gone awry' with sociological predictions:

> The first has been the persistent strength of what Max Weber called 'segregated status groups'—race, ethnic, linguistic, religious—whose loyalties, ties and emotional identifications have been more powerful and compelling than class at most times, and whose own divisions have overridden class lines.

It is not discussed further, but one immediately asks: "Why"? Race, country (region), language, religion: why do these have their 'persistent strength' that is so annoying to predictions stemming from the autonomy of institutions? I think I know. Bell lets it pass. But I'll make my own prediction: their 'persistent strength' will make a merry hash of the 'post-industrial society' too.

On the issue of the failure of rationality in industrial society, hear Bell:

> Traditional elements remain. Work groups intervene to impose their own rhythms and "bogeys" (or output restrictions) when they can. Waste runs high. Particularism and politics abound. These soften the unrelenting quality of industrial life. Yet the essential, technical features remain.

Where do 'their own rhythms' come from, that they are so intrusive? And by what standards do we judge that 'the quality of industrial life' is 'unrelenting' and needs to be 'softened'? Again, I think I know, but Bell just slips this one in with 'traditional elements remain.' But why do they remain? Why, as we have asked, if we can do anything, don't we just retrain people to find industry or bureaucracy satisfying? Perhaps we are just not very efficient or not ruthless enough (Skinner would say so). Perhaps. Again, on the literal 'inhumanity' of bureaucracy (a central theme in Tiger and Fox's *The Imperial Animal*) here is a remarkable statement by Bell (p. 119):

In the broadest sense, the most besetting dilemma confronting all modern society is bureaucratization, or the "rule of rules." Historically, bureaucratization was in part an advance of freedom. Against the arbitrary and capricious power, say, of a foreman, the adoption of impersonal rules was a guarantee of rights. But when an entire world becomes impersonal, and bureaucratic organizations are run by mechanical rules (and often for the benefit and convenience of the bureaucratic staff), then inevitably *the principle has swung too far."* (My emphasis)

'Has swung too far'? From what? We are not told. Again, if it's efficient why doesn't it just work? Why do intrusive elements 'persist'; how do we know it has 'swung too far'? I think Bell is unquestionably right—more right in fact when he exercises his sound human intuition than when he essays his complex analyses. 'Irrational' elements persist. We have gone too far. If we look at 'traditional societies'—those simple tribal and village people that are the stuff of anthropology—there is something quite striking that sociologists in their obsession with the torments of industrial society miss: they could go on forever. They are Lévi-Strauss's 'cool' societies, as opposed to the 'hot' societies that have entered the stream of historical change. If we look at the tribes, the bands, the small villages, it is obvious that they have not only existed from time immemorial, but could go on in the same way forever if they were not hit from the outside. Colin Turnbull's pygmies—existing as humanity in its most 'stripped-down' form—could clearly persist indefinitely if they were not dragged out of their forest, put in 'progressive' agricultural camps, and allowed to die off from the heat and epidemics.

It seems simple minded to say that they do not have the problems of our society—either the real problems of 'adjustment' or the intellectual problems of explaining it. But the annoying 'irrationalities' that 'persist'—these 'traditional elements'—and play havoc with our increasingly designed societies, are their 'irrationalities,' their elements: tribal loyalty identified with language, physical character, symbols, and beliefs. The 'natural rhythms of the work group' are their rhythms—the whole social entity is a work group with its internal reciprocities and rhythms. And if not disrupted, the traditional systems work. They just go on. It is not that they never change, but rather that change is not of their essence as it is with societies in the stream of history. As Tönnies was not afraid to conclude, Gemeinschaft is always more durable than Gesellschaft. Its life-style may not be wildly exciting compared with computer wars and disco bars (I'm not so sure) but it seems satisfying to the members, and it is not plagued with the problems that Bell needs so many pages to analyze.

These small-scale societies have their conflicts, of course. I am not saying that they are all peace and harmony. Conflict is part of life—in fact in trying to get rid of it we may do great damage. But that is not the point. The point is that they work, and they work in my estimation because their very scale is compatible with our 'environment of evolutionary adaptation'—the social environment for which we evolved and in which we are supposed to exist. Bell's 'intrusive' elements in the rapidly changing, ever rationalizing, increasingly bureaucratized societies, are precisely the elements that make small-scale, unhistorical, relatively unchanging societies work. When we have 'swung too far,' it is from this central point.

THE PIT AND THE PENDULUM

But what an abhorrent notion to the autonomists and the behaviorists. Since we can do anything, we can change society effectively as long as we can put our expert finger on just how to do it. But 'it' remains strangely elusive. I have another vision of what has happened in history. The successive stages of progress are simply different experiments in departing from the basic pattern (as outlined e.g., in chapter 6 of my *Red Lamp of Incest*). They are not in fact 'progressive stages' at all; it is simply that changes in technology allow us to try different experiments. The knowledge and technics used in trying these are cumulative, of course. But this only means that we can attempt even more bizarre designs for living than previously. But they never work, in the way that the primitive total societies work, because they can never be total societies: societies that tap the whole range of human needs and satisfactions for each and every member. These they fragment, and most so-called social pathologies are desperate attempts to heal the fragmentation or, if you like, the alienation and anomie.

In changing into Bell's post-industrial society, we are simply crawling to another part of the flypaper of history. We won't escape, and it won't work. But I shall repeat my solid sociological prediction: the traditional/irrational elements of the basic pattern of our social environment of evolutionary adaptation will persist and disrupt the new order. Orwell envisaged a 'total' totalitarianism as the only final (if not happy) answer to the agony of constant change. But Orwell's super bureaucratic state wouldn't work either, as David Ehrenfeld (*The Arrogance of Humanism*)—his great admirer—so forcefully points out. The 'inner party' themselves could never sustain their role. Hope did not lie, as Winston Smith thought, with the proles, but with the fallibility of the managers.

This view of history is close in some ways to the sociologies of change—deriving from certain philosophies of history—that see it as oscillating rather than progressing. (This is sometimes called the cyclical view of history, but I think oscillation—the swing of Bell's mysterious pendulum—is more adequately descriptive.) In the grand scheme of Sorokin (*Social and Cultural Dynamics*), cultures swing between two extreme commitments to conceptions of truth: the truth of the senses and the truth of faith. These are the 'sensate' and the 'ideational' extremes. Since each is only a partial version of truth, overwhelming commitment to either won't work, and the pendulum swings back the other way. The center of balance is 'idealistic'—those brief periods of history when the senses are idealized: the body in fifth-century Greek art, for example, and in the cathedral sculpture of the thirteenth century. It is a convincing scheme as far as it goes, but it only goes as far as 'theories of truth' in explaining the swing of the social pendulum.

If we take my 'scale of evolutionary adaptation' as the central point of rest, however, so much more follows. Swings of the pendulum can go in various extreme directions from this state, theories of truth being only one element. I would agree with

Sorokin that in the ideal state, 'truth' would be a judicious mixture of hard practical wisdom and an acceptance of the 'sacredness' (i.e., unquestionability) of certain key values. But there is so much more in the sheer content of social relations that can be derived directly from our knowledge of our evolutionary history of adaptation without hanging it all on abstract notions of truth. I confess I cannot—no one can—at this point detail all the content of the steady, central state. But that knowledge will come (although probably too late). In principle, however, it is only the properties of the total/small-scale society, with the added knowledge of its physiological and psychological underpinnings, that modern science is revealing.

In this respect, John Friedman (*The Good Society*) and other anarchists and quasi anarchists are interesting. For Friedman society oscillates between extremes of Individualism and Collectivism, with the 'Good Society' of Communalism lying at a kind of center. The communal society, however, can only ever be a kind of guerilla operation inside the extremist lunacies of the other types. But his theory is remarkably like Sorokin's in the sense that each of the supertypes tries to push to its extreme and breaks down. The communal society is a network of groups, each group having 'more than three, less than twelve' members, with '8+/−1' as the mode. This is about the average number of adult males in the Paleolithic hunting group. Add twice that number of child-bearing females and about twenty juveniles and infants (a typical demographic structure of a band) and you have the roughly forty persons of the organic group that we as a species evolved in. (It was in contact with many other similar groups of course.) I stress organic because Friedman's group is not: it is a parasitical ideological group.

Perhaps what we really need in order to recreate the 'communal good society' are organic extended kinship groups. But the bureaucracy hates them, which is why it enforces monogamy, restricts inheritance, encourages celibacy, and persecutes Mormons. Be this as it may, some theory of the basic nature of the organic group cannot be avoided.

And this brings me back to Bell and his ambivalence. Despite a theory of change based on institutional contradictions—the disjunction of culture and social structure, he is constantly forced back on the human creature and those limitations that Turner had borne home to him. Bell quotes with approval (p. 455) Rousseau's comment that the "universal desire for reputation, honors and preferences, which devours us all. . . . stimulates and multiplies passions . . ." and so on. "Vanity—or ego—can never be erased," Bell avers; "one of the deepest human impulses is to *sanctify* their institutions and beliefs . . ." (p. 480, his emphasis); "what does not vanish is the duplex nature of man himself—the murderous aggression, from primal impulse, to tear apart and destroy; and the search for order, in art and life, as the bending of will to harmonious shape."

Strong stuff! No. They do not vanish. And if in fact we take and put together all the social, emotional, and cognitive items that Bell finds so pervasive yet so destructive of the autonomy of institutions, we would come up with a pretty fair rendering of the basic human culture from which the successively more 'rational' permutations are disastrous departures.

So, I return to my point that these 'progressive' changes are illusory: they are merely oscillations about a point—swings of the pendulum further and further away from that naggingly persistent, irrational, but totally human central condition or basic state that is the community fitted to our environment of evolutionary adaptation.

THE DECLINE OF THE WEST

Where, in time, is this basic state to be found? The answer is straightforward: in the Late Paleolithic, some fifteen to forty thousand years ago. It is really that simple. We were fully formed modern *Homo sapiens sapiens;* we had reached the top of the food chain—we were doing quite a bit better than the other carnivores. Then, with a frightening rapidity, it all began to go wrong—or to go 'too far,' as Bell would have it. Population was squeezed into the Middle East and southwestern Europe by the ice, and the unprecedented social density thus created led to a burst of self-conscious activity evidenced by the fantastic art of the period (Bell's 'search for order in art'?). Hot on the heels of

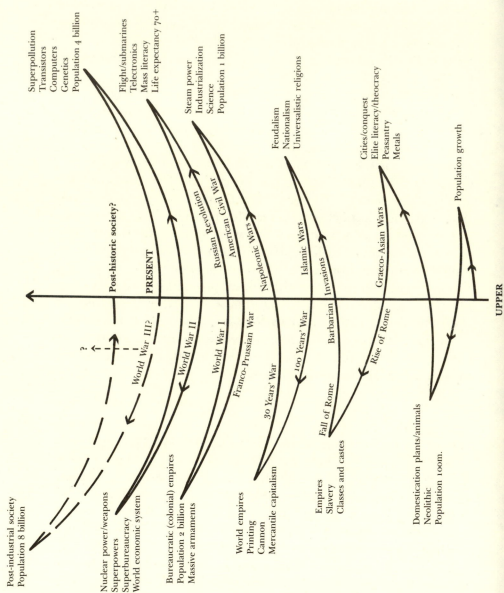

DIAGRAM 1

Post-industrial society
Population 8 billion

Nuclear power/weapons
Superpowers
Superbureaucracy
World economic system

World War III?

Post-historic society?

PRESENT

Superpollution
Transistors
Computers
Genetics
Population 4 billion

Flight/submarines
Telectronics
Mass literacy
Life expectancy 70+

Steam power
Industrialization
Science
Population 1 billion

Bureaucratic (colonial) empires
Population 2 billion
Massive armaments

World War II

World War I

Russian Revolution

American Civil War

Napoleonic Wars

Franco-Prussian War

30 Years' War

World empires
Printing
Cannon
Mercantile capitalism

100 Years' War

Islamic Wars

Barbarian
Invasions

Fall of Rome

Empires
Slavery
Classes and castes

Feudalism
Nationalism
Universalistic religions

Rise of Rome

Graeco-Asian Wars

Cities/conquest
Elite literacy/theocracy
Peasantry
Metals

Domestication plants/animals
Neolithic
Population 100m.

Population growth

UPPER

this came the warm interglacial in which we are still living (and which has almost run its course), and the first of the violent oscillations happened—the domestication of plants and animals. After that, the swings of the pendulum went on, sometimes at a leisurely pace, sometimes wildly. At the points between the wildest swings, we get the most terrible upheavals and carnage; and each huge swing has the effect of sending the pendulum wildly off in another direction. The only 'progress' in this view is the cumulative ability to indulge in even wilder and more rapid swings, aided by technology and rationality.

These swings are roughly illustrated in the accompanying diagram. The 'upward' movement is merely chronological and does not imply progress, except as cumulative technological change. Also, the extremes of the swings are simply my own highly condensed judgements; other observers will stress different ways in which the swings went (or will go) too far. For example, under blanket headings like Feudalism and Industrialism all the effects of these new systems of production have to be included. Thus, I have not included Industrial Capitalism or Socialism or Welfare Liberalism, and so forth under Industrialism, since these are all effects of the industrial revolution. Nor have I added refinements like Monopoly Capitalism or Multinational Corporations or Imperialism since these again are subdivisions of the more general headings. Again, the major wars I have indicated are those that have reflected or led to features of the major shifts. Thus the Fall of Rome and the Barbarian Invasions led to Feudalism; the Franco-Prussian War (see Michael Howard's excellent description of it) and the American Civil War reflect the impact of Steam Power which led to railways, and the 'nation in arms': universal conscription in France; the dominance of Ideology in America. These were the first great modern wars.

It should also be remembered that many cultures did not participate in these shifts, at least until the Western powers forced the results onto them. It can be argued that the picture is Euro-centered. True. We are not here presenting a scheme of world history, but a map of the major swings of the 'progressive' pendulum, and these mostly took place in Europe after the

Middle Ages; a fact that has obsessed modern social science. We cannot help but be centered on the West, and in consequence on the decline of the West, for this is where the pendulum did its latest and most damaging swinging. Bell is only pointing the way to another such swing, and at the same time realizing that something human is here being denied. I guess that all I want to do is keep calling attention to this humanity and to plead against its denial. If we can't go back to the 'Paleoterrific' then perhaps we can at least drop the nonsense about progress and rationality and start thinking about how we can serve that stubborn human core within the context of the inhuman super society. Perhaps it is only marginally possible. But it certainly won't be possible at all if we don't recognize the problems.

AS OTHERS SEE US

Doris Lessing says, in *The Sirian Experiments:*

> I think it is likely that our view of ourselves as a species on this planet now is inaccurate, and will strike those who come after us as inadequate as the world view of, let's say, the inhabitants of New Guinea seems to us. That our current view of ourselves as a species is wrong. That we know very little about what is going on.

It would be hard to press this view, I suppose, on all the Daniel Bells of the world who have written at such expert length about what is going on, has gone on, and is going to go on. That is what makes it hard for me to be a social scientist, for I agree with Lessing: our current view of ourselves as a species is wrong; we know very little about what is going on. But at least since Darwin we know a little more about ourselves as a species, and in another place I will have to analyze why the social sciences have spearheaded the refusal to acknowledge even that. But consider—what possible headway could the view that all 'history' is a series of wilder and wilder divergences from a Paleolithic norm make today in the world of behavioral science orthodoxy?

I am always amused at the 'Marxist' objection that the biological approach to social behavior, as they love to say, 'de-historicizes' man! What a puffed-up, pre-Darwinian, self-satisfied Enlightenment view of themselves these soi-disant 'Marxists' have! It is not biology that de-historicizes man but a view of him that would deny the relevance of *millions of years* of his history! What they call 'history' is a problematical blip at the end of this trajectory—the wild swings of the pendulum shown on the chart, swings that represent only a fraction of one percent of his history.

One part of the view of ourselves as a species that is wholly wrong, then, is the conventional time frame in which we choose to analyze ourselves: as though the last few thousand years are peculiarly privileged and the rest can simply be written off as 'pre-history'! This is pride, arrogance, hubris of a high order, and we are paying for it. Before Darwin, before we knew, it was perhaps forgivable. Now it is not even funny. It is the root of our self-destruction. Kenneth Bock can castigate 'sociobiology' for not being able to 'explain cultural diversity or recent history' without, apparently, any insight into the irrelevance of this claim. It is a measure of our lack of vision that an overwhelming majority of social scientists would agree with him. We have seen Bell's 'explanation' of 'recent history.' As an anthropologist I have spent my life 'explaining' cultural diversity. Blips on the end of the trajectory. In a thousand years those successors Lessing envisages will look back, (if there are any successors, of course) with some passing interest, on the phase called 'history' by those chrono-centric myopians who lived through it. The successors will be mildly amused by their arrogant pomposity but, we hope, will have learned never to repeat it.

ASIDE—FOR THE SOCIAL SCIENTIST

Let us, as a late and unlamented President said, get this perfectly clear. The Upper Paleolithic was in balance between the organism, the social system, and the environment. It got pushed off balance, probably by a sudden (in relative terms) increase of population density in southwestern Europe, the Middle East, and parts of Asia. Once the consequences of this density began to take hold, there emerged certain social properties that had not existed hitherto. And Durkheim was right that these were social properties, not individual. He was wrong, however, to divorce them from the biology of the organisms, for only this made them possible.

Thus, for example, religion in a small tribelet was one thing, but became something quite other when large numbers were involved with the concomitants of classes, religious castes, power elites, exploitation, and so forth. The raw material was the religiosity of the Paleolithic hunter: the 'new look' was the emergent properties of the new social density. Ever since, these emergent properties—seized as their subject matter by the social scientists—have been on a collision course with the social needs of the Paleolithic hunter. This is what we call 'history'; and 'cultural diversity' and 'recent history' are both but the latest set of examples of the collision course (for better or for worse, since some versions of culture are closer to the balance).

So to say that evolutionary biology cannot explain recent history is a totally empty claim. What could it mean? That it cannot account for specific series of events in recent time? Of course it can't. What can? This view entails a curiously nineteenth-century mechanistic version of 'explanation.' But if what we are after is understanding or perhaps interpretation, then only evolutionary biology can help us. The historians and social scientists are too trapped in the myopia of their short-term vision to help us. They have taken the emergent properties of the post-Paleolithic society as a reality sui generis. But they do not understand the genesis of this reality and therefore its ultimately fragile and dependent nature. For it is dependent on the continued acquiescence of the Paleolithic organism, and this, as Bell sees (but does not pursue his vision), it does not have. I would 'explain' recent history as an ever more desperate attempt to marry this precarious acquiescence to an ever more runaway technology. And that's from evolutionary biology!

If I can put this in a succinct phrase for the Bocks of this world to ponder: It is not so much that evolutionary biology explains what we do, as that *it explains what we do at our peril*. (End of aside.)

I don't want to trespass on Lessing territory, since while I certainly think the science-fiction writers often have a better grasp of things than the social scientists (Frank Herbert, for example) I don't aspire to their version of the vision. I am happier defending my own insistence on the virtues of the 'Paleoterrific.' (I don't know who coined the term—and I think it was meant sarcastically. But I don't care. I'll just reverse the sarcasm and shamelessly appropriate the lovely word.)

ET IN ARCADIA EGO

There is a reflex tendency to dismiss this view of the 'Paleoterrific' as romantic primitivism. But for me it is based on a hard-science view of the evolution of human behavior. It also gets around a common criticism: that those philosophers who advocate 'living in accordance with nature' have a hard time defining that very nature they are so fond of. (Thus for Diogenes it was living in a tub; for Aristotle it was living in a city.) I do not have that difficulty: my 'nature' is located during a specific era of evolution for specific reasons advanced above. This nature is not a vague conceptual state defined by whatever the philosopher feels is 'natural' and therefore by implication 'good.' It is a specific time and even place; and it is not 'good' because it embodies qualities I or any other philosopher admire necessarily. It was not, probably, according to most definitions so far advanced, very good at all. Life in it was not necessarily always nasty and brutish, but it surely was some of the time; and it was certainly short, by our standards, for most people. I would plead for a moratorium on the use of 'good' here, since it is very confusing. I am going to stress over and over again that I do not think we should hold to the Paleolithic model because it is some kind of utopian ideal, but because it is what we are and it worked because it stayed within those bounds. And that is all. Our notions of the good life are now so corrupted by all the paraphernalia of literate civilization that we have probably no way in which even to talk about the virtues of adaptation per se. That is, we cannot even conceive of approving a way of life simply because it worked, in turn because it was the way of life to which the creature had evolved. We see this for animals when we debate about keeping them in zoos that we 'reform' to approach the untouched grandeur of the natural surroundings of the incarcerated creatures. What I am asking is for a similar approach to ourselves. We have left that untouched grandeur and the life associated with it and have entered what Morris chose to call *The Human Zoo:* civilization. Can we, or can we not, reform that zoo so that it at least approximates the conditions from which the unfortunate animals were removed, or in this case, removed themselves? This is a crucial point in which we differ from the other animals, and I must return to it.

But before I do, let us consider the issue of the virtues of the 'Paleoterrific.' I will stick to my point that I am not looking at it as utopia or dystopia but simply as Paleotopia: as what it was. But I still feel inclined to ask: would life in the Upper Paleolithic have been so unsatisfactory for those of us nurtured in 'civilization'? We tend to view this from our softened position as inheritors of a gadget-ridden, mass-literate, high-technology culture. Let me do a little thought experiment here—a highly personal one, as a thought experiment has to be—and project myself back into that proto-culture.

When I view my own life, I find that many of the things that satisfy me most are not dependent on the high-technology culture, nor are they the things for which I receive reward and praise from that culture. On the other hand, some things for which I am rewarded have their Paleolithic counterparts. Thus, sitting on committees is equivalent to taking part in the councils of the tribe; teaching the young is part of the system of tribal initiation; and tending the myths and legends of the tribe (social theory) is pure Paleolithic—even if it then was solely oral rather than semiliterate. Literacy is a late intrusion which we have not properly understood or assimilated, which has some very bad side effects, and which is probably much overvalued. Most people get by without it, and many of those nominally 'literate' manage with a minimum and revert to orality (television) out of preference.

When I was young and poor I used to borrow books from the library, and, so that I would always have them to hand, committed to memory large parts of Pope's Homer, of *The Idylls of the King*, the *Lays of Ancient Rome*, *The Pied Piper of Hamelin* and so on. I can remember accurately the whole of many operas (particularly Gilbert and Sullivan), oratorios and cantatas, masses of Shakespeare, and much, much more. And I am here talking only of accurate memory, and only of a small part of it. My memory storage is nowhere near exhausted, and a whole mass of memorized songs (running into four figures) were learned orally. Given living poets and musicians rather than books and scores, I would have perhaps learned even more, and learned it more quickly. Literacy slows learning if anything. The Greek poets recited all of Homer by heart; the prodigies of memorization of the Celtic bards is legendary and is matched today by the reciters of folk epics in the Balkans; read Mark Twain on the memories of Mississippi steamboat pilots; look at the inventory of a Navaho singer. Mechanical devices make us lazy. My point is that I would have enjoyed a good intellectual existence in an oral culture without much loss, among people similarly well stacked with information, and even some division of intellectual labor. It is one of the things that can make growing old in such a culture so superior to growing old in our own: the old are the living libraries, the *bibliothèques nationales* of the tribe—and are often cherished accordingly.

I would have been valued for the lullabies I composed to quiet the children, and the songs I made up to amuse them. As to philosophizing, anthropologists now know that the myths and rituals of a tribe are just that. Fine-tuning of old myths to new social and cultural needs is what any ideological system— like 'social theory'—is about. I would have been good at that, along with tribesman Bell. I've always preferred couching ideas in story or verse rather than in 'rational' argument, anyway. (Another late and still unproven innovation.) I dropped music,

poetry, and art, at which I was also amateurishly good—to take
up science, thus losing the unity of art and science that is inherent in the logic of myth and ritual. How typical of our arrogance that we now honor a person who is good in many
fields—arts and sciences, sports and technologies—as a Renaissance Man; we never think to call him a Paleolithic Man! But
then, we haven't even absorbed the astonishment of Altamira
and Lascaux.

I could have been on the 'committee' that organized the incredible Lascaux ceremonial complex with its great halls, tunnels and side chapels, its crypts and vestries. (See John Pfeiffer's
The Creative Explosion.) If we look later, as Henry Adams did to
his central point of human unity, the eleventh, twelfth, and
thirteenth centuries, what do we find? We find again great ceremonial centers organized by committees at Chartres or Paris.
And what are they but huge, dimly lighted caves erected above
ground, with crypts, tunnels, side chapels, and wall decorations;
erected at huge expense of money, time and labor, and more
often than not to honor the Great Mother—Notre Dame—who
is Nature. Adams—who never really grasped Darwin, having
been sidetracked by Lyell—got as far as the eleventh century in
his search for the time of unity to compare with the time of
fragmentation he was living in. He was on the right track, but
he didn't know about Lascaux and Altamira.

Insofar as these were ceremonial centers (like later Stone-
henge) where many different people came for initiation into
the mysteries, I would have been good at picking up the foreign tongues and appreciating the power of the magic of alien
tribes. When it came to the hunt, I think I would have managed
once I knew that the ferocity of wild beasts could be countered
by the collective power of human imaginations and intellects. I
found this out directly when facing an enraged and dangerous
wild animal in an arena, armed only with these skills and a piece
of cloth.

As to war—or such skirmishing as passed for war then—well,
I am the son of a soldier, and I would have had something
worth fighting and dying for: my genetic investment in the little
tribe. Men do not really, except in heroic epics, die for the ashes

of their fathers and the temples of their gods, but for their living family of fellow creatures—as Macaulay, to his credit, has Horatius go on to recognize. They would really have needed me, in a way I find hard to believe that the 'Free World' needs me, or the United States, unless it is disguised as an 'uncle' to tap my Paleolithic kinship guilts. No. I don't think the Paleolithic would have been all that bad at all. It may well have been a short life, although it would have been free from epidemic, stress, and pollution-related diseases, as well as those diseases caused by 'progressive' changes in diet (see Eaton, Shostak and Konner, *The Palaeolithic Prescription*). But perhaps better that life, filled with immediate human and intelligible meaning, than a lingering, fragmented existence with less and less sense of worthwhileness as the species connives greedily in its own extinction.

Friends who have read the foregoing and who know my perhaps over-civilized tastes maintain that I must have my tongue in my cheek. Of course, this has been a 'thought experiment.' Of course, there would be much I would miss if thrust back now into a 'Paleoterrific' existence. But again, of course, I am not suggesting some such reversal—a sudden taking away of all we know and a thrusting of us back into the caves. I am assuming the position of someone like myself (a similar personality) who knows nothing other than the Paleolithic. What I am trying to convey is that such a person (and I take myself as an example precisely because I am over-civilized) could have lived a rich, full, meaningful, satisfying, exciting, and no less, perhaps even more HUMAN life in this period. That is all. I am trying to object at the personal level to the notion of 'progress': that because we are now surrounded by and totally accustomed to the paraphernalia of industrial civilization, that to be stripped of this would reduce us to the level of 'degraded savagery' or 'the stone age' or 'brutal barbarism' or something such.

We still automatically think in this way—this eighteenth/nineteenth century social evolutionary way, and no amount of enlightened social relativism cures us of it. (Although Jean Auel's *Earth's Children* series, and her charming creation, Ayla, seem to have gathered quite a following—but I suspect this is largely among environmentalists who mistakenly see Paleolithic man as the original conservationist, rather than among anthropologists who tend to be scornful of this, in fact quite interesting, exercise in conjectural history.) Indeed, my cultural-relativist anthropological colleagues are among the worst offenders. The notion that we have not only technologically but morally progressed since 'the caves' is deeply ingrained: "If it weren't for X, Y or Z we'd be back in the caves." And even if not morally then at least, they insist, intellectually. You could not really contemplate, they say, going back to a preliterate life—you're the most avaricious reader we know! And to abandon not only the literacy, but all that sheer knowledge—the rational scientific knowledge—and sink back into 'superstition.' It is no good pointing out to them again that this belies their relativistic premises. If the 'little society' or the 'savage mind' of which they write so eloquently and which they defend so passionately is as goddamned wonderful as they claim, then why be afraid of being part of it?

Is it not they who are pretending in fact? What it boils down to—what they really do not want to lose—are sheer material comforts that enable them to extol the virtues of the primitive state while keeping it at a vast distance with their gadgets and life-prolonging technologies. As a Paleolithic hunter-shaman-warrior I would know nothing of these things and hence could not miss them. Would I be less or more 'human'? Such a person transferred (like Tarzan or Ishi) to our own times would be suicidally nostalgic for his own way of life. It is all relative. It is nowhere written that it is better in any absolute way to be a Western Rational-Scientific-Literate person than to be a Paleolithic Hunter-Shaman-Warrior-Artist-Poet (oral). I am stuck with being the former, but I recognize this as an aberration, not a result of 'progress'—just a huge deviation.

I shall struggle, reproduce, and die just like my counterpart. I have a different set of artifacts to do it with, that is all. My word processor has not composed the *Iliad*. My acrylics have not painted the great bulls of Lascaux, and my camera only obediently reproduces them. My contemporaries are diverting the energy of the human population into the means of its own destruction. I have books and central air-conditioning and jet travel and a VCR. Medical science may well see to it that I and billions of others enjoy these until we are eighty or more. Wonderful.

For those more interested in the logic of this argument than its charm, I should emphasize again that I do not need this 'virtues of the Paleoterrific' premise. I only need that the Paleolithic (upper) is our Environment of Evolutionary Adaptation. I just think it should get a better press, that's all. A more serious criticism would be that even by the late Paleolithic we had passed the point of no return—with, for example, the invention of the bow and the destruction of the megafauna in Europe and North America. It could be argued that the EEA should be set earlier. But I would hate to give up the cave art and all it implies. I admit this as a weakness, and one that, if basically human and hence generalizable to our ancestors, may help explain the inevitable start-up of the pendulum swings.

THE REACH EXCEEDS THE GRASP

Which leads to the inevitable question: could we have stopped there? I very much doubt it. And that is the human tragedy and its grand paradox. I once asked an engineer why cars were built to achieve speeds (like 120 m.p.h.) that they almost never attained and couldn't use except for brief periods. He explained that if you wanted a car to have a cruising speed of, say, 85 m.p.h., then it had to have a capacity of 120 m.p.h.—to maintain the eighty-five. The problem is, with an ambitious driver, there is a temptation to want to cruise at higher and higher speeds.

Could it be that the Paleolithic brain (which is our brain, it hasn't changed) was geared to cruise at the 'Paleoterrific' level, but in consequence had to be capable of the industrial and post-industrial societies? That what we have done, post-Altamira, is put our foot (as it were) ever more firmly on the cerebral gas pedal simply because we *could* go faster? And that now we are trying to cruise at what were only intended as passing or emergency speeds? We are doing 110 in a car designed for 85, because we can do 120. But, I asked the engineer, for how long? Not very long, he said. It's all relative of course, but not very long.

We have never recovered the balance, never found (except in odd corners here and there) the cruising speed. We are roaring out of control—wild swings of the pendulum—but for how long? Can we retain the technology, but regain the cultural and social center? We scorn as 'savages' and 'backward' or 'under-developed' those who kept close to the balance, and we force the technology on them both to salve our guilt and extend our markets, and because we have persuaded them that they are chicken to be going at 65 when they can do 120. In their cruising state they are not necessarily 'noble'—but perhaps they are closer to being 'human' in a sense we may never again understand.

The anthropologists have partly understood it—but they are viewing it from the speeding car. Their applause, reward and symbolic immortality is located at one end of one of the wild swings of the pendulum—the extreme of rational, bureaucratic science; they cannot conceive of a return to the center, even if they see its virtues better than most. And as we keep observing, perhaps there is no return. But except in technology I do not see the 'progress.' And even that is not clear since the technology is destroying us; or we are destroying ourselves with the technology; or whatever.

In some sense then, we may be trapped. We—the creature—produce these fantasy structures—cultures, religions, laws, civilizations. We produce them out of the raw material of our speeding brains and ricocheting imaginations. So they correspond to something in the creature or they would not work at all. Humans are eternal adolescents: put them in a fast car and they'll speed. The raw material of testosterone and curiosity will see to that. And they do correspond to something: one dimension of our humanity is ingenuity and deceit. Capitalism saved itself (for a while) by appealing to the greed of its workers. Affluence bought them off. But the rest of the world, it appears, cannot be so easily bought and stagflation threatens capitalism again. Even the socialist world, however, seems glumly to accept that sheer repression cannot work and that it must appease the greed of the Paleolithic glutton. In the West we are back to bread and circuses. (Which only fail when the bread is mouldy and the circuses boring.) Television for all and electronic games for the children (with a return to low-key materialism) will buy them off—stem the dissatisfaction for a while.

But all these things appeal ever only to part of the creature's emotional and intellectual needs. We are greedy, certainly, but not endlessly greedy. We also have pride and a craving for attention, for example. Media society can buy us off here too, for a while. As Andy Warhol summed it up, this is a society in which everyone can be famous for fifteen minutes. But the nostalgia for wartime that continues to embarrass pacifists reflects a need to feel integrated into the group when it faces danger. (Now where could that need have arisen I wonder?) "We were all together then. People helped each other. We weren't going to let the bloody Huns get us down." This refrain as part of the very real nostalgia among civilians suggests the deep needs involved. Bureaucracy cannot provide for them. But the sociologists will not face these issues, except to take a passing glance and hurry back to the autonomy of institutions. This is probably why the sociologists, like the economists, are constantly being faced with mass phenomena they can't predict, can't explain (except with after-the-fact rationalizations), and wish would go away.

WORDS OF OUR FATHERS

Actually mine is not such an outrageous social-science notion as it may seem. I am only taking to a logical conclusion, and in the light of more recent information, the 'loss of community' theme running through much of modern Western social thought. It could perhaps be said to be *the* theme of modern sociology. But with the possible exception of Tönnies (and Kurt Vonnegut) few thinkers have wanted to push it this far; that is, to claim not just that we are losing—or have long ago lost—a more 'sociable' form of existence, but that we have lost this because we have lost our setting in nature. We have stepped irrevocably outside

the limits of our environment of evolutionary adaptation. Even
the anthropologists (like Redfield) saw the 'little society' as a cultural artifact, not as an 'organ' adapted to its evolutionary niche.
Max Weber, however, in his admiration of—and projected book
about—Tolstoy, came close to this point. This is the extra distance I am prepared to go. It is only a way of translating into
the language of social theory the not uncommon complaint that
the modern world is out of step with human nature.

It fascinates me that one of the most perceptive social ana-
lysts before Bell should have come close to this same conclusion. And Karl Polanyi, in 1944, was also writing of a major
shift in the swing of the pendulum—precisely the shift from
the preindustrial to the industrial-capitalist society (from which,
if Bell is correct, we are now lurching into the postindustrial
phase). Polanyi called this *The Great Transformation*, but throughout warned us that the transformation itself has muddied our
thinking (I quote from the Beacon Press edition of 1957):

> The habit of looking at the last ten thousand years as well as at
> the array of early societies as a mere prelude to the true history
> of our civilization which started approximately with the publica-
> tion of the *Wealth of Nations* in 1766, is, to say the least, out of
> date. (page 45)

This sentence could well have stood as an epigraph to this
argument. Except, of course, that I would have wanted to say
the last ten million years! But Polanyi had the point. He says,
on page 46:

> If one conclusion stands out more clearly than another from
> the recent study of early societies it is the changelessness of man
> as a social being. His natural endowments re-appear with a re-
> markable constancy in societies of all times and places; and the
> necessary preconditions of the survival of human society appear
> to be immutably the same.

Thus it is that 'traditional elements remain.' Thus it is that
the 'natural rhythms reassert themselves.' And so on. In his
great conclusion on the inherent inconsistencies in the 'market
mentality' Polanyi asserts it, once again having brilliantly ana-
lyzed the examples (p. 150, my italics):

For if the market economy was *a threat to the human and natural components of the social fabric,* as we insisted, what else would one expect than an urge on the part of a great variety of people to press for some sort of protection? This was what we found. Also, one would expect this to happen without any theoretical or intellectual preconceptions on their part, and irrespective of their attitudes towards the principles underlying a market economy. Again this was the case. Moreover, we suggested that comparative history of governments might offer quasi-experimental support of our thesis if particular interests could be shown to be independent of the specific ideologies present in a number of different countries. For this also we could adduce striking evidence.

Thus the 'free-market liberals,' he points out, were the first to cry out for protection against the consequences of their own theories with the enactment of anti-trade union and anti-trust laws. And thus again and again when the 'human and natural components of the social fabric' are threatened, natural and social humans recognize unconsciously that things 'have gone too far' and strive for redress even in the teeth of their own theories to the contrary.

A VIEW FROM THE BRIDGE

But despite such interesting insights—and there are many such in the history of Western thought—we are going to have to be ruthless in treating most views of man and society as largely beside the point and interesting mostly as data. They cannot be much use in the construction of a future adequate social theory because they all suffer from the same problem: they operate from inside 'history.' They have no view of the place of history in the total story of the human species. Anything before history is dismissed as 'pre-history' and its only interest is as a backdrop to the historical period. Various philosophies of history or works of political or social philosophy may well tell us important truths about this period, but they could not and cannot put the period itself in perspective since they have no idea what the perspective is or even that there is one! The 'State of Nature' was dealt with in a few (usually erroneous) sentences. Since

Darwin the possibilities of a longer perspective have been there and the 'early condition of mankind' got some attention. But even so, until very recently, no one knew the length of time that the so-called early period covered. We now know that it was at least five million years.

The Darwinian news that we must have emerged from the animal kingdom was shattering. But until we knew the time period involved (and it may go back much further) history could not be put in perspective. We now know that history is a brief episode in a temperate interglacial (which is coming to an end) and represents much less than one percent of real human history properly understood. We arrogantly refer to 'early man' in a few sentences, when it is ourselves—'late man'—who deserve a passing mention. As we have seen, Lessing prophesies that some historian of the future will look back with amusement at the pathetic pretensions of historic man, much as we now laugh at the superstitions of the savage, the ignorant peasant, or the Middle Ages.

The wisdom of the Greeks, of the Jews, and the Christian scholastics, the confident learning of the Renaissance and the Enlightenment, the turbulent self-assertion of the romantics and the triumphs of scientific method and technology, while full of insights, will have to be put on hold.

The new sense of ourselves as a problematical and experimental blip at the end of the trajectory of human history has to take hold and everything has to be recast in that perspective before we can even start to think sensibly and constructively about ourselves, our behavior, our values, our societies. All our assumptions—all that accumulated detritus on all those library shelves—will have to be re-examined and probably largely discarded. Discarded that is as truth. It is all useful as data on the aberrations of the historical period, and it is always, at least to me, interesting to see how close to a real insight into the human condition many thinkers and poets could come without the benefit of any knowledge other than their intuitive knowledge of their own fragile humanity. Which brings us back to Bell and my contention that he is closer to the truth when using that good intuition than when wielding the dubiously effective club of sociological theory.

THE COOL SOCIETY

What I see when I read the complexities of Bell's account is Society the Great Leviathan—the stranded beast thrashing and heaving in a desperate attempt to live, as it becomes massively bloated, poisoned, and tormented. Bad as its condition is, there is a resilience; there is endogenous healing power; there are social antibodies and a cultural immune system. Leviathan struggles to heal itself; struggles to restore the basic healthy condition it knew before its ambition brought about its near collapse. The healing process is itself painful and the beast suffers much. Now the problem is this: the diagnosticians of the wounded state have mistaken this state for normality. So they see the pains and suffering of the healing process as pathologies! (Such as the 'epidemics' of illiteracy, teenage pregnancy, divorce, juvenile delinquency, drug taking, and terrorism.)

The frightening situation therefore reveals itself: they rush to cure what they see as pathologies, but what they are doing is hampering the healing process! Those a little more perceptive say: Leviathan had become used to the wounded state, it wouldn't have killed him, but the healing process is too dramatic; he has to learn to live with the wounds (to 'adjust'); they are normality now. The metaphor breaks down because we diagnosticians are part of our own Leviathan. We may even be one of the pathologies. At least this can act as a cautionary tale: the physician may be part of the disease.

This view of the human condition is a version of what I and others have said often enough. The previous paragraphs are taken, in fact, from a previous book. There also I said that any of these diatribes are only contributions to a larger project, the aim of which is to free us from the intellectual shackles of the Enlightenment faith in reason, the romantic passion for the individual, and the nineteenth-century worship of progress. But it is worth saying over and over again because no one gets it the first time. The prejudices are too ingrained and the urge to kill the bearer of bad news too deep-rooted.

"But we can't go back!" Of course not. And I think like Friedman that we cannot successfully use our new knowledge to 'plan' perfect communities. Huge equations are involved and there are too many unknowns. In any case, we always have to start from where we are and tinker with that. (I suppose at heart I am a Burkean conservative, and shrink from radical-utopian solutions, including those embraced by the far right.) I was taught by Karl Popper and still believe in 'piecemeal social engineering,' but with a difference. We must do our patching and mending on some other basis than vague liberal-humanitarian notions of the good. These often result from a merely negative view, such as oppression is bad, and also often represent quite violent swings of the pendulum themselves—the obsessive stress on the individual, for example. No. We must start from what is a quite flexible basic model of the 'steady state' of human society (see *The Red Lamp of Incest,* chap. 6), and engineer our way as close to it as possible. The classical anarchists—Kropotkin particularly—saw this really quite clearly. They drew this and not the competitive/laissez-faire moral from Darwin! The 'small is beautiful' crowd see it too—but they have no basis in evolutionary biology to direct them positively. Small is beautiful, for them, simply because big is bad. But they have stumbled on part of the truth.

Is there any hope of restoring the basic pattern in the mass societies and coercive states of the postindustrial future? The optimist in me says: Yes—if we can hang on and assimilate the new knowledge, and if advanced technology can free us from total preoccupation with work, and if we can reduce and reverse population increase, and if we can obliterate the effects of pollution, for instance, then we can engineer small-scale polities (under the technological umbrella) that will be real experiments in social living within the basic pattern (not communes!). This is the dream of Lévi-Strauss. Rather engagingly he sees us going back to playing with very complex kinship systems, for example. This would indeed be close to the core of our Paleolithic social being—the assortative mating system!

But the pessimist in me says: No—we cannot stop the trends however pathetically we try to rebel. The pendulum will swing ever more wildly in our efforts to 'design' a livable environment from unlivable materials. We will poison ourselves, overcrowd and starve ourselves, or, more probably, blast ourselves out of existence, before we get a chance to try the piecemeal engineering that could lead us, not to utopia, but to a humane scale of social existence (violence and all).

RELIGIO LAICI

So far, and leaving socialism on one side for the moment, the ethical guidance we have leaned on most heavily is derived from the great universalistic religions. But the concerns of the founders of these universalistic religions seem strangely out of place in small tribal societies—anachronistic and irrelevant. Those concerns with sin and salvation, guilt and recompense, rejection of the world and self, brotherly love and moralistic neighborliness, self-sacrifice and communalism, temperance and abnegation: they are simply either out of place or totally unoriginal in Paleo-society. But we should note these two possibilities: where they are out of place it is because they are appealing to guilts and problems that scarcely exist in the small-scale society; and where they are unoriginal it is because they are asserting moral platitudes that would be unremarkable in such a society.

What we see in the great world religions then, is a kind of moral desperation at the state of man and the world—which is why they continue to appeal to us today. Faced with fragmented, alienated, self-seeking, individualistic, and guilt-ridden 'civilized' man, the great teachers—Buddha, Christ, Mohammed, Confucius, St. Francis, Thomas More, Rousseau, Tolstoy, Gandhi—regardless of their particular delusional systems, have issued *clarion calls for a return to Paleo-morality*. They have urged a return to the communal ethic of the tribelet. They have differed about where the boundaries of the tribe should be drawn. Of the great three, only Buddha seems to have been truly universalistic: the whole of mankind was his tribe. But the followers, with their proselytizing zeal, wished all mankind to be included, either voluntarily or if necessary by force. They are sad and moving, these desperate attempts to stem the progressive-historic tide. But why they are interesting for us is their key insight into the loss of the Paleo-morality and the urgency with which they used all the metaphysical armory at their disposal to fight for its reinstatement. On some things, for example pacifism, turning the other cheek, and loving one's enemies, they were way out of line with the Paleo-ethic. This is one of the instances where the tribesman would find them incomprehensible. But the pursuit of enemies and the exacting of vengeance are intermittent things with the tribe; they do not claim many victims and they do not threaten the social fabric. In the densely populated, stratified, colonial, and civilized societies of the Mediterranean, Middle East, India, and China, on the other hand, violence was rightly to be feared as a more total threat. The tribesman would not have understood. Mohammed, a tribesman speaking to tribesmen, would be, and has been, much more appealing. His legacy, when multiplied by millions, may well usher in the end, and this would be the ultimate paradox of consciousness out of context.

I have mentioned the zeal of the followers, and it is often stated that the followers 'betrayed' the founders and perverted their messages. The followers had no choice. They were caught up in the great oscillations of history and could no more resist those inexorable movements than we can for all our technological and rational-scientific sophistication. The followers were realists who knew that they must cooperate with the inevitable and hence adapt a morality and metaphysic that sought to oppose the inevitable. They held up the assertion of the Paleo-ethic as an ideal, but one which, given the sinfulness of mankind, they had little hope of achieving. Part of their embarrassment stems from the very absoluteness of the founders' ethics: it was all or nothing. And this is perhaps our lesson: we may perhaps hold up the Paleo-morality as an ideal, but we must try to restore such of it as we can in relatively limited circumstances, recognizing that we have long ago passed the point where we could insist on absolute and universal application. That point

lay in the very early Neolithic when smallness of scale still operated and still operates in those small-scale Neolithic survivals
studied by anthropologists.

This is not to say that communalistic ethics are universally
followed in small-scale societies. To say so is to make the same
error as to say these societies are free from conflict. We are not
talking here of little utopias or of noble savages at all. But we
are talking of what is accepted in such societies as a moral ideal,
either explicitly in codes or implicitly in custom and myth. No
society is known which does not have sanctions against wrongdoing. These would scarcely be necessary if there were no
wrongdoers. But the important thing is that the very institutional structure, plus the small scale, of these societies, makes
dangerous deviation difficult. In trying to restore the Paleo-
morality as much as possible then, we should ideally aim, not as
the great religious teachers have done, to impose explicit moral
codes through supernatural or other sanctions, but to build
compliance into the structure of our institutions; a compliance
that will be absorbed through socialization and flow from a free
acceptance of 'our station and its duties' (Bradley). This, rather
than either total disorder or total obedience, is the true dream
of the anarchists and the idealists. It would be a society, in other
words, where the rewards for communalism so outweighed
those for individual assertion that no reasonable person—and
most of us are reasonable most of the time—would even consider the alternative; it would not seem to exist.

This may be beginning to sound like a heady call for perfection of the kind I claim to eschew. But if the reader is really
aware of the argument here, then it should rather appear as
heavy realism. We cannot, I have insisted, create moral utopias
in our present circumstances. Nor should we try, for such utopias are foreign to our Paleo-nature, which is a mixture of good
and evil and must allow for the expression of both. We can
attempt a realistic, piecemeal social engineering of our over-
individualized, over-rationalized, over-bureaucratized, and altogether too large societies to produce small-scale institutional
settings where the Paleo-morality would have more chance to
flourish. Such settings will have conflict; they will have violence;

they will have wrongdoing; they will even have wars. But these will all be on a human scale; and while we will not eradicate conflict and evildoing, we can render these manageable in human terms. There may be killings, but there will be no Auschwitz; there may be wars, but there will be no Armageddon; there may be heresies, but there will be no Inquisition; there may be crime, but there will be no Syndicates; there may be repression, but there will be no Gestapo. Now, while I say this is hardheaded realism I do not say it can be achieved. I say it may be the best we can hope for, but I am totally pessimistic about its achievement. I doubt if we shall ever recover from our delusional systems (the 'disease of rhetoric' as Doris Lessing would have it) long enough ever to consider this alternative.

If we do, however, we must face a common criticism. It has often been observed that collectivism and individualism are in constant conflict, and that while extremes of either are bad, it is hard to strike a balance (Friedman, *The Good Society*). Although the moral problems of rampant individualism may be obvious, the soul-destroying alternatives of total collectivism are by now unthinkable to those of us who have tasted the very real joys of individual self-fulfillment. This is the terrible fear that lurks behind the tremendous response we have to Orwell and Kafka (among others). I have no easy answer. I would like to think that the Paleo-community was not totalitarian even though it was total. But our rejuvenated societies would perhaps be more like their Neolithic counterparts, and there are plenty of examples of these that are tyrannous and destructive of the individual—witchcraft obsessions and killings come to mind. This is truly always a possibility. I can only repeat that we are not looking for utopias. It is part of the human dilemma that communities can become rotten, repressive, and repulsive on any scale. Again, I can only argue that if the scale is indeed small, the damage is minimized. This point is absolutely basic. We should not be looking for the perfect community, but for one that is manageable on a human scale. Evil will exist on this scale as on any other. The only hope is that if the evil itself is small scale, it will indeed be more manageable, in my sense, than the large scale and totally destructive evils we are now faced with.

To be 'more human' is not to approach close to some ethical ideal of goodness in the usual sense. It is about scale versus survival, not about goodness versus evil. The argument then that Paleo-society can have evil anti-individual aspects is accepted. It is simply declared irrelevant to the present argument, which is not about social perfection. At its best, Paleo-society achieves the communalistic ideals while enhancing individual lives; at its worst it perverts both. In either case, it does not threaten the survival of the species or make social life an inhuman nightmare.

One of the most attractive of modern utopias, in Ursula LeGuin's *Always Coming Home,* does attempt to portray a small-scale social system deliberately based on the Neolithic model provided by the Pueblo Indians her father (A. L. Kroeber) knew so well. To their basic system of small, informally linked villages, with matrilineal clans and guild-like ritual and occupational groups, she adds electricity, a dash of geomancy, horse-drawn railways, and a kind of controlled literacy. While she does not make the error of having a society of total goodness, neither does she admit the possibility of true badness: there is no witchcraft, for example, without which the actual Pueblo societies would be unrecognizable. Hers is, after all, a frankly utopian picture, and if one wishes to see the best we could hope for, this is about as good as it could get.

WE HAVE MET THE ENEMY AND HE IS US

On balance? Taking a hard look at the situation I am more pessimistic than optimistic. The brain is in some ways its own worst enemy. Its capacity for illusion and self-delusion, while an evolutionary advantage to 'primitive' hunters (as Carveth Read saw in 1920), turns into a terrifying suicidal capacity in (post) industrial society. No wonder people turn again to cults, to astrology, to magic, to hedonistic forgetfulness, and to socialism. Socialism is, in its way, yet another cry for a return to the communal ethic. But it fails because like our other modern social philosophies it operates totally within the confines of history and even of industrial history. It has not—except in the insignificant agrarian and anarchistic versions—anything better to offer than

more and more industrial progress, with a more equitable sharing of the products of the rape of the earth. It is a prisoner
of the assumptions of progress and a leading example of the
power of technological hubris. It holds out millenarian hope,
and people will cling to this as they cling to the possibility of
intervention by benevolent aliens. Both are about as likely to
succeed in saving us from ourselves.

Since the beginnings of civilization we have known that something was wrong: since the Book of the Dead, since the Ma-
habharata, since Sophocles and Aeschylus, since the Book of
Ecclesiastes. It has been variously diagnosed: the lust for knowledge of the Judaic first parents; the hubris of the Greeks; the
Christian sin of pride; the Confucian disharmony with nature;
the Hindu/Buddhist overvaluation of existence. Various reme-
dies have been proposed: the Judaic obedience; the Greek
stoicism; the Christian brotherhood of man in Christ; the Confucian cultivation of harmony; the Buddhist recognition of
the oneness of existence, and eventual freedom from its de-
terminacy. None of them has worked. (Or as the cynic would
have it, none of them has been tried.) The nineteenth century advanced the doctrine of inevitable progress allied to its
eighteenth-century legacy of faith in reason and human perfectibility through education. We thought, for a brief period
('recent history'!) that we could do anything. We can't. But it
comes hard to our egos to accept limitations after centuries of
'progress.' Will we learn to read those centuries as mere blips
on the evolutionary trajectory? As aberrantly wild swings of the
pendulum? As going too far? Will we come to understand that
consciousness can only exist out of context for so long before it
rebels against its unnatural exile? We might, given some terrible shock to the body social of the species, as Marx envisioned
in his way. (Thus returning us to our state of Gattungswesen—
species-being—where we existed before the Greek invention of
the polis cut us off from nature in the first great act of alienation.) But we might also never recover sufficiently from the
shock to form the classless, nonindustrial communities that
were the—albeit vague—Marxian dream of the communalistic future; a dream which is as embarrassing to his followers

as Christ's egalitarian pacifist dream has been to the Christian nations.

Being on the side of man, unfortunately, requires more than just good will. And if man won't be on his own side, that's his privilege as an intelligent, rational, self-conscious, culture-bearing creature, who has passed beyond the grubby necessities of natural selection to bigger and better things. For as so many well-meaning commentators have so proudly and earnestly proclaimed, he is unique.

> O nimium caelo et pelago confise sereno,
> nudus in ignota, Palinure, iacebis harena.
> Virgil, *Aeneid* V

Notes and References

Chapter 1

This chapter was first delivered as a lecture at the Smithsonian Institution's Man and Beast Conference in Washington, D.C., 1970. Although it has been reprinted several times, this collection would have been incomplete without it.

Two works were very influential in the development of these ideas: Clifford Geertz, "The Transition to Humanity," in Sol Tax, ed., *Horizons of Anthropology* (London: Allen and Unwin, 1965); and C. H. Waddington, *The Ethical Animal* (New York: Atheneum, 1961.)

Further relevant bibliography can be found in L. Tiger and R. Fox, *The Imperial Animal* (New York: Holt, Rinehart and Winston, 1971; reissued, New York: Henry Holt, 1989), and in the author's *The Red Lamp of Incest: A Study in the Origins of Mind and Society* (Notre Dame: Notre Dame University Press, 1983). For a discussion of the "program" that a biosocial science might follow, see the introduction to R. Fox, ed., *Biosocial Anthropology* (London: Malaby Press; New York: Halsted Press, 1975).

REFERENCES

Chance, M. R. A. "The Nature and Special Features of the Instinctive Social Bond of Primates." In *Social Life of Early Man*. S. L. Washburn, ed. London: Methuen, 1962.

Chomsky, N. *Syntactic Structures*. The Hague: Mouton & Co., 1957.

———, *Current Issues in Linguistic Theory*. The Hague: Mouton & Co., 1964.

———, *Aspects of the Theory of Syntax*. Cambridge: MIT Press, 1965.

Keith, Sir A., *A New Theory of Human Evolution*. London: Watts & Co., 1948.

LaBarre, W., *The Human Animal*. Chicago: University of Chicago Press, 1955.

Le Gros Clark, W. E. *History of the Primates*. Chicago: University of Chicago Press, 1957.

Lenneberg, E. H. *Biological Foundations of Language.* New York: John
   Wiley and Sons, 1967.
Lorenz, K. *On Aggression.* London: Methuen, 1966.
Tiger, L., *Men in Groups.* New York: Random House, 1969.
Wynne-Edwards, V. C. *Animal Dispersion in Relation to Social Behavior.*
   London: Oliver and Boyd, 1962.

Chapter 2

In the original essay, in *Encounter* (1982), there were no references
given, since it was assumed that such an audience would know the
literature mentioned. Here a few items are given to benefit students
and general readers otherwise not acquainted with the material. This
is also an opportunity to say that while I here disagree with Ashley
Montagu on the subject of man's innate qualities, I have learned more
from my constructive dispute with him than from many an enthusiastic agreement. The book of his I cite (as an example, there are so
many) is dedicated to Morris Ginsberg, who, as the text here shows, is
one of my own heroes. Thus, we share some things while sticking to
our stubborn disagreements on others. From those works that do
agree with mine, however, I must single out as particularly useful
Peter Marsh's *Aggro: The Illusion of Violence* (London: J. M. Dent,
1978). This should be read by all those pundits deploring 'soccer
violence.'

This chapter first appeared as a speech on the occasion of the
fiftieth anniversary of the *Technion* (Israel Institute of Technology) in
Haifa in 1973. Extracts appeared under the title "Rational Ethics and
Human Nature" in M. Kranzberg, ed., *Ethics in an Age of Pervasive
Technology* (Boulder Colo.: Westview Press, 1980). During the Haifa
meetings I benefited greatly from conversations with Isaiah Berlin,
Stuart Hampshire, and Daniel Bell. The present title was suggested
by Mel Lasky, editor of *Encounter,* and is much better than the original. There were some footnotes with the earlier version, but I have
not reproduced them here, since the matters dealt with in them are
addressed in other chapters of this book.

REFERENCES
Burrow, J. W. *Evolution and Society.* Cambridge: Cambridge University
   Press, 1966.
Chomsky, Noam. *Reflections on Language.* New York: Pantheon, 1975.
Dubos, René. Foreword to Robert Claiborne. *God or Beast: Evolution
   and Human Nature.* New York: Norton, 1974.

Gellner, Ernest. *Words and Things: An Examination Of, And An Attack On, Linguistic Philosophy*. Rev. ed. London and Boston: Routledge and Kegan Paul, 1979.

Ginsberg, Morris. *Reason and Unreason in Society*. London: London School of Economics and Longmans, 1947.

Hobhouse, L. T. *The Metaphysical Theory of the State*. London: Allen and Unwin, 1918.

Hofstadter, Richard. *Social Darwinism in American Thought*. Philadelphia: University of Pennsylvania Press, 1944.

Lévi-Strauss, Claude. *Les structures élémentaires de la parenté*. Paris: Presses Universitaires de France, 1949.

Mill, John Stuart. *An Examination of Sir William Hamilton's Philosophy, and of the Principal Philosophical Questions Discussed in His Writings*. London and New York: Longmans Green, 1867, 6th ed. 1889.

Montagu, Ashley. Ed. *Man and Aggression*. New York: Oxford University Press, 1968.

Sartre, Jean-Paul. *Critique de la raison dialectique, precédé de question de méthode*, Paris: Gallimard, 1960.

Trilling, Lionel. *Beyond Culture*. New York: Harcourt Brace, 1965.

Chapters 3 and 4

No bibliography is given for these chapters since the references are in the text, are often generic, and refer to primary sources which are classical texts in easily available standard editions.

I have not cited a long list of secondary sources here since as far as I can tell the point I am making is entirely original and was developed from a re-reading of the primary sources. Both factors (empiricism versus nativism and collectivism versus individualism) have, however, been discussed separately at length, as have the ideas of the many philosophers and scientists I cite, and I have obviously learned a great deal from the discussion of other scholars. I list some of them here, although since this idea has been germinating for more than thirty years I am bound to forget a few: Gordon Allport, Noel Annan, J. W. Burrow, Ernest Becker, Tom Bottomore, J. B. Bury, Isaiah Berlin, Donald Campbell, Noam Chomsky, Stefan Collini, John Crook, Louis Dumont, John Pfieffer, Ernest Gellner, Morris Ginsberg, Paul Heyer, Clément Heller, Julian Huxley, Richard Hofstadter, Geoffrey Hawthorn, Elie Halévy, Julian Jaynes, Erich Kahler, Thomas Kuhn, David Lewis, Stephen Lukes, Claude Lévi-Strauss, Konrad Lorenz, Arthur Lovejoy, Donald Macrae, Roger Masters, Ernst Mayr, Alasdair MacIntyre, Jacques Monod, Edgar Morin, Jacques Mehler, Talcott

Parsons, Karl Popper, Gianfranco Poggi, W. van O. Quine, Cynthia Russet, Amelie Rorty, George Stocking, Leslie Stephen, Michael Taylor, Bernard Williams, Basil Willey, Gary Wills, John Yolton, J. Z. Young.

Chapter 5

This chapter was originally delivered as an inaugural address for the new Department of Anthropology at the University of Notre Dame in 1985. It was published in *Waymarks: The Notre Dame Inaugural Lectures in Anthropology* (K. Moore, ed., University of Notre Dame Press, 1987) along with the lectures by John Bennett, Victor Turner, Marvin Harris, and Eric Wolf. Since it was intended for a new department in a Catholic university, it started with the following, perhaps heartlessly irreverent, homily:

> It was with real pleasure that I accepted the honor of initiating the Department of Anthropology at Notre Dame. I have, however, the proverbial bad news and the good news. The bad news is that I want to argue that we do not need more departments of anthropology. The good news is that I would also like to argue that if we have to have more, then they should be in Catholic universities. This has to do with a complicated argument about original sin, innate ideas, and the downfall of empiricism. I wanted to call this talk "Putting sin back in." I was told that this would be an inappropriate and embarrassing subject at a Catholic university, where they prefer to think they are just like everyone else in the academic world. Contrariwise, I would argue that given the state of the academic world, one of the few things such institutions have going for them is that they are Catholic. And I say this as an unrepentant Protestant agnostic. (I stress *Protestant* agnostic because Catholics who become agnostic are different. They tend to be rather sad and troubled about it. Protestants, as is their wont, tend to be insufferably self-righteous.) But there it is. Since you want to be like everyone else, you'll never know why you are the potential *salvator anthropologiae*, you will only discover why you are superfluous. So be it.
>
> I must start, then, by confessing a certain ambivalence. It is no secret that I have opposed the rapid expansion of anthropology over the last two decades—even though I have been a not inconsiderable beneficiary of that expansion. So it is obviously hard for me to sing songs of praise to the opening of yet another department. I do not share the view of academic subjects as growth industries. To heed most of my colleagues would be to conclude that quantity was all, and that the army of unemployed Ph.D.'s now marching out into the real world represented a measurable loss to the discipline. But where is it written that we should have

been producing them in the first place? How do we measure the costs and benefits? By the number of Ph.D.'s produced, they reply—not always seeing the circularity of this reasoning.

Since this chapter covers the whole sweep of anthropology through its history, a list of references would be endless if I documented every point in detail. The classical works of Darwin, Durkheim, Boas, Kroeber, Tylor, among others referred to in the first part are all well known and available in standard editions. The work of Matthew Arnold referred to is, of course, his *Culture and Anarchy* (1869); the excellent commentary on this by George Stocking is in his *Race, Culture and Evolution* (Free Press: 1968). Herder's work is *Outlines of a Philosophy of the History of Man* (T. Churchill trans., 2nd. ed. 1803)—see also Stocking op. cit. for further commentary and also Isaiah Berlin, *Vico and Herder* (Chatto and Windus, 1976). Derek Freeman's criticism of Mead (and hence Boas) is in his *Margaret Mead and Samoa* (Harvard University Press, 1983). Clifford Geertz's treatment of the universals issue is in his collection *The Interpretation of Culture* (Basic Books, 1973), and F. H. Bradley's astonishing essay on "My Station and its Duties" in his *Ethical Studies* (Oxford, 1876). Ludwig Wittgenstein, to some people's satisfaction, settled the universals problem in his *Philosophical Investigations* (Macmillan, 1953).

For the second half of the essay readers should consult the extensive references in my *The Red Lamp of Incest: A Study in the Origins of Mind and Society* (Notre Dame University Press, 1983). Specifically, the interesting Guttman-like distribution of traits in boys' initiation ceremonies is discussed in J. W. M. Whiting, R. Kluckhohn, and A. S. Anthony, "The Function of Male Initiation Ceremonies at Puberty," in *Readings in Social Psychology*, ed. E. E. Maccoby, et al. (New York: Henry Holt, 1958). The concept of biomass is a commonplace of any ecology textbook, and kin selection has been well summarized in E. O. Wilson, *Sociobiology* (Harvard University Press: 1975), and given a sprightly and readable treatment in Richard Dawkins, *The Selfish Gene* (Oxford, 1976). Hormonal states and social status are best dealt with in *Hormones, Drugs, and Primate Social Behavior*, ed. H. Steklis and A. Kling (New York: Spectrum Publications, 1983). See especially the work of Steklis and Kling themselves and that of McGuire and Raleigh. More work in this area, including work on humans, continues to appear almost daily. The discussion of the relations of social states to brain, memory, categories, etc. is an extension of chapter 7 of *The Red Lamp of Incest* ("The Matter of Mind"), where the appropriate references can be found, especially to the ongoing work of

Jonathan Winson. Readers should consult the book by Winson titled *Brain and Psyche: The Biology of the Unconscious* (Doubleday, 1985) which gives his thesis in detail. And no one should miss the extraordinary essay by Victor Turner, "Body, Brain, and Culture" in *Zygon* 18, no. 3 (1983): 221–45. I quote his first sentences: "The present essay is for me one of the most difficult I have ever attempted. This is because I am having to submit to question some of the axioms anthropologists of my generation—and several subsequent generations—were taught to hallow. These axioms express the belief that all human behavior is the result of social conditioning. Clearly a very great deal of it is, but gradually it has been borne home to me that there are inherent resistances to conditioning." There follows a most brilliant discussion of the relation of the brain to culture and ritual by someone who must surely rank among the greatest of all 'symbolic' anthropologists. His death was not only a personal loss for many of us, and a sad day for anthropology, but was obviously keenly felt by those of us who have been working for twenty or more years to bring anthropology round to this point of view. We can only hope that others will have as much intellectual courage as he did.

Chapter 6

On the evolutionary argument behind the role of the neocortex as an inhibitor, as well as a facilitator, of not only the capacity but the *drive* to make rules about basic behaviors, see the author's *The Red Lamp of Incest.*

For further developments of the aggression argument see: R. Fox, "Aggression: Then and Now," in M. Robinson and L. Tiger, eds., *Man and Beast Revisited* (Washington, D.C.: Smithsonian Institution Press, 1989); and R. Fox, "The Seville Declaration: Anthropology's Auto-da-Fé," *Academic Questions*, 1:4 (1988): 35–47.

Chapter 7

This chapter was originally delivered as a lecture to the Oxford University Seminar on Social Rules and Social Behavior, organized by Peter Collett in 1974. It was delivered extempore from a few notes, apart from the actual description of the fighting, and was written up from a recorded version. It therefore preserves some of the oral character of its original. The footnotes were by way of asides.

An ethnographic account of Tory Island can be found in Fox (1978). Some of the present account of Tory Island fighting first appeared in

Fox (1973), but in a sufficiently different context to warrant the repetition. And in any case, the reader by now deserves a little light relief, albeit with a serious end in mind.

1. Throughout the nineteenth century there was no priest on the island. Occasionally, however, a visiting friar would go out to the island as a 'penance.' When there was no priest, they would conduct marriage services by lighting fires on the island and the mainland. The priest would stand on the mainland; as he read one part of the service he would cover the fire, and the people on the island would make the appropriate response. They would then cover their fire, and so it went on.

2. I was reading a book by Conor Cruise O'Brien (1957) on Parnell recently. He was quoting letters to the Irish Press during the Parnell scandal in which people were offering to take off their coats for Parnell, so this is obviously a pan-Irish thing, but in the fight context it becomes very important.

REFERENCES

Bergson, H. *The Two Sources of Morality and Religion.* Trans. R. Ashley Audra & C. Brereton. London: Macmillan, 1935.

Bradley, F. H. *Ethical Studies.* Oxford: Clarendon Press, 1876.

Darwin, C. *The Descent of Man.* London: Murray, 1871.

Espinas, A. *Des sociétés animales* (1877). Troisieme edition. Paris: Felix Alcan, 1924.

Fox, R. *Encounter with Anthropology.* New York: Harcourt Brace Jovanovich, 1973.

————. *The Tory Islanders: A People of the Celtic Fringe.* Cambridge: Cambridge University Press, 1978.

Gardiner R., and K. Heider. *Gardens of War: Life and Death in the New Guinea Stone Age.* New York: Random House, 1968.

Hansen, W. *The Peacock Throne: The Drama of Mogul India.* New York: Holt Rinehart and Winston, 1972.

Hume, D. *A Treatise of Human Nature.* London, 1739.

Lévi-Strauss, C. *Les structures élémentaires de la parenté.* Paris: Presses Universitaires de France, 1949.

O'Brien, C. C. *Parnell and His Party.* Oxford: Clarendon Press, 1957.

Chapter 8

Presented at the Thirty-first Annual Conference ("Recent Discoveries in Neurobiology—Do They Matter for Religion, the Social Sciences, and the Humanities?") of the Institute on Religion in an Age of Science, Star Island, New Hampshire, 28 July–4 August 1984.

1. I think I am closer to Winson's true argument in this paper than I was in *The Red Lamp of Incest* (1983), but in chapter 7 ("The Matter of Mind") I go into more detail than is possible here on the question of the theories of totemism, for example, and the problem with the Durkheimian theory of social categories, which I try to resolve in an evolutionary framework.

2. The best contemporary discussion is in Berger and Luckman (1967). It is interesting in view of the anthropological insistence on maintaining the nature-culture dichotomy (which Victor Turner was so anxious to break down) that they conclude that the tendency to so structure the world must be a 'basic feature of the organism.'

3. The following is my own interpretation of Winson's argument, and I am responsible for any errors or misunderstandings. The necessary references can be found in Winson (1985).

4. Striking confirmation of Konner's hunch about the ability of the brain to 'file through' a series of remembered faces comes from the work of, among others, Perrett and Rolls (1983), which shows that primate neural mechanisms exist in specific regions of the temporal lobe which are specialized to process the complex visual patterns of faces.

REFERENCES

Berger, Peter L. and Thomas Luckman. *The Social Construction of Reality*. New York: Doubleday, 1967.

Berlin, Isaiah. *Against the Current: Essays in the History of Ideas*. Ed. Henry Hardy. New York: Viking Press, 1980.

Douglas, Mary. *Purity and Danger*. London: Routledge, 1969.

———. *Natural Symbols*. New York: Academic Press, 1973.

Durkheim, Emile. *The Elementary Forms of the Religious Life*. Trans. J. Swain. London: Allen & Unwin, 1915.

Durkheim, Emile and M. Mauss. *Primitive Classification*. Trans. Rodney Needham. Chicago: University of Chicago Press, 1963.

Eibl-Eibesfeldt, Irenäus. *Ethology*. New York: Holt, Rinehart & Winston, 1982.

Fox, Robin. "Kinship Categories as Natural Categories." In *Evolutionary Biology and Human Social Behavior*, ed. N. Chagnon and W. Irons, 132–44. North Scituate, Mass.: Duxbury Press, 1979.

———. *The Red Lamp of Incest: An Inquiry into the Origins of Mind and Society*. Notre Dame, Ind.: Univ. of Notre Dame Press, 1983.

Konner, Melvin. *The Tangled Wing: Biological Constraints on the Human Spirit.* New York: Holt, Rinehart & Winston, 1982.

Leach, Edmund R. "Anthropological Aspects of Language: Animal Categories and Verbal Abuse." In *New Directions in the Study of Language.* Ed. E. Lenneberg, Cambridge, Mass.: MIT Press, 1964.

————. *Lévi-Strauss.* London: Fontana Books, Modern Masters Series, 1970.

Lévi-Strauss, Claude. *Le totémisme aujourd'hui.* Paris: Presses Universitaires de France, 1962.

————. *The Savage Mind.* Chicago: Univ. of Chicago Press, 1963.

————. *Mythologiques: L'homme nu.* Paris: Plon, 1971.

Mark, Vernon H., and Frank Ervin. *Violence and the Brain.* New York: Harper & Row, 1971.

Ojemann, G. A. "Correlations between Specific Human Brain Lesions and Memory Changes: A Critical Survey of the Literature." *Neurosciences Research Progress Bulletin,* no. 4, 1966, supplement: 1–70.

Perrett, David I. and Edmund T. Rolls. "Neural Mechanisms Underlying the Visual Analysis of Faces." In *Advances in Vertebrate Neuroethology,* ed. Jörg-Peter Ewert, Robert R. Capranica, and David J. Ingle, New York: Plenum, 1983.

Turner, Victor. "Body, Brain, and Culture." *Zygon: Journal of Religion and Science* 18 (September, 1983): 221–245.

Tylor, E. B. "Remarks Concerning Totemism with Especial Reference to Some Modern Theories Concerning It." *Journal of the Royal Anthropological Institute* 28 (1899): 138–148.

Whorf, Benjamin Lee. *Language, Thought and Reality.* Cambridge, Mass.: MIT Press, 1956.

Winson, Jonathon. *Brain and Psyche: The Biology of the Unconscious.* New York: Doubleday, 1985.

Chapter 9

This chapter was first prepared as a report for a committee of the American Academy of Arts and Sciences, then published in Chagnon and Irons (1979).

1. But see his modified position in the introduction to the English translation: *The Elementary Structures of Kinship,* trans. J. H. Bell and J. R. von Sturmer, ed. and trans. R. Needham (Boston: Beacon Press, 1969).

2. The literature on kin selection (and inclusive fitness generally) is

now very large. See the works cited in Chagnon and Irons (1979), E. O. Wilson (1975), and Fox and Fleising (1976).

3. See D. Schneider (1964) and the references therein to the debate among Gellner, Needham, Barnes, and Beattie.

REFERENCES

Bischof, N. "The Comparative Ethology of Incest Avoidance." In *Biosocial Anthropology.* Ed. R. Fox, pp. 37–67. London: Malaby Press, 1975.

Chagnon, N. A., and Irons, W. *Evolutionary Biology and Human Social Behavior.* North Scituate, Mass.: Duxbury Press, 1979.

Fox, R. "Demography and Social Anthropology." *Man* 65 (1965): 86–87.

———. "The Cultural Animal." In *Man and Beast: Comparative Social Behavior.* Ed. J. F. Eisenberg, pp. 273–296. Washington, D.C.: Smithsonian Institution Press, 1971.

———. "Primate Kin and Human Kinship." In *Biosocial Anthropology.* Ed. R. Fox, pp. 9–35, London: Malaby Press, 1975.

——— and U. Fleising "Human Ethology." In *Annual Review of Anthropology.* Vol. 5: 265–88. Eds. B. J. Siegal, A. R. Beals, and S. A. Tyler, Palo Alto: Annual Reviews, 1976.

Lévi-Strauss, C. *Les structures élémentaires de la parenté.* Paris: Presses Universitaires de France, 1949.

———. *La pensée sauvage.* Paris: Plon, 1962.

Morgan, L. H. *Systems of Consanguinity and Affinity of the Human Family.* Washington, D.C.: Smithsonian Institution, 1870.

Murdock, G. P. *Social Structure.* New York: Macmillan, 1949.

Needham, R. "Remarks on the Analysis of Kinship and Marriage." In *Rethinking Kinship and Marriage.* Ed. R. Needham. London: Tavistock, 1971.

Sahlins, M. *The Uses and Abuses of Biology: An Anthropological Critique of Sociobiology.* Ann Arbor: University of Michigan Press, 1976.

Schneider, D. M. "The Nature of Kinship." *Man* 217 (1964): 180–181.

Tax, S. "Some Principles of Social Organization." In *Social Anthropology of the North American Tribes.* Ed. F. Eggan, pp. 3–32. Chicago: University of Chicago Press, 1955.

Chapter 10

This chapter was first delivered as the annual spring lecture of the Committee for the Study of Individual and Society at the University of Virginia in 1987. I should like to thank Professor Robert Scharlemann and the committee for the invitation, and the three members who made formal comments on the paper: Professor Hartt, Professor Handler, and Professor Klosko.

REFERENCES

(Where the reference to a writer's work is generic, no citation is included; only works specifically referred to in the text are listed here.)

Adams, Henry. *Mont St. Michel and Chartres.* Privately printed by the author, 1904; first published edition, Boston: Houghton Mifflin, 1913.

Bell, Daniel. *The Coming of Post Industrial Society.* New York: Basic Books, 1973.

Bock, Kenneth. *Human Nature and History: A Response to Sociobiology.* New York: Columbia University Press, 1980.

Bradley, A. H. *Ethical Studies.* Oxford: Oxford University Press, 1876.

Eaton, S. B., M. Shostak, and M. Konner. *The Palaeolithic Prescription.* New York: Harper and Row, 1988.

Ehrenfeld, David. *The Arrogance of Humanism.* New York: Oxford University Press, 1978.

Fox, Robin. *The Red Lamp of Incest: An Inquiry into the Origins of Mind and Society.* Notre Dame: University of Notre Dame Press, 1983.

Friedman, John. *The Good Society.* Cambridge Mass.: The MIT Press, 1979.

Geertz, Clifford. *The Interpretation of Cultures.* New York: Basic Books, 1973.

Goodman, Paul. *Growing Up Absurd.* New York: Random House, 1960.

Havelock, Eric. *Preface to Plato.* Cambridge Mass.: Harvard University Press, 1963.

Howard, Michael. *The Franco-Prussian War.* London: Rupert Hart-Davis, 1961.

Kropotkin, Prince Peter. *Mutual Aid: A Factor of Evolution.* New York: McClure Phillips and Co., 1903.

LeGuin, Ursula K. *Always Coming Home.* New York: Harper and Row, 1985.

Lessing, Doris. *The Sirian Experiments.* New York: Knopf, 1987.

Lévi-Strauss, Claude. *The Scope of Anthropology.* London: Cape Editions, 1967.

Morris, Desmond. *The Human Zoo.* London: Cape, 1969.

Orwell, George. *1984.* New York: Harcourt Brace, 1949.

Pfeiffer, John. *The Creative Explosion.* New York: Harper and Row, 1982.

Polanyi, Karl. *The Great Transformation* (orig. pub. 1944). Boston: Beacon Press, 1957.

Read, Carveth. *The Origin of Man and His Superstitions*. Cambridge: Cambridge University Press, 1920.

Redfield, Robert. *The Primitive World and its Transformations*. Ithaca: Cornell University Press, 1953.

Sorokin, Pitirim. *Social and Cultural Dynamics*. 4 Vols. New York: American Book Co., 1937–1941.

Tiger, Lionel, and Robin Fox. *The Imperial Animal*. New York: Holt Rinehart and Winston, 1970.

Tönnies, Ferdinand. *Gemeinschaft und Gesellschaft*. Leipzig: Fues Verlag (R. Reisland), 1887.

Turnbull, Colin. *Wayward Servants*. London: Eyre and Spottiswoode, 1965.

Turner, Victor. "Body, Brain and Culture." *Zygon: Journal of Religion and Science*. 18 (1983): 221–245.

Index